War and Revolution in South China

Royal Asiatic Society Hong Kong Studies Series

Royal Asiatic Society Hong Kong Studies Series is designed to make widely available important contributions on the local history, culture, and society of Hong Kong and the surrounding region. Generous support from the Sir Lindsay and Lady May Ride Memorial Fund makes it possible to publish high-quality works that will be of lasting appeal and value to all, both scholars and informed general readers, who share a deeper interest in and enthusiasm for the area.

Recent titles in the series:

The Lone Flag: Memoir of the British Consul in Macao during World War II (2014)
John Pownall Reeves
Edited by Colin Day and Richard Garrett, with a biographical essay by David Calthorpe

Portugal, China and the Macau Negotiations, 1986–1999 (2013)
Carmen Amado Mendes

Custom, Land and Livelihood in Rural South China: The Traditional Land Law of Hong Kong's New Territories, 1750–1950 (2013)
Patrick H. Hase

Scottish Mandarin: The Life and Times of Sir Reginald Johnston (2012)
Shiona Airlie

Governors, Politics and the Colonial Office: Public Policy in Hong Kong, 1918–58 (2012)
Gavin Ure

《東江縱隊：抗戰前後的香港游擊隊》 (*East River Column: Hong Kong Guerrillas in the Second World War and After*) (2012)
Chan Sui-jeung (陳瑞璋)

War and Revolution in South China

The Story of a Transnational Biracial Family, 1936–1951

Edward J. M. Rhoads

HKU
PRESS
香港大學出版社

Hong Kong University Press
The University of Hong Kong
Pokfulam Road
Hong Kong
https://hkupress.hku.hk

ISBN 978-988-8528-66-0 (*Hardback*)

British Library Cataloguing-in-Publication Data
A catalogue record for this book is available from the British Library.

10 9 8 7 6 5 4 3 2 1

Printed and bound by Paramount Printing Co., Ltd. in Hong Kong, China

In loving memory of my daughter

Jennifer R. White

路明洁

(1975–2019)

Contents

Illustrations

Maps

Note on the Spelling of Chinese Names and Terms

In general, Chinese names and terms are rendered in pinyin according to their Putonghua (or Mandarin) pronunciation. Thus, specifically, all places within Guangdong Province at or above the county (*xian*) level, all places outside of Guangdong, and names of all Chinese individuals of national or post-1949 renown are rendered in pinyin. Examples: Guangzhou rather than Canton, Qujiang rather than Kukong, Chongqing rather than Chungking, and Luo Ren rather than Law Yan.

Exceptions to the pinyin rule are sub-county places within Guangdong Province, places in Hong Kong, and names of locally known Chinese in the pre-1949 era. These are generally spelled according to their Cantonese pronunciation, though the spelling can sometimes be rather idiosyncratic. Examples: Hong Lok rather than Kangle, Ngan Bin Tsuen rather than Yanbiancun, Kowloon rather than Jiulong, and Ngan Heung Cho rather than Yan Xiangchu.

I have, at the same time, generally kept the spelling of personal names as they appear in the documents or as they are (or were) preferred by the individuals. Examples: Y. L. Lee rather than Li Yinglin, Chen Su-ching rather than Chen Xujing, and Chi-tung (C. T.) Yung rather than Rong Qidong.

Abbreviations Used in the Notes

AFSC   American Friends Service Committee
CKR   Chi Kit (Ngan) Rhoads
ER   Edward Rhoads
HGR   Howard G. Rhoads
INS   Immigration and Naturalization Service
ODW   Olin D. Wannamaker
OWI   Office of War Information
TLUA–HYL   Trustees of Lingnan University Archives, Harvard-Yenching Library
USNA–CP   US National Archives, College Park, MD
USNA–NY   US National Archives, New York City
USNA–S   US National Archives, Seattle, WA
YDSL   Yale Divinity School Library

Introduction

In recent years there has been a remarkable upsurge of interest in the Second World War among Western historians of China. This follows, and indeed is most likely a consequence of, a change of attitude toward the war within post-Mao China. As historian Parks Coble has observed, "for much of the early history of the People's Republic of China—the Maoist years—mention of the anti-Japanese war of resistance almost vanished from view. . . . Maoist China largely lacked memorials, museums, and historical writing and literature devoted to the war." Instead, "the party mandated a historical narrative that privileged the revolution and the leadership of the Communist Party."[1] It was only in the 1980s that, as part of Deng Xiaoping's new strategy of "reform and opening out," the party decided to rewrite history; it began to downplay the narrative of revolution in favor of the narrative of war, including the party's long-suppressed collaboration with Chiang Kai-shek and the Nationalists against the Japanese. As Rana Mitter gratefully acknowledges, his book of 2013, *Forgotten Ally: China's World War II, 1937–1945*, "is a beneficiary of [this] remarkable opening-up process in China."[2] Similar beneficiaries are the many other English-language books on the war published in the past decade.[3]

The War of Resistance against Japan, as the war is known in China, began in north China in July 1937, then quickly spread southward to the border of French Indo-China. Yet, with few exceptions (notably the books by Macri and Zhu), the above-mentioned publications all tend to focus on the war in North and Central China and largely ignore what went on in South China. Thus, there are accounts of battles on the North China Plain and at Shanghai, of the breeching of the Yellow River dikes and the Henan famine of 1942–1943, of Wuhan and Chongqing as refugee capitals, of Shanghai as a "solitary

---

1. Parks M. Coble, *China's War Reporters: The Legacy of Resistance against Japan* (Cambridge, MA: Harvard University Press, 2015), pp. 140–143.
2. Rana Mitter, *Forgotten Ally: China's World War II, 1937–1945* (Boston and New York: Houghton Mifflin Harcourt, 2013), pp. 11–12.
3. These include the following monographs (listed in chronological order of publication): Stephen R. MacKinnon, *Wuhan, 1938: War, Refugees, and the Making of Modern China* (2008); Diana Lary, *The Chinese People at War: Human Suffering and Social Transformation, 1937–1945* (2010); R. Keith Schoppa, *In a Sea of Bitterness: Refugees during the Sino-Japanese War* (2011); Franco David Macri, *Clash of Empires in South China: The Allied Nations' Proxy War with Japan, 1935–1941* (2012); Micah S. Muscolino, *The Ecology of War in China: Henan Province, the Yellow River, and Beyond, 1938–1950* (2015); Pingchao Zhu, *Wartime Culture in Guilin, 1938–1944: A City at War* (2015); and Hans van de Ven, *China at War: Triumph and Tragedy in the Emergence of the New China, 1937–1952* (2017). Yet other recent English-language publications on the war are compilations of essays, such as Stephen R. MacKinnon, Diana Lary, and Ezra F. Vogel, eds., *China at War: Regions of China, 1937–1945* (2007); James Flath and Norman Smith, eds., *Beyond Suffering: Recounting War in Modern China* (2011); Mark Peattie, Edward J. Drea, and Hans van de Ven, eds., *The Battle for China* (2011); and Joseph W. Esherick and Matthew T. Combs, eds., *1943: China at the Crossroads* (2015).

island," of the terror bombing of Chongqing, of the "scorched earth" policy in North China, and of refugees in Zhejiang. But what of South China, here defined as "Lingnan" 嶺南, the region "south of the mountain range" that separates the West River from the Yangtze? What of the battle for Hong Kong, or the famine of 1943–1944 in Guangdong, or Qujiang as the wartime capital of Guangdong Province, or Hong Kong as another "solitary island," or the terror bombing of Guangzhou, or the "scorched earth" policy and refugees in South China? These events hardly figure, or figure not at all, in the above publications.

Also, most of the above publications tend to be macro-histories, viewing the war from above and describing it in broad strokes. With rare exceptions (notably the books by Lary, Muscolino, and Schoppa), they downplay the effect of the war on individual people on the ground. Yet, as Parks Coble has also observed, "Millions were displaced by the Sino-Japanese War, but it is clear that there is no one, no master narrative of this experience. . . . The diverse range of experiences of mobility during the war reflects the complex reality of wartime China."[4] To capture that "complex reality of wartime China," a micro-history might work better than the macro-histories that are offered to us.

There is, thus, much to gain from looking at the Sino-Japanese War from the perspective of South China and from the perspective of an individual family. This book tries to remedy the shortcomings in current scholarship by answering two questions: How did the war affect South China? And, more specifically, how did it affect one particular family in South China? In this account I go along with Hans van de Ven's idea that for the Chinese the war did not end in 1945 but continued through the postwar civil war between the Nationalists and the Communists up to Communist China's intervention in the Korean War.

The family whose experiences I have chosen to examine is my own. I was born in 1938 in Guangzhou (Canton), and, except for one year in Chongqing and one year in the United States, I lived in South China for the first thirteen years of my life. My mother, a Chinese from a well-to-do family with a middle-school education, was a trained stenographer-typist; my father, an American college professor. What they and I, together with our nanny Ah Hoh, went through from 1936 to 1951 forms part of "the complex reality of wartime China" to which Coble referred. This is history from the bottom up. However, though it's a micro-history (down to the level of local street addresses), it is written within the framework of the macro-history. My family's wartime experiences were not necessarily typical, but neither were they atypical.

The happenstance of my birth and upbringing led me to study modern Chinese history, with a particular interest in the South. Thus, my first scholarly publication was a case study of the Revolution of 1911 in Guangdong Province. Though I have always been curious about my Chinese past, I—like many children—was never curious *enough* to interrogate my parents, and my parents themselves hardly ever talked about their past either. My younger sister and I were never told, for example, that my mother had been divorced before she married my father. As a recent family historian wrote, "Maybe all fathers [and mothers too] are unknowable. Maybe all families are mysterious. If we're lucky, we get interested in ours before it's too late. Memories silt over, lives are cut short. By the time we've come up with the questions, there's no one left to answer."[5]

4.   Coble, *China's War Reporters*, p. 103.
5.   Janny Scott, *The Beneficiary: Fortune, Misfortune, and the Story of My Father* (New York: Riverhead Books, 2019), p. 26.

About fifteen years ago, long after the death of both my parents and following my retirement from the University of Texas at Austin, I set out more systematically to learn what they (and thus, coincidentally, I) had been doing in China. At the time, I knew the basic story but not the details. My father was from Philadelphia and went to China in 1936 to teach at Lingnan University in Guangzhou. There he met my mother, a native Cantonese. They married and, in 1938, had me. (Though employed at one of China's ten-plus "Christian" colleges, my father was never a missionary, and thus I was never, technically, a "mish kid.") Soon after I was born, the Japanese invaded and occupied Guangzhou, at which point we, along with the university, relocated to Hong Kong. Three years later, when the Japanese overran the British colony, my father, as an enemy alien, was placed in an internment camp in Hong Kong, while my mother and I sought refuge in what was called "Free China" in northern Guangdong Province. After my father was repatriated to the US, he managed at some point to rejoin his family in northern Guangdong. Sometime later, we had to flee once again—this time to Chongqing (Chungking), the wartime capital of Nationalist China, where my father found employment with the Office of War Information, an American propaganda agency. Following Japan's surrender in 1945, we were able to return to Guangzhou and to Lingnan University. In 1948–1949 my father took a year's furlough (or sabbatical), which we spent in Philadelphia. By then the anti-Japanese War of Resistance had given way to the Revolutionary Civil War between the Nationalists and the Communists, and the Communists were winning. Nevertheless, at a time when other foreigners were fleeing China, we went back. But in February 1951, after more than a year under the Communists, we were forced to leave China for good. Altogether we were refugees not once, not twice, but four times—in 1938, in 1942, in 1944, and, finally, in 1951.

Written history depends upon sources. What sources were there for a fuller account of my family's experiences in China? Unfortunately, not many. Hardly anything that my parents might have written about their wartime experiences—for example, letters to family members—survived. There are no reminiscences (written or otherwise), no family papers. What might be considered the Rhoads family archive consists of my father's US passport, my mother's Chinese passport, my father's insurance policy, my mother's divorce paper, my parents' marriage certificate, my birth certificate and that of my sister, my baptismal certificate, my mother's application for a US visa, some of my Chinese school report cards, some family photographs, and the deed to a cemetery plot in Philadelphia (where my parents are buried).

Though I shared many of my parents' experiences in wartime and revolutionary China, I myself am not much of a source either. I was thirteen years old when we left China in 1951, and it might be thought that I would have been old enough to remember a fair amount of what had gone on, particularly toward the end of our stay in China. But perhaps because we had had to move around a lot during those thirteen years, what I do remember is very confused in my mind. On the one hand, I am not at all sure that what I think may have happened actually did happen. For example, I think I hid under the bed when my father showed up in northern Guangdong in 1943 after having been gone for a year and a half; but did that really happen? There is no way of knowing. On the other hand, there are things I now know happened to me that I have no recollection of at all. Such as the first time I went to school, usually a memorable event in one's life. This was in the fall of 1944, soon after we arrived in Chongqing, when as a six-year-old I enrolled in the Chee Min Boys' School. The only reason I know this is that among the documents in the small collection of family papers is my report card from the school. Yet armed with this information, I still have no memory of this event. In short, this book is, most definitely, not a memoir. It is, rather, a document-based history, or so I intend.

If I myself don't remember much and if there are few family papers, how then is it possible to write a history of my family in wartime China? More generally, how much can one learn about the past when sources are scarce? The answer, in this case, is, quite a lot. As with any historical research, I have gone in search of other documents. My initial and principal source of information was the archive of the Board of Trustees of Lingnan University, a New York–based organization that hired my father to teach at Lingnan and that for all but one year of his stay in China was, technically, his employer. The original hardcopies of these papers are at the Harvard-Yenching Library at Harvard (with a set of microfilm copies at the Divinity School Library at Yale). Another important archival source was the Records of the Office of War Information at the US National Archives at College Park, Maryland: the OWI was the American agency for which my father worked for the two years before and after the end of the war. Additionally, I have sought out and found, at various university libraries, the papers of some of my father's colleagues at Lingnan (notably William W. Cadbury, Henry Brownell, and Gilbert Baker) and with the OWI (Christopher Rand, William L. Holland, and Everett Hawkins). Yet other archives that yielded pieces of useful information include the Maritime Customs Service Archives at the Second Historical Archives of China at Nanjing, the Needham Research Institute in Cambridge, England, the American Friends Service Committee Archives in Philadelphia, the Presbyterian Historical Society also in Philadelphia, and the Yale Divinity School Library. For information about my mother's family and upbringing, I have learned much from one of my maternal uncles, several of my cousins, and a nephew and also from the Records of the US Immigration and Naturalization Service, in Seattle and in New York City.

On the basis of all this archival research, I now have a much better understanding of our family's experiences in wartime China than when I first began the project. Does this mean that I now know all that I would like to know? Not quite. I don't know why my father chose to go to China in the first place. I don't know, aside from his name, who my mother's first husband was. I don't know how exactly my mother, together with me (then four years old) and Ah Hoh, made our way from Japanese-occupied Hong Kong into Free China in early 1942. I sketch out the three escape routes taken by other refugees, but I don't know which one we ourselves took. Also, while I now know how my mother was employed once we reached Free China (she worked for the Maritime Customs Service in Qujiang), I have no idea where exactly we lived for the year and a half that my mother and father were separated. Regrettably, I know very little about our amah (or nanny), Ah Hoh, though she was very much a part of our family once she came to live with us in Hong Kong in 1939 (or perhaps 1941). Because of the near absence of family papers, I know very little about what my parents felt about all that they were experiencing. I have been able, I believe, to reconstruct their lives but not their thoughts.

Finally, what did I learn from this research? Two things. One, I learned that the war in South China was no less turbulent than it was in North and Central China. And two, I came to appreciate the important role that my mother, as one of China's New Women, played in the history of our family during the war. The following account is as much her story as it is my father's.

1

My Mother

My mother, Ngan Chi Kit 顏志潔, was born near the end of the Qing dynasty (1644–1912), three years before it was overthrown in the Republican Revolution. The birthdate she always gave in later years was 26 November 1909. It is possible, however, that she was actually born a month and a half later. Since China did not utilize the Gregorian (or solar) calendar until after the revolution, it is likely that at her birth her parents were still using the traditional lunar calendar. In which case, my mother's birthdate might well have been the twenty-sixth day of the eleventh month in the *siyou* 己酉 year, which in the Gregorian calendar was 7 January 1910. Either way, she was born in the first year of the reign of Puyi, China's last emperor.

My mother was a native of Ngan Bin Village 顏邊村 in Nanhai County, Guangdong Province, in southern China. Ngan Bin is now, administratively, part of the city of Guangzhou (or Canton); when my cousin, Ngan Cheong Shun 顏昌順, and I visited in January 2016, it belonged to Hexi Village 河西村, Dali Township 大瀝鎮, Nanhai District 南海區 of Guangzhou Municipality. Back in the nineteenth century, however, it was still a separate rice-growing village, situated in Im Po Township 鹽步堡, near the mid-point of what an old county gazetteer called the "Guangzhou-Fat Shan highway" (*Sheng-Fo tongqu* 省佛通衢), running from the West Gate of the provincial capital to Fat Shan 佛山, a commercial and industrial city ten miles to the southwest.[1] Ngan Bin, as its name suggests, was a predominantly single-clan village, a common feature of rural society in South China. Most inhabitants of the village shared my mother's surname, and in the community today there are no fewer than three standing ancestral halls dedicated to members of the Ngan lineage. One is the main ancestral hall—Yanshi dazongci 顏氏大宗祠—and two others are smaller branch halls, Zhenyu Yan gongci 鎮宇顏公祠 and Xiangting Yan gongci 向亭顏公祠. There are remnants of a fourth ancestral hall, Chujing Yan gongci 處靜顏公祠, as well.

The Ngan 顏—or Yan in Mandarin—is an ancient and illustrious lineage. At the main shrine in Ngan Bin Village is a picture gallery of notable ancestors, the oldest of whom (sixth century BC) is Yan Zhengzai 顏徵在, the birth mother of the great sage, Confucius. However, the lineage also traces its ancestry to Yan Hui 顏回 (d. 481 BC), the favorite disciple of Confucius, who was much admired for his love of learning and his virtuous behavior. Given their shared surname, it is likely that Yan Hui was somehow related to Confucius's mother. The principal tenet of the "family instruction" (*jiaxun* 家訓) of the Ngan lineage, as spelled out by my mother's father, was to emulate Yan Hui. In particular,

---

1. *Nanhai xian zhi* (Nanhai County gazetteer: 1835 ed.), *juan* 3, pp. 3b–4a, 36b–37a.

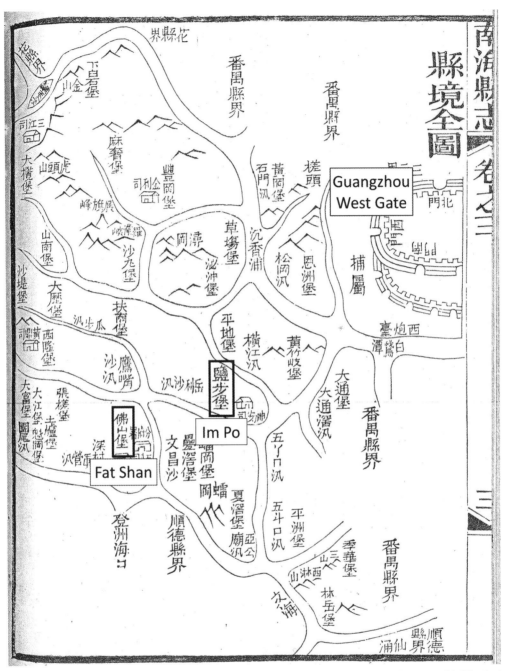

Map 1.1: Nanhai County, Guangdong Province, 1835 (detail). From *Nanhaixian zhi* (Nanhai County gazetteer; Daoguang 15 [1835] edition), *juan* 3, p. 3b.

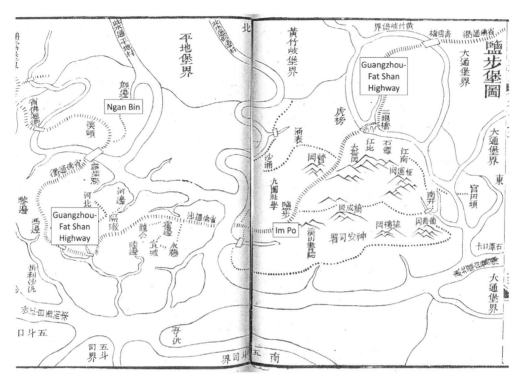

Map 1.2: Im Po Township, Nanhai County, 1835. From *Nanhaixian zhi* (Nanhai County gazetteer; Daoguang 15 [1835] edition), *juan* 3, pp. 36b–37a. The Guangzhou–Fat Shan Highway is the hatched path that runs across both leaves of the Im Po Township map.

Figure 1.1: Gateway to Ngan Bin Village, with my seventh uncle, Ngan Po Ming, and his son, Cheong Shun, 1988. Photo courtesy of Cheong Shun Ngan. The gateway was no longer standing during my visit in 2016.

Figure 1.2: The main ancestral hall of the Ngan lineage, Ngan Bin Village, 2016.

members of the lineage were admonished to take heed of what Confucius said of his disciple: "Admirable indeed was the virtue of Hui! With a single bamboo dish of rice, a single gourd dish of drink, and living in his mean narrow lane, while others could not have endured the distress, he did not allow his joy to be affected by it. Admirable indeed was the virtue of Hui!"[2]

Ngan Bin Village itself dates back to the beginning of the second millennium. It was founded by Yan Guangxian 顏光先, a high official of the Northern Song dynasty (960–1127). Around AD 1000, according to the historical marker in front of the Ngan ancestral hall, he was sent as an Investigation Commissioner (Lianfangshi 廉訪使) from the imperial capital, Kaifeng, to Guangdong, on what was then the southern frontier of the Song empire.[3] Though Yan Guangxian himself was a native of Jiangxi Province, he and his family relocated to Nanhai County and settled in Ngan Bin. The main ancestral hall at Ngan Bin, which was built in the Ming period (1368–1644) and rebuilt in the 1830s, commemorates Yan Guangxian and all his (male) descendants, who are collectively known as the Kefutang 克復堂. (The other ancestral halls in the village presumably honor branches, or sub-lineages, of the main lineage.) It is unclear how my mother's

---

2.   Ngan Ki Ping, "Zi Yuan" [Predestined toward words], an autobiographic sketch written for Queen's College 1952 Certificate Form Association, *Diamond Jubilee Album*, Hong Kong, 2012. Confucius's quotation is from *The Analects*, Book 6, Chapter 9; the translation (slightly modified) is that of James Legge.

3.   Charles O. Hucker, *A Dictionary of Official Titles in Imperial China* (Stanford: Stanford University Press, 1985), p. 312.

immediate family fit into the larger Ngan lineage; efforts to locate a lineage genealogy or clan book during my visit to the village were unsuccessful.

My mother's father was Ngan Sai Wing 顏世榮 (1873–1958), who was better known in later life by his "literary name" (*zi* 字), which was Ngan Heung Cho 顏向初. He was born in Ngan Bin in 1873 or possibly a year earlier.[4] Once upon a time, perhaps in the 1830s, when the main ancestral hall was rebuilt, the village had been a prosperous place, a thriving commercial center with pawnshop operations extending to neighboring Guangxi Province. However, by the time Ngan Sai Wing was born, in the late nineteenth century, it had become, according to a contemporary French missionary, quite "poor and in debt."[5]

About all that is known about Sai Wing's early life is that he was the offspring of Ngan Wing Cheung 顏永暢, who evidently had some wealth and most likely multiple wives. According to Ngan Ki Ping 顏其平, my maternal uncle, Sai Wing was "the only son of a young widow who got deprived of [her share of her husband's] assets." Sai Wing's mother, nevertheless, managed to take him to nearby Hong Kong and to enroll him in St. Joseph's College, "one of seven boys from China wearing their pigtails." On their departure from Ngan Bin Village, Sai Wing supposedly promised his mother that he would one day recover the properties in the village that had been stolen from her.[6] He was to make good on this promise.

Ngan Sai Wing's move to Hong Kong may also have been due to the Sino-French War of 1884–1885. China had gone to war to oppose French encroachments in Vietnam, which at the time was a vassal state of the Qing dynasty. The result was a defeat for China, which was forced to give up all claims to Vietnam. The war, however, had stirred up anti-foreign sentiment in Guangdong Province, which then bordered on Vietnam and where some of the fighting took place. The popular hostility was directed at the Christian missionaries—principally French Catholic missionaries—and their native converts. The missionaries were particularly disliked because they often intruded into local disputes on behalf of their converts and because they forbade their Chinese followers from participating in key communal activities that they regarded as idolatrous. There was a significant Catholic presence in Ngan Bin: among its population of about 3,000 were 105 Christians, including Ngan Sai Wing and his mother. In the fall of 1884, at the height of the anti-foreign movement, their village came under assault for two days by so-called bandits. According to the local French missionary, M. Delsahut, the Christian villagers "were all robbed and nearly all of them had to exile themselves to [Portuguese] Macao or [British] Hong Kong."[7] It was probably at this time and under these circumstances that Ngan Sai Wing—who in 1884 would have been twelve years old—was taken to Hong Kong.

St. Joseph's College, founded in 1875 and staffed by De La Salle Christian Brothers, was the oldest Catholic boys' secondary school in the British colony. At the time, it was

---

4. Ngan Heung Cho's gravestone, in St. Michael's Catholic Cemetery, Happy Valley, Hong Kong, gives his birthdate as 18 April 1873; his US immigration papers, however, give it as 24 May 1872. See American Consulate General, Canton, "Precis in re Ngan Heung Cho," 2 December 1926, Case File 6500/4-3 (Ngan Heung Cho), RG 85, Records of the Immigration and Naturalization Service, USNA–S. As with my mother's birthdate, there may be a (partial) explanation for this discrepancy. 24 May 1872 turns out to be, in the lunar calendar, the eighteenth day of the fourth month (whence, perhaps, "18 April") in the *renshen* 壬申 year; the *renshen* year, however, was 1872, not 1873.

5. Adrien Launay, ed., *Histoire des missions de Chine: Mission du Kouang-tong, Monographies des districts par les missionaires* (Paris: Anciennes Maisons Douniol et Recani, 1917), p. 16.

6. Ngan Ki Ping, personal communications, 2 September and 8 November 2014, and "Memo #4," 10 June 2015.

7. Launay, *Histoire des missions de Chine*, pp. 16–17; Jean-Paul Wiest, "Catholic Activities in Kwangtung Province and Chinese Responses, 1848–1885" (PhD diss., University of Washington, 1977).

located on Robinson Road in the Mid-Levels of Hong Kong Island. It offered an English-language curriculum that prepared its students to work as translators in the colonial government and foreign trade firms. It had about three hundred students, two-thirds of them Europeans (mostly Portuguese) and one-third Chinese. Ngan Sai Wing, if he had stayed for the full course of study, would have graduated around 1891.[8] It was undoubtedly because of this schooling that he acquired an excellent command of English, especially written English.

He, predictably, became a treaty port merchant, a common occupation along the South China coast in the late nineteenth and early twentieth centuries. According to my uncle, Ngan Sai Wing (now more commonly known as Ngan Heung Cho) started out as a cargo inspector for the Kowloon Wharf group in Hong Kong; later he worked for an unidentified foreign firm in Taiwan, "before beginning [around the turn of the century] the saga of his life as an entrepreneur in Canton."[9] When, in November 1926, he applied to go to the United States, he stated that he had worked as a "clerk in various foreign firms" in Guangzhou from 1897 to June 1924, at which point he became a "merchant" in the Wing Tai Loong Silk Company 永泰隆絲莊. According to his US immigration file, he was, in 1926, the "general manager" of the Wing Tai Loong Company; at the same time, he "represented," in some unspecified capacity, "the well known firm of Li & Fung," 利豐公司, an import–export company founded in Guangzhou in 1906 by Fung Pak Liu 馮柏燎, who like Ngan Heung Cho was Hong Kong–educated and Catholic.[10]

By the 1920s, raw silk had replaced tea as China's leading item of export, and the Canton delta was, along with the Shanghai region, its major producing area. Wing Tai Loong was a silk "commission house" (*sizhuang* 絲莊), which meant that it acted as an intermediary between the domestic filatures, which reeled the silk thread from the cocoons, and the foreign (mostly US and French) export firms. There were twenty or thirty such commission houses in Guangzhou at the time, of which Wing Tai Loong was one of the largest. The company had been founded around 1919 by Shum Kwok Wah 岑國華, a native of Shunde County who, like Ngan Heung Cho, had risen from poverty to commercial success.[11] My grandfather, according to his visa application, had a big stake in the company; his investment of $90,000 (gold) accounted for about two-thirds of the firm's total value. The Wing Tai Loong office was on Sun Hing Street 新興街, adjacent to

---

8. On St. Joseph's College, see Thomas F. Ryan, *The Story of a Hundred Years: The Pontifical Institute of Foreign Missions (P.I.M.E.) in Hong Kong, 1858–1958* (Hong Kong: Catholic Truth Society, 1959), pp. 82, 87, 88. I have not been able to confirm Ngan Sai Wing's attendance at St. Joseph's. School records do not go back that far, and his name does not appear among the lists of college prize winners for 1880, 1884, 1886, 1888, and 1890 as published in the *China Mail* and the *Hong Kong Daily Press*. These newspapers are available online at Old HK Newspapers, Digital Collection, the Multimedia Information System of the Hong Kong Public Libraries, http://mmis.hkpl.gov.hk (last accessed 14 November 2017).

9. Ngan Ki Ping, personal communications, 8 and 9 November 2014.

10. Ngan Heung Cho's application for a US visa, Canton, 26 November 1926, courtesy of Ngan Ki Ping; American Consulate General, Canton, "Precis in re Ngan Heung Cho," 2 December 1926, Case File 6500/4-3 (Ngan Heung Cho), Chinese Exclusion Case Files, RG 85, Records of the INS, USNA–S. On the Li & Fung Company, see Feng Bangyan, *Bainian Lifeng* [A hundred years of Li & Fung], enl. ed. (Hong Kong: Sanlian shudian, 2011).

11. C. W. Howard and K. P. Buswell, *A Survey of the Silk Industry of South China* (Guangzhou: Ling Nan Agricultural College, Canton Christian College, 1925), pp. 147–149; "Siye juzi Cen Guohua zhi nü Cen Yufang huiyi fuqin shengping" [Cen Yufang, daughter of the silk industry giant, Shum Kwok Wah, remembers her father's life], *Zhujiang shangbao*, 9 June 2014; "Fuhao pian—Cen Guohua: Guangdongren cong chipin dao haofu de zaoqi renzheng" [Annals of the rich and powerful—Shum Kwok Wah: The authentication of the early life of a Cantonese who rose from abject poverty to power and fame], *Nanfang dushi bao*, 29 August 2008.

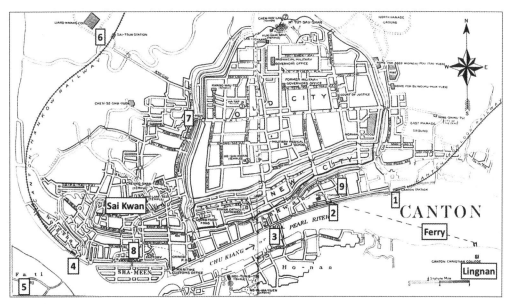

Map 1.3: Guangzhou, 1920. From Wikipedia, map in public domain. #1 = Da Sha Tou (Guangzhou-Hankou) railroad station; #2 = Tin Tze Wharf; #3 = site of Pearl River Bridge (built 1933); #4 = Wong Sha (Canton-Kowloon) railroad station; #5 = Fa Ti 花地 (site of True Light Middle School); #6 = Sai Tsuen (site of Union Normal School); #7 = West Gate; #8 = No. 10 Sap Sam Po Street (Ngan Heung Cho's home); #9 = No. 15 Man Tak East Road (my mother's home with Chan Cheuk Ming).

the Anglo-French settlement on Shameen Island, where the foreign export firms were located.[12]

"To sell the silk," according to a 1925 report, "the commission house secures a 'merchant,' who has had some training in English, to deal with the foreign exporters in Shameen. . . . Each day the 'merchant' [*mazhan* 仔毡] visits the offices of the foreign exporters . . . The 'merchant' of the commission houses ascertains whether any orders have been received [from] abroad and whether exporters wish to buy any silk. The amount as well as the price offered for each order is [*sic*] noted and reported to the commission house." In view of his competence in English—something that Shum Kwok Wah perhaps lacked—Ngan Heung Cho may have been Wing Tai Loong's "merchant."[13] At some point, in addition to the silk company, Shum Kwok Wah founded an import–export firm (*yanghang*) of the same name—永泰隆洋行—located in the French section of Shameen Island. Wing Tai Loong seems to have been the only silk commission house in Guangzhou that handled its own exports. And after 1927 it was the only Chinese firm to be a member of the Silk Association of America.[14]

The reason Ngan Heung Cho went to the United States was to set up Wing Tai Loong's American office in New York. This was during the period of Chinese Exclusion (1882–1943), when most Chinese were prohibited from entering the United States;

---

12. Ngan Heung Cho's application for a US visa, Canton, 26 November 1926, courtesy of Ngan Ki Ping.
13. Lei Yue Wai and Lei Hei Kit, "Report on a Steam Filature in Kwangtung," *Lingnaam Agricultural Review* 3, no. 2 (1925): 111–112.
14. "Siye juzi Cen Guohua zhi nü Cen Yufang huiyi fuqin shengping"; Silk Association of America, *56th Annual Report* [1927–1928], p. 115.

however, businessmen like Ngan Heung Cho were classified as "Section 6 Merchants" and were exempt from the prohibition. He arrived at Seattle aboard the US passenger liner *President Grant* on 30 January 1927.[15] In New York City he set up an "office" for Wing Tai Loong by renting a desk in a commercial building at 450 Fourth Avenue; from there, he sought out buyers of raw silk. Over the following year, he sold between four and five hundred bales of raw silk with a total worth of $160,000 to $200,000. He was listed in the telephone directory for 1927–1928 as living at 138 East 28th Street in the Kips Bay neighborhood of Manhattan.[16]

Ngan Heung Cho went to America also on behalf of the Guangdong Silk Industry Research Institute (Guangdong siye yanjiusuo 廣東絲業研究所), probably in an effort— ultimately unsuccessful—to beat back the competition from Japan and to maintain the province as a major exporter of raw silk.[17] In its report for 1926–1927, the Silk Association of America mentioned to its members that "a number of [Chinese] filature owners have visited this country, and through your Association have been able to meet the silk men in this market who are potential buyers. . . . In answer to inquiries from Canton, the Association has outlined the popular complaints on silk from this district, and filatures have sent representatives here to investigate the situation." One of these representatives sent by filatures in Guangdong was undoubtedly Ngan Heung Cho.[18]

Ngan was in the US for slightly over a year. In February 1928 he made plans to go home to China for a short visit. He would travel by way of Europe, perhaps with the idea of visiting France, which was another leading importer of Guangdong silk. He petitioned the US Immigration Service for a "return permit" that would allow him to reenter the country without having to reapply for a visa as a Section 6 Merchant. Though granted a hearing at Ellis Island on 7 March, his petition was ultimately denied; he was told that "his admission in 1927 cannot be said to be for permanent and unrestricted residence."[19] It seems that he left the US soon afterwards, never to return. In 1928 he was no longer listed in the Manhattan telephone directory, and though Wing Tai Loong remained a member of the Silk Association of America, its American office had closed. There is, however, no official record of Ngan Heung Cho's departure from the US, though it is likely that he did as he had intended, which was to go home by way of Europe. Once back in Guangzhou, he presumably continued his business association with Wing Tai Loong.

Ngan Heung Cho, as a silk man in the mid-1920s, may have achieved his greatest economic and social success at this time. As befit a Chinese man of substance, and not-withstanding the teachings of the Catholic Church, he had four wives (not all of them simultaneously), who between 1900 and 1940 bore him eighteen children (not all of whom survived into adulthood). The names of these children, arranged by gender and then by birth order, are carved on his gravestone.

---

15. See his immigration case file, 6500/4-3, RG 85, Records of the INS, USNA–S.
16. "In re Ngan Heung Cho, an applicant for an Immigration Return Permit," Ellis Island, 7 March 1928, Case File 125/225 (Ngan Heung Cho), Box 367, Chinese Exclusion Case Files, RG 85, Records of the INS, USNA–NY; *New York City Telephone Directory*, Manhattan, White Pages, Winter 1927–Summer 1928, p. 996.
17. This information comes from an undated and unsourced newspaper clipping, titled 絲商請減輕稅餉 [Silk merchants request a reduction in taxes], sent to me by Ngan Ki Ping, 8 November 2014; see also Li Weishi, "Lingnan daxue gailiang Guangdong siye de yishu" [Recollections of Lingnan University's improvements to the silk industry], *Guangzhou wenshi ziliao*, no. 13 (1964): 191, where Ngan Heung Cho is misidentified as 顏少初.
18. Silk Association of America, *55th Annual Report* [1926–1927], p. 20.
19. Case File 125/225 (Ngan Heung Cho), Box 367, Chinese Exclusion Case Files, RG 85, Records of the INS, USNA–NY.

According to the testimony that he gave to the US immigration authorities in 1928 when he applied for a return permit, Ngan Heung Cho married his first wife around 1897, when he was twenty-four years old and just beginning his business career. Her name was Ng Shee 吳氏 (that is, "a woman of the Ng [or Wu] clan or lineage"). She was almost certainly Catholic and from "a rather well off family." One of her relatives, Wu Zhitao 吳志滔, who was perhaps a younger brother, seems to have remained close to the Ngan family thereafter.[20] Almost nothing else is known about Ng Shee. This is not so surprising, for in the patriarchal society of China in the late nineteenth and early twentieth centuries, a married woman was absorbed into her husband's family and had no independent social standing, especially outside the home. Ng Shee was the mother of Ngan Heung Cho's first six children (including my mother). She died in 1914, four or five years after my mother was born.

About a year after the death of Ng Shee, when Heung Cho said he was forty-two years old, he married his second wife, Low (or Lao) Shee 劉氏, whose Christian name was Mary Lao 劉瑪利亞.[21] She had one son (Kei Chee 其之, no. 7 in birth order), who was Heung Cho's oldest surviving son. Reportedly in poor health, Low Shee died in 1925.

Ngan Heung Cho's third marriage, to Wong Shee 黃氏, took place, he told his interrogators in 1928, "fifteen years ago," which would place it around the same time as his marriage to Low Shee. Wong Shee was twenty years younger than Heung Cho; in 1926, when he applied to go to the United States, he was fifty-four and she was thirty-four. As of 1928, she had given birth to three children (nos. 8 to 10 in birth order)—two sons (one of whom died) and a daughter. The fact that for about ten years Ngan Heung Cho seemingly was married to two women greatly troubled the US immigration officials at Ellis Island, who accused him of practicing polygamy. He, however, denied that he ever had more than one "wife" at the same time. Breaking into English—he had been interrogated in Cantonese up to this point—he explained that "in China you can't have two proper wives at the one time" and that therefore so long as Low Shee and Wong Shee were both alive, "one [Low Shee] was my wife and one [Wong Shee] was my concubine." Indeed, in late traditional times and continuing into the early Republican era, a man could have only one principal wife at a time, and this wife could not be discarded or demoted. If he were wealthy enough, however, he could have a number of secondary wives, or concubines, whose legal and social status was entirely legitimate and whose children were supposed to be treated the same as those of the principal wife.[22]

Sometime after his return from the United States, Ngan Heung Cho married yet again, this time to an even younger Taiwanese woman, Ho Mo Kun 何慕勤 (1898–1985). She, too, must have come from a rather well-to-do family. Her older sister supposedly married a *xiucai* 秀才, holder of the lowest of the three degrees in the traditional civil service examination system; a younger sister married a railway inspector.[23] She succeeded Low Shee as the principal wife, while Wong Shee remained as a concubine. Thus, within the Ngan family, Ho Mo Kun, as Heung Cho's third "wife," was addressed as "Sam Gwu"

20. "In re Ngan Heung Cho, an applicant for an Immigration Return Permit," Ellis Island, 7 March 1928, Case File 125/225 (Ngan Heung Cho), Box 367, Chinese Exclusion Case Files, RG 85, Records of the INS, USNA–NY; Ngan Ki Ping, personal communication, 1 August 2016.

21. Christine Pang, personal communications, 12 November and 29 December 2014; Tony Cheong Shun Ngan, personal communications, 4 and 6 June 2016. Christine and Tony are Mary Lao's grandchildren.

22. "In re Ngan Heung Cho, an applicant for an Immigration Return Permit," Ellis Island, 7 March 1928, Case File 125/225 (Ngan Heung Cho), Box 367, Chinese Exclusion Case Files, RG 85, Records of the INS, USNA–NY.

23. Ngan Ki Ping, personal communication, Memo #2, 12 April 2015.

三姑 (Third Lady), whereas Wong Shee, the concubine, was referred to as "Wong Sam Mui" 黃三妹 (Third Sister Wong). Together the two of them produced eight more children, three more by Wong Sam Mui (nos. 11, 12, and 16) and five by Sam Gwu (nos. 13–15, 17–18). These two women and their respective offspring maintained separate residences and evidently kept their distance from each other.[24]

My mother, Ngan Chi Kit, was the fourth of Ngan Heung Cho's eighteen children, a daughter of his first wife, Ng Shee. Though officially a native of Ngan Bin Village, she was, most likely, born in Guangzhou city, where her father was working. Among her many siblings and half-siblings, she was closest to her two older sisters, Chi Kin 志堅 and Chi Ying 志英, who were born of the same mother as she and who were nos. 2 and 3, respectively, in birth order. They had an older brother named Kei Lok 其樂, who was no. 1 but had died by the mid-1920s. (In the extended Ngan lineage, the boys in the same generation as my mother all shared the character 其 in their given name, and the girls the character 志.) The three sisters also had two younger brothers by the same mother, but they too seem to have died young. With Ng Shee dead by around 1914, the three girls grew up essentially motherless and may have had to look after one another. They were quite close in age, about five or six years apart; according to their father's immigration papers in 1926, Chi Kin was then twenty-one, Chi Ying eighteen, and Chi Kit (my mother) sixteen. At that time, they, together with their father, their stepmother (Wong Shee), and three half-siblings, all lived together at No. 10 Sap Sam Po Street 十三甫路, in Sai Kwan 西關, the "Western Suburbs" of Guangzhou city.[25] Sai Kwan was the bustling area outside the West Gate of the Old City (though the city walls themselves had been torn down a few years earlier, in 1919), and it lay just north of the Anglo-French leasehold of Shameen Island. Nearby was the office of Wing Tai Loong. Until the development of Tung Shan 東山 in the 1920s and early 1930s at the eastern end of the city, Sai Kwan was thought to be the most desirable residential neighborhood in Guangzhou.[26]

Ngan Heung Cho was wealthy and enlightened enough to give all three of his eldest daughters a formal education, at least through middle school. Though born in the last years of the empire, my mother and her two sisters came of age in the 1920s, when China, as a new republic, was undergoing profound cultural and political changes, and Guangzhou, their hometown, was at the forefront of the political and cultural revolution. Women were stepping out from behind the curtain of anonymity that had obscured their mothers. By then foot-binding was no longer practiced, at least among urban elite families like the Ngans; women were bobbing their hair; and formal education for women was beginning to be socially acceptable. In Guangzhou the first middle schools for girls were founded in the mid-1910s.

The Ngan sisters were among the first to attend these new schools for women. Chi Kin (ca. 1903–1972), the eldest of the three, attended Union Normal School (Xiehe shifan xuexiao 協和師範學校) and is listed among the first twenty-one students who graduated in or before 1924. Founded in 1916 in Guangzhou city and relocated in 1922 to Sai Tsuen 西村 in the northern suburbs, Union Normal School was operated by Protestant missionaries from the United States, Canada, and New Zealand. It offered a three-year course to

24. Ngan Ki Ping, personal communications, 17 November and 22 December 2014 and 24 July 2016; Cheong Shun Ngan, personal communication, 18 August 2020.

25. American Consulate General, Canton, "Precis in re Ngan Heung Cho," 2 December 1926, Case File 6500/4-3 (Ngan Heung Cho), Chinese Exclusion Case Files, RG 85, Records of the INS, USNA–S.

26. Edward Bing-Shuey Lee, *Modern Canton* (Shanghai: Mercury Press, 1936), pp. 11, 25, 29.

Figure 1.3: Shameen Island, Sai Kwan, and the Pearl River, June 1932(?). From Folder 7, Box 306, RG 8, Special Collections, YDSL.

Figure 1.4: The Ngan sisters—Chi Kin (front right) and, perhaps, her younger sisters Chi Ying (left) and Chi Kit (right)—and unidentified friends, Guangzhou, early 1920s. Photo courtesy of Luo Ji'er.

prepare graduates to teach in elementary schools.[27] According to one of her sons, Chi Kin, following her graduation, taught at a kindergarten.[28]

My mother, and evidently Chi Ying as well, attended another of Guangzhou's missionary schools, True Light Middle School (Zhenguang zhongxuexiao 真光中學校). This was a boarding school for girls founded in 1917 by American Presbyterian missionaries and located on a new, twelve-acre hilltop campus in the Paak Hok Tung 白鶴洞 suburb, southwest of Guangzhou. It had grown out of a primary day school for girls founded by Harriet (Newell) Noyes in 1868; known as the True Light Seminary, the primary school had remained behind in downtown Guangzhou when the middle school was established at Paak Hok Tung. The social background of most True Light students was like that of my mother; their fathers were generally merchants or businessmen.[29]

True Light was reputedly the premier girls' high school in Guangzhou, perhaps in all of South China. With John W. Creighton as its founding principal, it offered a five-year program divided into three groups of courses: college preparatory, education, and domestic science (or home economics). Its fifth-year class was supposed to be equivalent to the first year of college. In 1923–1924, the middle school enrolled 135 students, with another 145 girls in the Higher Primary Department.[30] A year earlier, one of the first-year middle-school students was named "Ngan Chi Ying," who was identified in the school's YWCA quarterly newspaper as a representative of her class.[31] This "Ngan Chi Ying" was almost certainly my mother's older sister. She is not listed, however, among the school's graduates. Chi Ying may have been a sickly child; according to my father's handwritten genealogy of the Ngan family, she died at age seventeen, which would have been around 1925. This is clearly wrong, but as we shall see, perhaps by only four or five years. My mother did graduate from True Light, in 1927, at age seventeen. If my mother attended the full five years (as was most likely), she would have enrolled at the school in 1922, the same year as Chi Ying.

The years 1922–1927, when my mother was at True Light, were tumultuous ones in the history of Guangzhou and China. Though the Qing dynasty had been overthrown in 1912, the republic that took its place had fallen apart. China was politically and territorially divided among competing warlords and dominated directly and indirectly by various foreign powers. In the early 1920s the Nationalist Party (Guomindang or, formerly, Kuomintang), under Sun Yat-sen, had joined forces with the newly-formed Communist Party to combat these twin evils of warlordism and imperialism. Together the two political parties carved out a foothold in Guangzhou and began under the leadership of Chiang Kai-shek to train and indoctrinate an army. In 1927 the National Revolutionary Army set

27. Mary Raleigh Anderson, *A Cycle in the Celestial Kingdom: Protestant Mission Schools for Girls in South China (1827 to the Japanese Invasion)* (Mobile, AL: Heiter-Starke Printing Co., 1943), pp. 262–264; Guangzhou Xiehe High School, "Xiehe zhi you" 協和之友 [List of graduates], at www.gzxhhs.net/item/131.aspx (last accessed 28 August 2013). In May 2020, the list was no longer accessible to the general public.

28. Luo Ren, "Huan wo fan tanfu de ziyou" 還我反貪腐的自由 [Please restore my freedom to oppose corruption], 16 January 2016, p. 3. This is a draft of a letter (in my possession) addressed to leaders of the Chinese Communist Party; in it he, inter alia, talks about his family background.

29. "The True Light Middle School, Canton China" (a prospectus from late 1921), in Folder F NT6.3 T766p, Presbyterian Historical Society, Philadelphia, PA; Anderson, *A Cycle in the Celestial Kingdom*, p. 202.

30. Anderson, *A Cycle in the Celestial Kingdom*, pp. 99–106, 203–204; J. W. Creighton to Arthur J. Brown, Canton, 2 March 1918, and "Mission Report of True Light Middle School Year of 1923–1924," Folder 12, Box 15, RG 82, Secretaries' Files: China Mission, Presbyterian Church in the USA, Board of Foreign Missions, National Archives of the Presbyterian Church in the USA, Presbyterian Historical Society, Philadelphia, PA.

31. *True Light Y.W.C.A. News Letter*, Vol. 4, No. 1 (November 1922), p. 2, in Folder F NT6.3 T766, Presbyterian Historical Society.

Figure 1.5: True Light Middle School campus, Paak Hok Tung, early 1920s. Photo by Elsie Anderson. From Folder 109a, Box 17, RG 175, Special Collections, YDSL.

Figure 1.6: Some True Light students in the early 1920s. Photo probably by Elsie Anderson. From Folder 109a, Box 17, RG 175, Special Collections, YDSL.

out for the north to defeat the warlords; by 1928 it had nominally reunified the country. By then, however, Chiang and the Nationalists had turned against their Communist allies.

Until then, in Guangzhou itself the Nationalists and the Communists together had been mobilizing the local population against the various manifestations of exploitation by the foreign powers. The missionaries and the churches, schools, and hospitals the foreigners founded and operated were one highly visible set of symbols of their special presence in China, particularly since their nationals at that time enjoyed the privilege of "extraterritoriality"; that is, though living and working in China, they were subject to their home countries' laws and not those of China. Another locally visible symbol of foreign imperialism was Shameen, the small man-made island adjacent to the commercial heart of Guangzhou, which was governed and policed by the British and the French and over which the Chinese had no control. Though often described as a foreign "concession" (like the International Settlement in Shanghai), Shameen was technically a leasehold. For, as journalist Edward Bing-Shuey Lee observed in 1936, "a small ground rent is paid annually by [Shameen's] landowners to the Chinese government, although it has its own bye-laws, municipal council and police." Moreover, unlike in Shanghai's International Settlement, Chinese were barred from buying or renting property on Shameen.[32]

The high point of this anti-imperialist nationalism came in the middle of 1925 with the May Thirtieth Movement, a response to the shooting of several dozen unarmed Chinese protesters by the British police in Shanghai. A month later, on 23 June, at a

Figure 1.7: Anti-British demonstrations, Guangzhou, 23 June 1925. Students marching down the Bund on their way to Shameen. Note the numerous sampans moored along the shore of the Pearl River. From Folder 642, Box 57, RG 14, Special Collections, YDSL.

---

32. Johnathan Andrew Farris, *Enclave to Urbanity: Canton, Foreigners, and Architecture from the Late Eighteenth to the Early Twentieth Centuries* (Hong Kong: Hong Kong University Press, 2016), ch. 2 and pp. 190–204; Lee, *Modern Canton*, p. 28.

large and noisy sympathy demonstration in Guangzhou, yet more Chinese (including a professor and a student from Lingnan University) were shot and killed by the British and French as they marched down Shakee Road 沙基路 (now renamed 六二三路 or June 23rd Road) opposite Shameen Island. This Shakee Massacre led to a year-long strike-boycott in the Guangzhou–Hong Kong region against the British and, more generally, against all foreigners.[33]

Despite its remote location in the southwestern suburbs, True Light Middle School was not immune from the political turmoil in Guangzhou city. In 1925, after the initial shooting incident in Shanghai at the end of May, the school moved up the commencement ceremony and hurriedly sent the students home. A month later, after the Shakee Massacre, the school closed up altogether and all the foreign teachers left the country; the school would not reopen until the end of October. Even then the school continued to be hit by strikes. In late November 1925, home economics teacher Jean Macpherson (1916–1980) wrote to her mother, "*All* our servants left today. It leaves us with a great deal of work—dishes, meals, laundry etc. . . . Every servant in P.H.T. [Paak Hok Tung] left— forced out by the Strike Union in Canton. . . . It will be good practice for us to cook and take care of ourselves again. It will . . . also show the students we aren't afraid of work." The school's principal summarized the situation at the end of the 1925–1926 school year: "General unrest, anti-Christian tendencies, anti-foreign propaganda, a labor movement influenced if not actually directed by extreme radicalism have produced a situation trying in the extreme."[34] My mother, who would have been a middle school junior then, could not have been unaffected by all these disturbances. However, she was most likely not a political activist.

In addition to political revolution, the 1920s were a decade of intellectual and cultural revolution, at least in urban areas, where the hegemony of Confucianism was being overthrown and replaced by "Mr. Science and Mr. Democracy." This was the May Fourth Movement, sometimes referred to as the Chinese Enlightenment, one key aspect of which was the emancipation of women. As described by historian Wang Zheng, "the proposed norms for an emancipated woman—that is, the new woman . . . included an education that would make her a conscious modern citizen as well as secure her an occupation; an independent personhood, which meant financial self-reliance and autonomy in decisions concerning marriage, career, and so on; a capacity to participate in public life; and a concern for other oppressed women."[35] My mother attended True Light at precisely the time when these new, revolutionary ideas were percolating. Many of the attributes of the emancipated woman definitely applied to her. She would have been among the "new women" who were beginning to emerge in the 1920s.

---

33. Michael Tsin, *Nation, Governance, and Modernity in China: Canton, 1900–1927* (Stanford: Stanford University Press, 1999), pp. 151–156; "Memorial Minute on the Death of Professor Au Lai Chau and Student Hui Su Cheung Killed in a Patriotic Procession, Canton, June 23, 1925," Minutes of a Special Meeting of the Trustees of Lingnan University, 10 September 1925, Folder 3229, Box 178, China College Files—Lingnan University, RG 11, United Board for Christian Higher Education in Asia Archives, Special Collections, YDSL.

34. Jean Macpherson, [Paak Hok Tung], to Mother, 8 June 1925, to Father and Mother, 14 June 1925, to Mother, Thanksgiving Day 1925, Folder 9, Box 1, RG 193, Pommerenke Family Papers, 1907–1980, Presbyterian Historical Society; "The True Light Middle School, The Report of the Principal, June 1926," Folder 12, Box 15, RG 82, Secretaries' Files: China Mission, Presbyterian Board of Foreign Missions, Presbyterian Historical Society. Macpherson later married Presbyterian missionary Herbert H. Pommerenke.

35. Wang Zheng, *Women in the Chinese Enlightenment: Oral and Textual Histories* (Berkeley: University of California Press, 1999), p. 16.

Figure 1.8: Western teachers at True Light, early 1920s. Photo probably by Elsie Anderson. From Folder 109a, Box 17, RG 175, Special Collections, YDSL Jean Macpherson is #4; Sarah ("Sally") Flaniken is #2.

    The teaching staff at True Light Middle School included a number of young American women. In 1923–1924, out of twenty-seven teachers, nine were Americans (of whom five were full-time).[36] Except for courses in Chinese literature, the language of instruction at the school was English. Though my mother had probably begun the study of English with her father, it was most likely at True Light, studying with the American instructors, that she acquired her proficiency in spoken and written English. The school taught typing and probably stenography as well; my mother took the school's course in typewriting in her last two years.[37]

    True Light was well-known for its music program. It was among "the first mission institutions in Canton to stress training in music." The glee club as well as piano recitals arranged by its music department were well attended by "music lovers from various parts of the city."[38] One such concert, in March 1925, presented the Latvian pianist Harry Ore and an unidentified Russian cellist. Ore had studied piano and composition at the Conservatory in Saint Petersburg, Russia, where he was a schoolmate of the composer Sergei Prokofiev. In the late 1910s he had come to China and East Asia on tour, and there he stayed, living in Hong Kong after 1921.[39] My mother would later study with Ore and was a competent pianist. It is possible that she had begun to play the piano at True Light and that her association with Harry Ore dated from that time.

36. "Mission Report of True Light Middle School Year of 1923–1924," Folder 12, Box 15, RG 82, Secretaries' Files: China Mission, Presbyterian Board of Foreign Missions, Presbyterian Historical Society.

37. "Mission Report of True Light Middle School Year of 1923–1924" and "Some Things We Teach at the True Light Middle School," Folder 12, Box 15, RG 82, Secretaries Files: China Mission, Presbyterian Board of Foreign Missions, Presbyterian Historical Society; CKR's application for librarian training, East Longmeadow, MA, 26 October 1964, in my sister's possession.

38. Anderson, *A Cycle in the Celestial Kingdom*, p. 103; "Some Things We Teach," Folder 12, Box 15, RG 82, Secretaries' Files: China Mission, Presbyterian Board of Foreign Missions, Presbyterian Historical Society.

39. Jean Macpherson, [Paak Hok Tung], to Mother and Father, 5 March 1925, and to Mother, 23 March 1925, Folder 9, Box 1, RG 193, Pommerenke Family Papers, Presbyterian Historical Society; on Harry Ore, see "HK's Top Musician is Dead," *South China Morning Post,* 7 April 1972, p. 1, and Maksis Čulītis, "No Pēterpils Līdz Hongkongai" [From St. Petersburg to Hong Kong], *Jaunā Gaita* [The New Course], no. 80 (1970). This last article is available online and translated by Google from Latvian.

Figure 1.10: A student in typing, probably Guangzhou, early 1920s. Photo by Elsie Anderson. From Anderson Photograph Collection of YWCA in China, 1920s–1940s, East Asian Library Special Collections, Stanford University.

Figure 1.9: "A Student in Shorthand," probably Guangzhou, early 1920s. Photo by Elsie Anderson. From Anderson Photograph Collection of YWCA in China, 1920s–1940s, East Asian Library Special Collections, Stanford University.

True Light was a Protestant school whose stated purpose was "to train Chinese young women for christian [*sic*] lives of service in the home and society." Most of the students were said to come from Christian homes and were themselves Christians. "Christian" here, most likely, meant Protestant, yet my mother had been raised a Catholic. Father Joseph A. Hahn (1912–1993), a Maryknoll priest who taught at Lingnan between 1948 and 1951, mentioned in passing that my mother along with an unnamed sister had been "baptized in their village near Fatshan [referring, undoubtedly, to Ngan Bin] many years ago," but that both had "left the Church" later on.[40]

It is possible that my mother "left the [Catholic] Church" while at True Light, for those students who were not Protestant were subjected to enormous peer pressure to convert. The school's principal noted that "all girls attend Bible classes on Sunday,

40. "The True Light Middle School, Canton China [1921]", in Folder F NT6.3 T766p, Presbyterian Historical Society; Anderson, *A Cycle in the Celestial Kingdom*, p. 202; Joseph A. Hahn, Diary Report for December 1950 (also first part of January 1951), p. 10, Folder 2, Box 1, Series 1: China, Mission Diaries, 1918–1969, Maryknoll Mission Archives, Maryknoll, NY.

although they are not compelled to do so. Public opinion, overwhelmingly favorable to these meetings, exerts the pressure." The school also held, near the end of each academic year, a campus-wide Decision Week, during which the students were encouraged to "sign their cards." Regarding one such occasion, in early June 1925, home economics teacher Jean Macpherson wrote that of the six Third Year middle-school girls with whom she had been meeting, only two had signed. Of the four holdouts, she was hopeful "if we pray earnestly enough that some day they will be won."[41] My mother would have been a member of the Third Year class in June 1925, and perhaps she was one of the students with whom Macpherson had been meeting. If so, would she have signed her card and been "won"? Or would she have been among the holdouts? It was not until 1930, after the Nationalists had come to power nationally and True Light had registered with the Chinese government, that "religious instruction in the school was forbidden."[42]

In 1927, the year her father traveled to the United States on behalf of the Wing Tai Loong Silk Company, my mother graduated from True Light Middle School, one of twenty-one graduates in her class.[43] Previously, young women from well-to-do families had not pursued professional careers; instead they married and produced children to perpetuate the husband's family line. The "new women" of the 1920s, by contrast, were stepping out into the world. According to a contemporary survey of the roughly 262 graduates of True Light from 1919 to 1933 (with overlapping statistics), 159 had continued their studies, either abroad or in China; 76 were teaching; 9 had done social work; 18 had done secretarial work; and 57 had married.[44] My mother did not go on to college, nor did she, unlike her older sister, Chi Kin, take up teaching. Instead, she became a secretary.

In the summer of 1933, six years after graduation, my mother, then twenty-three years old, found herself working at Lingnan University. Lingnan was an English-language institution founded in 1888 by American Presbyterian missionaries. Originally called (in English) Canton Christian College, it began offering true college-level courses in 1916, and in 1918 it granted its first degrees, which were formally issued by the Regents of the University of the State of New York, by which the college was accredited. In 1927, in response to the rise of Chinese nationalism, the Americans who heretofore had run the school yielded formal control to Chinese administrators and the school was renamed Lingnan University 嶺南大學. Thereafter the president of the university was Chinese, while an American (James M. Henry [1880–1958]) served as the provost and concurrently the resident representative of the New York–based Board of Trustees of Lingnan University. Known in China as the American Foundation (Meiguo jijinhui 美國基金會), the Board of Trustees held title to the campus land and buildings, but had leased them to

---

41. "Mission Report of True Light Middle School Year of 1923–1924," Folder 12, Box 15, RG 82, Secretaries' Files: China Mission, Presbyterian Board of Foreign Missions; Jean Macpherson to Mother, [Paak Hok Tung], 1 June 1925, Folder 9, Box 1, RG 193, Pommerenke Family Papers, both in Presbyterian Historical Society; Muriel Lockwood Refo, "Midwest China Oral History Interviews" (1980), *China Oral Histories*, Book 94, http://digitalcommons.luthersem.edu/china_histories/94 (accessed 17 October 2019), pp. 13–14. Muriel Lockwood taught at True Light from 1927 to 1931.

42. "True Light Middle School, Canton Station, South China Mission, September 1932 [Annual Report]," Folder 12, Box 15, RG 82, Secretaries' Files: China Mission, Presbyterian Board of Foreign Missions, Presbyterian Historical Society.

43. Guangzhou True Light High School, "Xiaoyou zhi jia" 校友之家 [List of graduates], http://www.gztims.com/140/newsdis.asp?id=62 (last accessed 29 August 2013). In May 2020, the school's website was no longer accessible to the general public.

44. Anderson, *A Cycle in the Celestial Kingdom*, p. 205; see also Muriel Lockwood Refo, "Midwest China Oral History Interviews," pp. 15–16.

a local Board of Directors that was predominantly Chinese for a nominal rent of one US dollar per year. The administrative head of the Board of Trustees in New York, otherwise known as the American Director, was Olin D. Wannamaker (1875–1974), who had taught English at Lingnan from 1902 to 1908.[45]

Putting to use the English-language and typing and stenographic skills she had acquired at True Light, my mother was hired to be James Henry's secretary in the office of the American Foundation. Up until then, the American trustees had sent out an American woman to serve as the resident director's secretary. But with the onset of the Great Depression they had turned to a less expensive local hire. My mother's senior colleague at the American Foundation was Tong Fuk Cheung 唐福祥 (1893–1953), who was the *de facto* office manager. Famed as a soccer player—he was the captain of China's first national team and later the team's coach—Tong also headed Lingnan's Department of Physical Education.[46]

The first letter that my mother typed for James Henry and which carried the typist tag "JMH/CKN" was dated 17 July 1933. For the next six months, Henry's correspondence with New York usually carried this tag or was signed for him "Per C. K. Ngan." But then this stopped: his subsequent letters carried no tag at all. The reason why is not known; nevertheless, it is clear that my mother continued as Henry's secretary for at least the next three years. She would take dictation from him, type up a draft of the letter, show it to him to make revisions and correct typographical errors, and then type up the final letter for signing and mailing. As he explained in a handwritten postscript to one of his letters, "When I can reread Miss Ngan's letters long enough ahead [of time] I can avoid a good deal [of mistakes] but sometimes as in this case it's impossible & the corrections (some I fear) have to be made in the final letter."[47] As the secretary to James Henry, she was privy to much that was going on at the university. The annual salary of the resident director's secretary, which though staffed locally was paid by the New York trustees, was HK$1,500 (or US$600), which was not much less than my father's salary of HK$1,800 (US$720) when he was hired in 1936 as an English professor.[48]

At some point in the mid-1930s my mother got married. By then, as a consequence of the ongoing cultural revolution, it was no longer the norm, at least among the urban elite, for marriages to be arranged by families without regard to the preferences of the bride and groom. That said, the interests of the respective families could not be ignored; in particular, the two families had to be social equals. In 1929, for example, my mother's older sister Chi Kin had married into the family of Loh Keng Chuen 羅鏡泉 (1861–1932) of neighboring Panyu County. Loh Keng Chuen, much like Chi Kin's own father, through

---

45. On the history of Lingnan University, see Charles Hodge Corbett, *Lingnan University: A Short History Based on the Records of the University's American Trustees* (New York: Trustees of Lingnan University, 1963) and Dong Wang, *Managing God's Higher Learning: U.S. China Cultural Encounter and Canton Christian College (Lingnan University), 1888–1952* (Lanham, MD: Lexington Books, 2007); on Wannamaker, see Henry Barnes, *Into the Heart's Land: A Century of Rudolph Steiner's Work in North America* (Great Barrington, MA: SteinerBooks, 2005), ch. 8.
46. Xie Dingchu, "Lingda 'Meijihui' de Tang Fuqiang" [Tong Fuk Cheung at Lingnan University's American Foundation], *Guangzhou wenshi ziliao*, no. 13 (1964): 125–128; JamesTalk, "Zhongguo guojiadui shouren duizhang, Li Huitang zhiqiande 'Yuandong qiuwang', Tang Fuxiang" [The first captain of China's national team and Li Huitang's predecessor as "Football King of the Far East," Tong Fuk Cheung] (2019), https://www.dongqiudi.com/archive/953232.himl (accessed 20 October 2019).
47. James M. Henry to ODW, Canton, 17 July 1933, Box 58, and 20 February 1934, Box 60, TLUA–HYL.
48. "Field Budget 1936–1937: Salaries, Allowances, Etc.," 13 May 1936, Box 148, TLUA–HYL, where my father's line in the budget was as Ruth McCullough's replacement. His compensation, however, also included an annual "reserve" of US$100 as well as other benefits.

Figure 1.11: Ngan Chi Kin and Loh Ying Ho's wedding, Guangzhou, 30 September 1929. Photo courtesy of Luo Ji'er.

frugality and hard work had famously parleyed a paltry bequest of twelve copper coins into a vast business network. Indeed, he and Ngan Heung Cho were business associates in the Wing Tai Loong Silk Company. No less famously, Loh Keng Chuen had fathered forty children (by three wives and, possibly, a few other women).[49]

Ngan Chi Kin's fiancé Loh Ying Ho 羅英豪 (1901–1972) was Loh Keng Chuen's thirteenth child. A returned student, he had been sent abroad in 1922 to study, initially in Germany. Because of the chaotic conditions in postwar Europe he had moved to the United States after one year. (Students, like merchants, were exempt from the Chinese Exclusion laws.) He started out at the University of Illinois, then in 1925 transferred to the University of Michigan, from which he graduated in 1927 with a bachelor's degree in mechanical engineering. Soon after returning to China, Loh Ying Ho went to work for his father and his future father-in-law at the Wing Tai Loong Silk Company as an "investigator." He and Ngan Chi Kin were married two years later, on 30 September 1929, after her father had returned from his 1927–1928 business trip to the United States. Later, when she was asked about the wedding, Chi Kin described it as "partly new and partly old": two elderly gentlemen—one of whom was Shum Kwok Wah, the founder of Wing Tai Loong—had "officiated at the ceremonies," after which "we went home and I worshipped at my husband's ancestors."[50]

---

49. He Xuehua, "Guangdong yijiazu liangdai chule 65-ge daxuesheng 4-wei kang-Ri jiangling" [A Guangdong family in two generations produced 65 university students and 4 anti-Japanese military leaders], *Xinxi shibao* [Information times], 31 August 2003, news.eastday.com (last accessed 3 June 2020); Luo Ren, "Huan wo fan tanfu de ziyou," p. 3.

50. American Consulate General, Canton, "Precis in re Loh Ying Ho," 28 October 1930, Case File 7029/19 (Loh Ying Ho), and transcript of hearing, "in the Matter of Ngan Chi Kin and Loh Chee Man," Seattle, 29 November 1930, Case File 7031/149 (Ngan Chi Kin), Chinese Exclusion Case Files, RG 85, Records of the INS, USNA–S; Luo Ren, "Huan wo fan tanfu de ziyou," p. 3. On Loh Ying Ho's arrival in the US in 1923, see Passenger Search at the website

Figure 1.12: The groom and bride and her two bridesmaids, Chi Ying (left) and Chi Kit (detail).

The photograph of Ngan Chi Kin and Loh Ying Ho's wedding is a fascinating document. The bride is wearing a Western-style white wedding gown, with a crown of flowers and a veil, and holding a floral bouquet; the groom is dressed in a tuxedo with a boutonniere on his lapel and is clutching a pair of white gloves and a top hat. Standing next to her, also dressed in white and holding bouquets, are her two bridesmaids: the one slightly toward the back is my mother, and the other in front is most likely their sister Chi Ying. Also in the photograph are the fathers of the wedding couple; they are the two older men seated in the front row on the groom's side, with Ngan Heung Cho on the outside and Loh Keng Chuen on the inside. Seated in the front row on the opposite side should have been the two mothers, but both Chi Kin's mother, Ng Shee, and Ying Ho's mother, Woo Shee, were dead by then. So, who are the two elderly women sitting there? A marked-up copy of the wedding photograph in the possession of the Loh family identifies the woman sitting on the inside, the place for the mother of the groom, as "3 祖母" (*san zumu*, or third granny), that is, Loh Keng Chuen's third (and last) principal wife, hence Loh Ying Ho's stepmother. This suggests that the other woman might be Wong Shee, Ngan Heung Cho's thirty-seven-year-old concubine and Chi Kin's step-mother, except that the woman in the photograph looks to be a much older person. Nor does the woman look like Ho Mo Kun, Ngan Heung Cho's fourth wife, which indicates that they were not yet married as of Chi Kin's wedding in 1929. In short, it is unclear who that woman is. Finally, the young boy in the front row standing next to Ngan Heung Cho is probably Kei Chee (better known in later life as Ngan Po Ming 顏寶明), his oldest surviving son; born in 1917 and no. 7 in birth order, Kei Chee would then have been about eleven years old. The little girl standing in front of Loh Ying Ho's stepmother is Loh Keng Chuen's fortieth child.[51]

---

of the Statue of Liberty–Ellis Island Foundation, libertyellisfoundation.org (last accessed 4 June 2020); and on his attendance at the Universities of Illinois and Michigan: Cara Setsu Bertram, of the University Archives at the University of Illinois at Urbana-Champaign, to ER, 21 November 2014, and University of Michigan, *Register* (Ann Arbor) for 1924–1925, 1925–1926, and 1926–1927.

51. On Loh Ying Ho's mother, see transcript of hearing, "in the Matter of Ngan Chi Kin and Loh Chee Man," Seattle, 29 November 1930, Case File 7031/149 (Ngan Chi Kin), Chinese Exclusion Case Files, RG 85, Records of the INS, USNA–S; on Kei Chee, Ngan Ki Ping, personal communication, 29 March 2015.

Figure 1.13: Fathers of the groom and bride, Loh Keng Chuen (left) and Ngan Heung Cho (detail).

Figure 1.14: "Mothers" of the groom and bride (detail).

Other members of the Loh and Ngan families make up most (perhaps all) of the rest of the people in the photograph.

In 1930, a year after his wedding, Loh Ying Ho was sent by Wing Tai Loong to New York City to reopen the company's American agency. That agency, founded by his father-in-law, had ceased operations on Ngan Heung Cho's return to China; nevertheless, in the intervening couple of years Wing Tai Loong had kept up its membership in the Silk Association of America. In 1931–1932, Wing Tai Loong had an address at 152 East 27th Street, which was also Loh Ying Ho's address in the telephone directory. (This was a block away from where Ngan Heung Cho had lived.) Ying Ho's wife Chi Kin and their infant son Luo Wen 羅文 (1930–2015) accompanied him to New York. (As the wife and child of a "Section 6 Merchant," they too were exempt from Chinese Exclusion Laws.) A year and a half later, mother and son returned to Guangzhou, where Chi Kin gave birth to her second son, Luo Ren 羅仁. Loh Ying Ho, travelling home by way of England and Europe (as his father-in-law probably had done), rejoined them in 1933.[52] A third child, Luo Ji'er 羅季兒 (d. 2018), was born, in Guangzhou, in 1934. Chi Kin's three children were to be very close to my family and to me.

In contrast to Chi Kin's wedding, practically nothing is known about my mother's; there are no photographs, no family memories. The only thing known is the name of the groom, Chan Cheuk Ming. He would likely have had a similar family and educational background and employment as Chi Kin's husband. The first character in his given name—爵 written with a "standing heart" 忄 radical—is so arcane that it cannot be found in most dictionaries, which suggests that he came from a literary family.[53] (His name

---

52. Case Files 7029/19 (Loh Ying Ho) and 7031/149 (Ngan Chi Kin), Chinese Exclusion Case Files, RG 85, Records of the INS, USNA–S; Silk Association of America, *60th Annual Report* (1931–1932), p. 39; *New York City Telephone Directory*, Manhattan, White Pages, 1931–1932, p. 606; United Kingdom, Incoming Passenger Lists, 1878–1960, under Loh Ying Ho (available at ancestry.com).

53. The character appears in the authoritative Kangxi Dictionary, where its pronunciation is given as *jiao* and not, as one might have expected, *jue* [or *cheuk* in Cantonese], which nevertheless is how it seems to have been pronounced.

is sometimes written with the more common "fire" radical: 陳爛明.) Depending on her in-laws' social and economic status, my mother too may have had a big, formal wedding like Chi Kin's. On the other hand, Chi Kin had married just as the Great Depression was about to hit—her wedding on 30 September 1929 took place almost exactly one month before the stock market crash on Wall Street—and by the early 1930s the Great Depression had seriously crimped their father's silk business. Ngan Heung Cho was never to recover fully from these financial losses. Presumably his associates, including perhaps Chan Cheuk Ming's father, had been similarly affected. So it is also possible that my mother, unlike Chi Kin, did not marry well and did not get a big, formal wedding.

It is also unclear precisely when the wedding took place. It undoubtedly would have been held after her eldest sister Chi Kin's wedding in 1929 and probably after elder sister Chi Ying's early death around 1929–1930. When Chi Kin was interrogated by US immigration officials in November 1930, she was asked if she had any siblings; she replied, "One younger sister," whom she identified as "Ngon Gee Git, 20 years old, not married." In other words, by then Chi Ying was no longer alive.[54] My mother still may not have been married in 1933 and 1934, when she began working at Lingnan. At the office, she was known as "Miss Ngan," and in the university's staff directory for October 1934 she was listed as unmarried and living in the northeastern section of the campus in Building no. 53, or Bradley House, which accommodated single women among the faculty and staff.[55]

By August 1935, however, my mother was being called "Mrs. Chan," and in the October 1936 staff directory for the university she was described as living, presumably with her husband, off campus in Guangzhou city at 15 Man Tak East Road 文德東路, 4/F. Conveniently located near the foot of Man Tak Road was the Tin Tze wharf 天子碼 頭, which was served by the motor launch that ferried passengers across the Pearl River between the city and the Lingnan campus. (There were also plenty of sampans—small wooden boats propelled manually by poles and oars—that offered ferry service on demand.) Finally, in the 1936–1937 bilingual yearbook for the Women's International Club of Canton, a city-wide social organization to which my mother belonged, she was listed as both "Mrs. Chan Ngan Chi Kit" (in English) and Mrs. Chan Cheuk Ming 陳爛明 夫人 (in Chinese). According to historian Wang Zheng, a compound last name such as "Chan Ngan" was another sign of the "progressive" new woman.[56] It thus appears that my mother's marriage to Chan Cheuk Ming took place sometime in 1934–1935.

The marriage did not last. Perhaps it had been an arranged marriage after all, and one that had not worked. Divorce in traditional Chinese society was rare. When a marriage was troubled, the husband was not supposed to cast aside his principal wife, but he could take one or more concubines. The wife, by contrast, was stuck. As sociologist (and Lingnan professor) C. K. Yang explains, "there was no institutional ground upon which a woman could obtain a divorce. Should she become dissatisfied with the marriage, even on justifiable grounds such as extremely cruel treatment, she was advised to tolerate the

---

54. Transcript of hearing, "in the Matter of Ngan Chi Kin and Loh Chee Man," Seattle, 29 November 1930, Case File 7031/149 (Ngan Chi Kin), Chinese Exclusion Case Files, RG 85, Records of the INS, USNA–S.
55. "List of Staff, Lingnan University," 1 October 1934, Folder Miscellaneous–Lingnan University 1/3, Box 66, Collection No. 1192, William Warder Cadbury & Catherine Jones Cadbury Papers, Quaker Collection, Haverford College Library, Haverford, PA.
56. Henry S. Frank to ODW, Canton, 19 August 1935, Box 64, TLUA–HYL; "List of Staff, Lingnan University," 12 October 1936, Folder Miscellaneous—Lingnan University 1/3, Box 66, and "The Women's International Club of Canton, Year Book for 1936–1937," in Folder International Women's Club of Canton, Box 67, Collection No. 1192, Cadbury & Cadbury Papers, Haverford College Library; Wang, *Women in the Chinese Enlightenment*, p. 136, n. 23.

situation and preserve family unity by exercising forbearance and self-sacrifice and by resignation to fate." By the early 1930s, however, as another outcome of the family revolution and the emancipation of women, divorce, while still rare, was now possible. "After half a century of agitation and struggle," Yang writes, "the right of divorce for both men and women had gained acceptance at least among the new intelligentsia." This right had been incorporated into the kinship law promulgated by the new Nationalist government in 1930. Indeed, according to historian Lynn Pan, "the Chinese divorce law surpassed the German and Swiss codes after which it was modelled, as well as the codes of contemporary England, France and the United States, in having a 'no fault' mutual consent provision in addition to the usual grounds."[57]

An American lawyer in Shanghai, Norwood F. Allman, described the separation process: "If a Chinese husband and wife can't agree to live together they simply agree to disagree. They can obtain a divorce by a simple written agreement to that effect without any court action whatsoever." This is precisely what my mother and her husband did. On 22 February 1937, in the presence of two (named) witnesses, Ngan Chi Kit and Chan Cheuk Ming signed a short document stating that for the duration of their marriage there had never been any feeling of affection between the two of them and that they feared it would be difficult for them to grow old together. Accordingly, they had agreed, voluntarily and without conditions, to terminate their relationship as wife and husband and to go their separate ways. The document, of which there were two copies, one for each party, was affixed with four ten-cent "revenue stamps" of the National government, as if it had been registered with some government agency.[58]

They had been married no more than two or three years. There were no children from the marriage. My mother's previous marriage was never mentioned in our family. I did not find out about it until after my parents had died, when I was going through some of her papers and came upon the divorce agreement.

---

57. C. K. Yang, *The Chinese Family in the Communist Revolution* (Cambridge: MIT Press, 1959), pp. 64–67; Lynn Pan, *When True Love Came to China* (Hong Kong: Hong Kong University Press, 2015), p. 232.

58. Norwood F. Allman, *Shanghai Lawyer* (New York and London: McGraw-Hill, 1943), p. 187; CKR's divorce paper, 22 February 1937, in my personal collection.

2

My Father

My father, Howard Garrett Rhoads, was nine years older than my mother. Born in Philadelphia, Pennsylvania, on 27 July 1900, he was the only child of John Franklin Rhoads (1866–1926) and Annie Louisa Garrett (1866–1935). He was always proud to claim descent from Dr. Thomas Wynne, a Quaker from Flintshire, Wales, who was the personal physician of William Penn, the founder of Pennsylvania. Charles II of England, in part as a reward for meritorious services that Penn's father, an admiral, had rendered the king during the Restoration, had granted him a vast tract of land in America in the Delaware River region, to be called the "province of Pennsylvania." Wynne and other Quakers fleeing religious persecution in Britain had come with Penn in 1682 aboard the ship *Welcome* to take possession of that land. The basis of my father's claim is that Dr. Thomas Wynne was the great-great-great-grandfather of Elizabeth Wynne (1792–1874), whose daughter, Ann Davy Rose (1833–1898), was Annie Garrett's mother.[1] Annie's father was Thomas Garrett (1829–1877), a blacksmith who at least in his later years may have worked in the car shop of the Pennsylvania Railroad.[2] Annie was not yet a teenager when her father died in 1877. She and her older sister, Sarah Elizabeth (1860–1931), were brought up by their widowed mother.[3]

On his paternal side, my father came from a large, relatively well-to-do family in Harrisburg, the capital of Pennsylvania. His father, John Franklin Rhoads, was the third child—and second son—of John Rhoads (1839–1896) and Elizabeth (Cummings) Rhoads (1842–1901), who went on to have altogether nine children.[4] The senior John Rhoads was a veteran of the American Civil War, who had enlisted not once but three separate times to fight for the Union; as he wrote later on, "the Battle of Fredericksburg Virginia

---

1. On Dr. Thomas Wynne and his descendants down to Elizabeth Wynne and her husband William Rose, see George E. McCracken, *The Welcome Claimants, Proved, Disproved and Doubtful, with an Account of Some of their Descendants* (Baltimore: Genealogical Publishing Company, 1970), pp. 561–587, and Lynn Larsen and Becky Thill, *Dr. Thomas Wynne's Legacy* (New York: TFG Press, 2002), esp. pp. 125–132. The line of descent is as follows: Dr. Wynne (b. 1627) → Jonathan Wynne (b. 1669) → Thomas Wynne (b. 1695) → Lt. Thomas Wynne (b. 1733) → Thomas Wynne (b. 1763) → Elizabeth Wynne (b. 1792) → Ann Davy Rose (b. 1833) → Annie L. Garrett (b. 1866) → HGR (b. 1900).
2. US Federal Census, Pennsylvania, Philadelphia County, for 1850 (West Philadelphia, p. 509B), 1860 (5th Precinct of 24th Ward, p. 36) and 1870 (District 78, p. 39); *Philadelphia City Directory*, 1855 to 1876; "Died [Thomas Garrett]," *Public Ledger* (Philadelphia), 15 November 1877, [p. 2].
3. US Federal Census, 1880, Pennsylvania, Philadelphia County, District 497, p. 15. An older sister, Emma (born ca. 1856), died sometime before the 1870 census.
4. Ray Rhoads, "Pennsylvania Family Group Record for Daniel Rhoads (1815–1872) and Susan Russel (1821–1881)," http://www.fgs-project.com/pennsylvania/r/rhoads-d.txt (last accessed 24 May 2020). Daniel Rhoads was John Rhoads's father.

J. R. LAUGHLIN, 3518 MARKET ST., WEST PHILAD'A

Figure 2.1: The Garrett sisters, Annie Louisa (left) and Sarah Elizabeth ("Sallie"), ca. 1873. Studio photograph, J. R. Laughlin, West Philadelphia.

[in December 1862] was the most important event in the history of my service."[5] In civilian life John Rhoads was a businessman with wide-ranging interests. His first two sets of discharge papers from the Pennsylvania Volunteers, in 1861 and 1863, state that he was a confectioner, as does the 1880 federal census. His 1865 discharge papers and the 1870 census describe him, however, as a "car inspector," while the Harrisburg city directories in the late 1870s list his occupation as a "transportation master."[6] Whatever a "transportation master" is, it suggests that (like his son's future father-in-law, Thomas Garrett) he too may have worked, though in an administrative capacity, for the Pennsylvania Railroad, which was a major employer in the state. In addition, John Rhoads was an inventor; between November 1865 and 1895, he patented at least eight inventions, all of them relating to railroad cars.[7] Sometime in the early 1880s, John and Elizabeth Rhoads and their growing

5. *Personal War Sketches, Grand Army of the Republic, Courtland Saunders Post No. 21, Department of Pennsylvania*, 3: 68, Collection No. 1574, Historical Society of Pennsylvania, Philadelphia.

6. Ray Rhoads, personal communication, 8 August 2013; US Federal Census, 1870, Pennsylvania, Dauphin County, p. 78, and 1880, Pennsylvania, Dauphin County, District 90, p. 47; *Harrisburg City Directory*, 1876–1877, p. 270, 1878–1879, p. 228, and 1880–1882, p. 234, ancestryheritagequest.com.

7. See the US Patent and Trademark Office, "USPTO Full-Text and Image Database," http://patft.uspto.gov (last accessed 4 June 2020), for patents no. 51,093 (1865), 105,980 (1870), 164,330 (1875), 184,664 (1876), 290,356 (1883), 298,298 (1884), 442,238 (1890), and 552,448 (1895).

family moved from Harrisburg to Philadelphia, where he became, according to the city directories, a "superintendent" of an unnamed organization, possibly the Penn Gas Coal company, a subsidiary of the Pennsylvania Railroad. He also founded, in 1886, a carpet cleaning and storage company named after himself.[8]

John Franklin Rhoads, then twenty years old, went to work for his father's new carpet cleaning company as a "clerk" and "bookkeeper." He was to be associated with the John Rhoads Company for the rest of his life. After the death of his father in 1896 and his mother in 1901, ownership of the company passed jointly to him and his older brother, Daniel Carson Rhoads (1860–1927). He became the company's manager and, later, around 1908, its proprietor, while his brother served as an "estimator."[9]

Annie Louisa Garrett and John Franklin Rhoads, both twenty-four years old, were married on 24 June 1890 at her mother's home. For the first years of their marriage—until John Franklin Rhoads had become manager of the carpet cleaning and storage company, or possibly even until Ann Davy (Rose) Garrett's death in 1898—they lived with Annie's widowed mother at her house.[10] My father was born ten years after his parents' marriage. Of his grandparents, only Elizabeth (Cummings) Rhoads was alive at the time of his birth, and she died less than a year later.

Philadelphia at that time was the third-largest city in the United States.[11] My father grew up in West Philadelphia, the part of the city across the Schuylkill River from downtown. West Philadelphia today is one of the poorer sections of the city, with 75 percent of its population African-American, a consequence of the Great Migration from the southern United States. At the turn of the twentieth century, however, it was a "streetcar suburb" populated by white professional and middle-class families.[12] Annie Garrett had grown up on the first (or "unit") block of North 41st Street, while John Franklin Rhoads, after his family's relocation from Harrisburg, had lived at 4003 Spring Garden Street. The John Rhoads Company was located in the 700 block of North Holly Street. The modest two-story rowhouse my father lived in for most of his early life—a typical middle-class residence in West Philadelphia—was at 769 North 44th Street. It was a house that his mother bought in 1904 and held until after her husband's death. (The deed unambiguously states that the owner of the house was Annie Louisa Garrett Rhoads, not her husband and not jointly.)[13] All of these places were located within a small area of Philadelphia's Twenty-Fourth Ward—bounded by Market Street on the south, Lancaster Avenue on the north, 40th Street on the east, and 44th Street on the west. Lancaster Avenue—known locally as the Lancaster Pike or, simply, the Pike—and Market Street

8. *Philadelphia City Directory*, 1884 and 1886, 1891, 1895 and 1896; "Mrs. Stephen J. Kollar," *Philadelphia Inquirer*, 9 August 1947, p. 18. Sara Jane Bing Kollar was a younger sister of John Franklin Rhoads.

9. Ray Rhoads, personal communication, 31 July 2013; *Philadelphia City Directory*, from 1887 onward; US Federal Census, Pennsylvania, Philadelphia County, 24th Ward, for 1900 (District 568, Sheet 4B), 1910 (District 521, Sheet 2A), and 1920 (District 728, pp. 11A–11B).

10. "Marriages [Rhoads-Garrett]," *Public Ledger*, 28 June 1890, p. 4; *Philadelphia City Directory*, 1891 to 1898.

11. See John Henry Hepp IV, *The Middle-Class City: Transforming Space and Time in Philadelphia, 1876–1926* (Philadelphia: University of Pennsylvania Press, 2003).

12. See "West Philadelphia: The History, A Streetcar Suburb in the City, 1854–1907," at westphillyhistory.archives. upenn.edu (last accessed 20 May 2020); for a memoir of middle-class life in West Philadelphia at the beginning of the twentieth century, see John Cecil Holm, *Sunday Best: The Story of a Philadelphia Family* (New York: Farrar & Rinehart, Inc., 1942).

13. *Philadelphia City Directories*; Deed abstracts for 769 N. 44th St., Plan Book No. 59N, p. 17, Lot No. 95, Philadelphia City Archives.

Figure 2.2: My father and his parents, John Franklin Rhoads and Annie Louisa (Garrett) Rhoads, West Philadelphia(?), ca. 1905.

were both commercial thoroughfares; both were served by trolley lines, as was 41st Street between the two avenues. This was the heart of West Philadelphia.[14]

Though my father had many cousins on his father's side, he seems to have been distant from them all. The one relative he was close to throughout his life (as we shall see) was his maternal first cousin, Anna Eckfeldt Davis (1903–1997), the daughter of Sarah Elizabeth ("Sallie") Garrett and A [no period] Eckfeldt Davis (1860–1951). Anna had an older brother, Walter (b. 1893), but after his early death in 1911, when she was eight years old, she too was effectively, like my father, an only child. She and my father were roughly the same age, and their homes were near each other. In 1910, the Davises lived at 733 North 43rd Street, the next block over from the Rhoads's on 44th Street. Also, their mothers, Sallie and Annie, were very close.

As was common then, my father was brought up in a Christian environment. According to one of his college schoolmates, George Brandon Saul, his parents "were lovable folk of the old school who reared him in an atmosphere of genuinely Christian piety." Though Dr. Thomas Wynne had been a devout Quaker and though Philadelphia

---

14. See J. L. Smith, *Atlas of the 24th, 34th & 44th Wards of the City of Philadelphia* (1911), https://westphillyhistory. archives.upenn.edu/maps/1911-atlas-smith (last accessed 11 March 2019).

Figure 2.3: The rowhouse in West Philadelphia where my father grew up, 2013. 769 North 44th Street is the fourth house from the end, with the white screen door.

two centuries later continued to be a Quaker stronghold, my father's family were not Quakers but Methodists. John Franklin Rhoads and Annie Louisa Garrett had been married by a Methodist minister, and their son was baptized, on 10 September 1903, by another Methodist minister.[15] According to another college schoolmate, Frank Prentzel Jr., who grew up in the same West Philadelphia neighborhood as my father and who himself became a Methodist minister, "We were raised in the same church as boys."[16] (It should be noted that both Saul and Prentzel were writing in support of my father's application to teach at missionary-founded Lingnan University, so their statements may have unduly stressed his Christian upbringing.) While, as historian Thomas Rzeznik has found, "Quakers, Episcopalians, and Presbyterians [were] the three denominations that claimed the greatest loyalty among members of [Philadelphia's] upper class," it seems that it was the Methodist church that had the greater appeal for middle-class business owners like my father's parents and grandparents.[17]

---

15. George Brandon Saul, 4 May 1936, in HGR's Placement File, Alumni Records, University Archives, University of Pennsylvania; on HGR's parents' marriage, see *Public Ledger*, 28 June 1890, p. 4, and on HGR's baptism, see Sarah D. Cooper Memorial United Methodist Church Records, Record of Baptisms, Archives of the Eastern Pennsylvania Conference of the United Methodist Church, St. George's United Methodist Church, Philadelphia, PA.
16. Frank Prentzel Jr., 30 April 1936, in HGR's Placement File, Alumni Records, University Archives, University of Pennsylvania.
17. Thomas F. Rzeznik, *Church and Estate: Religion and Wealth in Industrial-Era Philadelphia* (University Park: Pennsylvania State University Press, 2013), p. 36.

In 1913, when he was thirteen years old, my father graduated from the Belmont Boys Grammar School, at 41st and Brown Streets, in West Philadelphia, after which he enrolled in the West Philadelphia High School for Boys, at 4901 Chestnut Street. The school, which had opened just the year before, offered three types of courses, Academic, Commercial, and Manual Training. He was enrolled in the Academic Course. The school was blessed with some extraordinary teachers, as the actor and playwright John Cecil Holm, who came along three years after my father, recalled with enthusiasm and gratitude: "There was Irvin W. Anthony teaching English. 'Rise and Shine,' he'd say. And John Dennis Mahoney—why, he made people come to life! Shakespeare and Chaucer and Johnson and Boswell! They breathed and walked right through the classroom. And there was Roy Helton, tall and angular with his easygoing speech, why, poetry wasn't any sissy thing for only girls to know!"[18] It was perhaps because of these teachers that my father became interested in English literature. He graduated from the West Philadelphia High School in June 1917.

My father may have been the first in his family to go to college. As did many of his West Philadelphia High School classmates, he attended the University of Pennsylvania, which in 1871 had relocated to its present campus in West Philadelphia, about two miles from his parents' home. With a total enrollment in 1917 of around nine thousand, it was, at the time, an all-male school at the undergraduate level.[19] As an undergraduate at Penn from 1917 to 1921, my father was enrolled in "The College," the liberal arts core of the university, majoring in English. In addition to English (32 credits), he took courses in Latin (18 credits), French (12), Greek (6), German (6), Philosophy (12), History (12), Geography (2), Psychology (10), Mathematics (4), Chemistry (6), Physics (6), and Physical Education (8). He evidently was a very good student, and in recognition of his academic achievements he was elected to the Phi Beta Kappa honor society.[20]

In April 1917, just as my father was about to graduate from high school, the United States had finally entered the Great War, or the First World War, on the side of the Allies. Thus, when my father turned eighteen in the summer of 1918, he was required to register for the newly instituted draft.[21] Soon afterward, on 1 October, the day it was founded at Penn, he joined the Students' Army Training Corps. "Members were considered to be part of the United States Army. . . . Students of the S.A.T.C. lived on a military schedule and in military housing, ate in military-style mess halls, and participated in drill and athletics every single day." Happily, the Germans surrendered six weeks later. The training corps was demobilized in December 1918, and my father was discharged. According to the War Service Record he subsequently submitted, he had held the rank, while in the S.A.T.C., of "corporal, acting sergeant."[22]

---

18. HGR's Registration Blank, University of Pennsylvania Placement Service, 4 September 1934, Alumni Records, University Archives, University of Pennsylvania; *History of the West Philadelphia High School, Prepared on the Occasion of Its Fiftieth Anniversary, 1912–1962* ([Philadelphia]: West Philadelphia High School Alumni Association, [1962]); Holm, *Sunday Best*, p. 258.
19. Edward Potts Cheyney, *History of the University of Pennsylvania, 1740–1940* (Philadelphia: University of Pennsylvania Press, 1940).
20. *Catalogue of the University of Pennsylvania*, 1917–1918 to 1920–1921; HGR's Registration Blank, University of Pennsylvania Placement Service, Alumni Records, University Archives, University of Pennsylvania; *The Record* [Yearbook of the University of Pennsylvania], vol. 21 (1921), p. 436.
21. US World War I Selective Service System Draft Registration Cards, 1917–1918, Pennsylvania, Philadelphia County, Draft Board 19, ancestry.com.
22. HGR's file, Alumni Records, University Archives, University of Pennsylvania; "Penn in the Great War: The University's Role in a Critical Time" (2013), The United States Goes to War and Penn Follows, 1917–1918, archives.

In addition to the Students' Army Training Corps, my father, whose college nickname was "Howdy," was active in a number of other student organizations. He was a member of the Arts Association all four undergraduate years and was on its executive committee his junior and senior years; the association organized "get-together smokers" and lecture series and promoted "all-round good fellowship among the student body." He also belonged to the Sophomore Dues Committee, the Junior Prom Committee, and in his senior year the Ivy Week Committee.[23] However, the two most meaningful of his college associations were his social fraternity and the student newspaper. He was a member of Delta Sigma Phi, and for his last two years as an undergraduate, he lived at the fraternity house at 202 South 36th Street. (For his first year, he may have lived at home; for his second year, when he was with the S.A.T.C., he presumably lived on campus in military housing.) Some of his closest friends, including the above-quoted Frank Prentzel and George Brandon Saul, were Delta Sigma Phi fraternity brothers.[24] No less important to him was the student newspaper, *The Pennsylvanian*, which he joined as a sophomore. He

Figure 2.4: My father's entry in Penn's 1921 yearbook.

upenn.edu (accessed 19 June 2018); US World War I Selective Service System Draft Registration Cards, 1917–1918, Pennsylvania, Philadelphia County, Draft Board 19, and Pennsylvania, WWI Veterans Service and Compensation Files, 1917–1919, Pennsylvania State Archives, Harrisburg, PA (both at ancestry.com).

23. *The Record*, vol. 51 (1921), pp. 109, 402–403; on the Arts Association, see *The Record*, vol. 50 (1920), p. 169.

24. Cheyney, *History of the University of Pennsylvania*, p. 380; for HGR's residential addresses, see the *Catalogue of the University of Pennsylvania* for the respective years.

was a member of its editorial board from then on, first as a night editor, then as an associate editor, and finally (in his senior year) as an editor.[25]

Following his graduation from college in 1921, my father set out to become an English professor.[26] At first he remained at Penn, where for one year he pursued graduate studies and also taught as an assistant in English. Then for two years (1922–1924) he was an instructor at the College of Wooster in Ohio, making $1,500 a year. In 1924 he went back to school, enrolling at Harvard, where he earned a master's degree in 1925 and was a teaching assistant in 1925–1926. He might have continued his studies at Harvard, but in January 1926 his father died, and as a single child it fell to him to look after his mother, who may not have been in the best of health. He returned to Pennsylvania and took a full-time job as an instructor at Lehigh University in Bethlehem, fifty miles north of Philadelphia. He was at Lehigh for six years (1926–1932), rising in 1929 to the rank of assistant professor and earning a salary of between $1,900 and $2,800. While at Lehigh he assisted a senior colleague, Robert Metcalf Smith, in editing a seven-volume anthology of plays titled World Drama Series, which was published in 1928 by Prentice-Hall. In 1930, according to the census, he (along with five other single men) was living in a boarding house in Bethlehem at 34 Wall Street run by the family of F. Roycroft Croll, a draftsman in a steel mill.[27]

My father left Lehigh in 1932, perhaps because of the Great Depression, and returned to the University of Pennsylvania to work on his doctorate in English literature, which he received two years later. His dissertation was a textual analysis of an early seventeenth-century play, *Apollo Shroving* by William Hawkins. As his former colleague and collaborator at Lehigh, Robert Smith, wrote for his placement file, "We should have liked to reappoint him after he attained the [doctoral] degree, but retrenchment because of the depression worked har[d]ship in his case." Moreover, as another Lehigh colleague wrote, "a greater handicap was the long and eventually fatal illness of his mother forced him to sacrifice all opportunities that would take him away from the immediate vicinity of Philadelphia." For the next couple of years (1934–1936) he was first a research assistant at Penn to English Professor A. C. Baugh and then an assistant professor at Beaver College (now Arcadia University) in Jenkintown, a Philadelphia suburb.

Annie Louisa's death in March 1935, however, left him free to look farther afield. It so happened that in 1936 the Board of Trustees of Lingnan University in New York was desperately looking for an English teacher for the university's Department of Western Languages and Literature. And it preferred someone who was single (to avoid having to pay the travel expenses of a spouse) and male (to offset the number of women in the department). He applied for the job.

Why did he choose to go to China? There is no indication that he had any prior interest in the country. And he was almost certainly not motivated by religion. Unlike the founders of Lingnan or some of his future colleagues, he was not a missionary, and though he was nominally a Christian he was not particularly religious, despite his upbringing as a Methodist. For his placement file at the University of Pennsylvania, he had listed "none" for church membership. In any case, Lingnan in 1927 had been required to sever

---

25. *The Record*, vol. 51 (1921), pp. 264–267.
26. On HGR's career from 1921 to 1936, see his University of Pennsylvania placement file, 4 September 1934, and his "Curriculum Vitae and testimonials," 28 December 1951, both in HGR's file, Alumni Records, University Archives, University of Pennsylvania.
27. US Federal Census, 1930, Pennsylvania, Northampton County, Bethlehem City, Electoral District 20, Sheet 12B.

its institutional ties to foreign missionary bodies and become not only Chinese but also secular. It is most likely that my father's motivation for going to China was economic. He had inherited some money from his mother: the family's carpet cleaning and storage company had continued to operate for some years after John Franklin Rhoads' death. Still, my father was hardly wealthy, and at the depth of the Great Depression teaching opportunities in the US were few and far between. In a similar situation, Franklin G. Wallace (1909–1995), a zoologist, when asked years later why he had gone to teach at Lingnan in 1933, replied, "It was a job and a chance to see another part of the world."[28]

My father's job interview, in May 1936, was with William W. Comfort, president of nearby Haverford College and a member of the Lingnan Board of Trustees. Afterwards Comfort wrote that he thought "well of him and the spirit in which he is approaching a position at Lingnan." My father was offered the job, but then, oddly, he turned it down![29] Almost immediately, however, he changed his mind and agreed to a three-year contract at an annual salary of $720. (While this was one-third of what he had earned at Wooster and Lehigh, at Lingnan his housing and medical and dental benefits would have been provided for.) Everything moved quickly after that. On 24 June he received his passport; on 16 July, eleven days before his thirty-sixth birthday, he took out a $2,000 life insurance policy (which the trustees evidently paid for); soon afterward he was off to China.[30]

My father probably made his way to China by train across the continent and then by ship across the Pacific; years later, he mentioned having visited Tokyo in 1936.[31] The ship he took was, most likely, the *President Jackson*, which arrived in Hong Kong from Seattle on 5 September, around the time that he was expected. Met by Provost James Henry, he was taken immediately to Guangzhou.[32] He was to spend most of the next fifteen years of his life associated with Lingnan.

28. Franklin Wallace, "Midwest China Oral History Interviews" (1977), *China Oral Histories*, Book 76, p. 28, http://digitalcommons.luthersem.edu/china_histories/76 (accessed 17 October 2019).
29. W. W. Comfort to ODW, Haverford, PA, 20 May 1936, and ODW to Comfort, New York, 22 May 1936, Box 68, TLUA–HYL.
30. "Field Budget 1936–1937: Salaries, Allowances, etc.," 13 May 1936, Box 148, TLUA–HYL; HGR's application for Manufacturers Life insurance policy, 16 July 1936, and ER's Report of Birth, Canton, 13 June 1938, both in my personal papers.
31. HGR to James M. Henry, Yokohama, 6 September 1949, Box 125, TLUA–HYL.
32. James M. Henry to ODW, Canton, 1 September and 10 September 1936, Box 68, TLUA–HYL; "Shipping News—Arrivals," *Hong Kong Daily Press*, 7 September 1936, p. 15.

3

The War Comes to South China (1936–1941)

My father arrived in China, in September 1936, at a seemingly most hopeful time. This was during the "Nanjing decade" (1928–1937), when Chiang Kai-shek and the Nationalist Party had nominally unified the country, whose new capital was located at Nanjing. Chiang had driven his Communist rivals out of their rural bases in south-central China and forced them to retreat to the barren northwest, where they barely survived under their new leader, Mao Zedong. Chiang had also overcome various factional opponents in South China, including Chen Jitang 陳濟棠, who had ruled Guangdong as an autonomous region from 1929 to 1936. Referring to Chen's fall from power, James Henry, Lingnan's provost (and my mother's boss), wrote in September 1936, "This is a crowning achievement on the part of Chiang Kai-shek and those associated with him . . . China can now face her internal problems with new assurance and her external problems with a courage and determination that have not heretofore been possible."[1]

The Nanjing decade was also an era of railroad and highway building. Chen Jitang's overthrow coincided with the long-delayed completion of the Guangzhou–Hankou railroad. As Henry wrote, "The opening, within the last few days, of the through train to Hankow [now a part of Wuhan] is symbolic of the new unity which has been brought about."[2] One could now go by train from Guangzhou to Beijing and, indeed, all the way to Europe via the Trans-Siberian Railway. In addition to 3,300 kilometers of railroad lines, the Nationalists, in the regions they controlled, also built 6,000 kilometers of public highways. Chen Jitang in Guangdong had been even more productive. Between 1929 and 1935 he added 14,000 kilometers of highways, making Guangdong, according to historian Alfred Lin, "first among all provinces in length of highways completed." As the medical missionary Dr. Frank Oldt (1879–1976) later observed, "It was fortunate that these roads were built before the War. It made possible the great refugee treks. The transportation facilities were a big factor in resistance against the Japanese, not only from a military standpoint but also for civilian life." Both railroads and highways were to play important roles in our family's wartime experiences.[3]

1. James M. Henry to Members of the Lingnan National Advisory Council, 11 September 1936, Box 68, TLUA–HYL.
2. James M. Henry to Members of the Lingnan National Advisory Council, 11 September 1936, Box 68, TLUA–HYL.
3. Van de Ven, *China at War*, p. 38; Alfred H. Y. Lin, "Building and Funding a Warlord Regime: The Experience of Chen Jitang in Guangdong, 1929–1936," *Modern China* 28 (2002): 179; "Frank Oldt, Medical Missionary: His Story," p. 965, in Dr. Frank Oldt Papers, HC-48, The Center for the Evangelical United Brethren Heritage, United Theological Seminary, Dayton, OH.

As to what Provost Henry called China's "external problems," the main one was Japanese expansionism. Since taking control of Manchuria in the northeast in 1931, Japan had been encroaching steadily on adjacent areas of North China. Chiang Kai-shek's reluctance to confront the Japanese led eventually to his being "kidnapped" in Xi'an in December 1936 by his own generals, who forced him to stop battling the Communists and instead form a "united front" with them against the Japanese. Paradoxically, upon his release from captivity, Chiang was hailed as the one person around whom all Chinese, including the Communists and other erstwhile domestic enemies, could rally. China, for the first time in a quarter-century, was united and at peace.

With the departure of Chiang Kai-shek's Northern Expedition in 1927, Guangzhou had "receded from the center of national politics and resumed its status as a provincial capital." Nevertheless, the city was prospering, as a consequence of Chen Jitang's reformist efforts. "With Guangzhou as his base, Chen [had] embarked upon an ambitious modernization program for the province, emphasizing industrialization, educational reform, infrastructural development (including plans for a province-wide road network), cooperatives, and the urban renewal of Guangzhou and other urban centers." With a population of over a million, Guangzhou had become, next to Shanghai and Hong Kong, probably the most modern city in China. Emblematic of the "New Canton" was the completion in 1933 of the Pearl River Bridge (now known as the Haizhu Bridge 海珠橋), a drawbridge linking the city's downtown with Ho Nam Island to the south.[4] Ho Nam now is largely urbanized, but in the 1930s, except for the bund along its north shore, it was "a large piece of farmland with a collection of small villages."[5] It was here that Lingnan University was located.

Figure 3.1: The Pearl River Bridge in the mid-1930s. From Folder 3, Box 306, RG 8, Special Collections, YDSL.

4. Shuk-wah Poon, *Negotiating Religion in Modern China: State and Common People in Guangzhou, 1900–1937* (Hong Kong: Chinese University Press, 2011), p. 8; Graham E. Johnson and Glen D. Peterson, *Historical Dictionary of Guangzhou (Canton) and Guangdong* (Lanham, MD, and London: Scarecrow Press, 1999), p. 128; Lee, *Modern Canton*, pp. 20–21, 24.

5. Lee, *Modern Canton*, pp. 12, 26.

Lingnan was one of thirteen colleges founded by Western (mostly American) Protestant missionaries in China, and it was one of the three best (along with Yenching in Beijing and St. John's in Shanghai). Alone among the Christian colleges, it was non-denominational. All the others were affiliated with one or more mission boards (Episcopalians in the case of St. John's, Methodists and three other denominations in the case of Yenching). In contrast, Lingnan, although founded by Presbyterians, was financially and administratively independent of the Presbyterian Church, as was its Board of Trustees in New York City.[6]

Moreover, according to historian Peter Tze Ming Ng, "Lingnan University was probably the first Christian University that was turned over directly to Chinese control." This took the form of a local and predominantly Chinese Board of Directors, headed by Sun Yat-sen's son, Sun Foh 孫科, that was separate from the American Board of Trustees.[7] Also, when it registered with the National government in 1926, James Henry, son of the university's co-founder, B. C. Henry (1850–1901), had stepped down as its president and been replaced by a Chinese, Chung Wing Kwong 鍾榮光 (1866–1942), who, though a Christian, was a Confucian scholar as well. (In the old civil service examination system, Chung was a *juren* 舉人 [provincial degree holder] of 1894.) And when President Chung resigned in 1937, he was succeeded by another Chinese, Lee Ying Lam 李應林 (or Y. L. Lee, 1892–1954), an Oberlin graduate (BA, 1920) and a former secretary of the YMCA in Guangzhou. (Lee's lack of an advanced degree troubled some on his academic staff; this shortcoming was somewhat mitigated in 1939, when he was awarded an honorary LLD by his alma mater.)[8] In the meantime, James Henry (College of Wooster BA, 1901; Union Theological Seminary DD, 1924) had stayed on in an ostensibly subordinate position, as provost (or adviser [*guwen* 顧問], as he was known to the Chinese). In contrast, Yenching, though it registered with the Chinese government in 1928, continued to be run by a foreigner, John Leighton Stuart, before he was ousted by the Japanese. St. John's, too, was headed by a foreigner, Francis Lister Hawks Pott, until 1939, and it did not register until after the war.

Another consequence of registering with the National government was that Lingnan became nominally a secular school. It could no longer propagate religion, nor could it include religious instruction among its required courses.[9] Nevertheless, Lingnan remained in spirit a Christian school. Thus, at his installation ceremony in 1927, President Chung Wing Kwong had defined the educational objective of Lingnan as follows: "to equip Chinese leaders with the application of a scientific mind and the Christian spirit of service and sacrifice, so that those who are educated will continue to serve the community and the nation in the spirit of selflessness and the Christian love." A couple of years later,

---

6. Ng Tze Ming, "Cong Guangzhou sili Lingnan daxue kan jidujiao daxue ying yi hezhong xingshi wei guojia jiaoyu shiye fuwu" [How should Christian colleges serve the nation's educational enterprise, as viewed from Guangzhou's Lingnan University], in *Zhongxi wenhua yu jiaohui daxue* [Christian universities and Chinese-Western cultures], ed. Zhang Kaiyuan and Arthur Waldron ([Wuhan]: Hubei jiaoyu chubanshe, 1991), pp. 242–245.

7. Peter Tze Ming Ng, "Nationalism, Democracy and Christian Higher Education in China: A Case Study of Lingnan University, Canton (A Preliminary Report)," a paper prepared for the Workshop on the History of Christian Higher Education in China, Yale University, New Haven, 17 February 1990.

8. For a brief biography of Y. L. Lee, see Xie Qiongsun, "Li Yinglin xiaozhang yu Lingda" [President Y. L. Lee and Lingnan University], *Zhujiang yiyuan* (March 1985): 33–43, in Folder 92, Box 14, RG 175, Sarah Refo Mason Papers, Special Collections, YDSL.

9. Corbett, *Lingnan University*, p. 105.

the school's mission statement was boiled down to four words: private, Christian, international, and Chinese.[10]

At the time of my father's arrival in 1936, the penultimate year of Chung's presidency, Lingnan University had four colleges: Arts and Sciences, Agriculture, Engineering, and Medicine. The first three schools were located on the university's main campus at Hong Lok Village 康樂村 on Ho Nam 河南 Island; their total enrollment was 560 (one-quarter of whom were women). Also in attendance were thirty American students, who were spending their junior year at Lingnan. (This was called an "exchange program," even though Lingnan sent hardly any students to the US.) The medical school, known as the Sun Yat-sen Medical College, was located in Guangzhou city; its enrollment was forty-two. In addition to these four colleges, the university operated at the main Hong Lok campus a Middle School (444 students), an "Overseas Section" (79), a Primary School (185), an Agricultural Vocational School (54), and a Western School for the children of the foreign staff and other foreigners in Guangzhou.[11] As a private institution, Lingnan was widely viewed as an "aristocrats' school" (*guizu xuexiao* 貴族學校). Many students were the pampered sons and daughters of wealthy merchants in Guangzhou and Hong Kong and among the overseas Chinese; in the opinion of one of the American exchange students, they were "decidedly spoiled."[12] Few of its students came from other provinces of China.

The main campus of Lingnan University, designed by American architects and modeled on New England liberal arts colleges, was among the most attractive in China. Occupying six hundred acres, it was, as described by another of the exchange students in 1936–1937, "a well-planned university grounds, with a hundred modern buildings in modified Chinese style, and with a great variety of different trees, shrubs and flowers. There were walks lined with banyans, palms, and eucalyptus; hedges of hibiscus and banks of flame-colored azalea; dormitories surrounded by gardenia bushes; and gardens displaying orchids and the exotic night-blooming cereus." The layout of the campus was, in the words of an architectural historian, "a typically Beaux-Arts scheme with a grand central axis and a series of cross-axes giving a formal, processional aspect to the whole." Thus, a promenade with parallel walkways ran the length of the campus from a wharf on the Pearl River on the north to a bus stop at the South Gate. The buildings ranged along this promenade included Swasey Hall, "an auditorium used for Sunday morning church services and college entertainments," the university infirmary, and Blackstone Lodge (the president's house). Bisecting the central axis was a crosswalk, along which was located "Grant Hall (administration, bank and store), the provost's house and the American Foundation," where my mother was employed. "On the western branch of the cross walk were . . . a cluster of residences used by the Chinese faculty." This would have been the Model Village (Mofancun 模範村), with fourteen smallish two-story houses, which accommodated not only Chinese faculty (like my mother's colleague, Tong Fuk Cheung) but several Western faculty members as well. To the east, atop a small hill (Ma Kong Ding 馬崗丁), were a "group of American residences." These latter residences, built

---

10. Ng, "Nationalism, Democracy and Christian Higher Education," p. 3; Wang, *Managing God's Higher Learning*, p. 8.

11. James M. Henry to ODW, Canton, 1 October 1936, "Enrolment All Schools," Box 69, TLUA–HYL.

12. D. Thurston Griggs, *One Man's Window on the 20th Century* (2002), Chap. 10, China Diary – 1935–1936 (Excerpts), userpages.umbc.edu/~tgriggs/autobio.html (last accessed 3 June 2020); for another account of life at Lingnan by a Chinese undergraduate in the mid-1930s, see Wang Yidun, "Lingda shenghuo sinian de huiyi" [Recollections of four years of life at Lingnan University], *Guangzhou wenshi ziliao*, vol. 13 (1964): 203–212.

Figure 3.2: Aerial view of the Lingnan campus at Hong Lok, June 1932, looking south along the central axis. From Folder 573, Box 51, RG 14, Special Collections, YDSL. #1 = Swazey Hall; #2 = Model Village; #3 = Grant Hall; #4 = Residence No. 47; #5 = Primary School; #6 = Wing Kwong Hall.

and maintained by the American Foundation, were set aside for the "permanent" expatriate faculty with families.[13]

As a recent hire without family, my father was instead given a room on the third floor in one of the men's dormitories, Wing Kwong Hall (named for President Chung), situated along the central axis and north of the crosswalk. For his meals he usually dined with Gilbert Baker (1910–1986), an Oxford-educated Anglican missionary, who likewise had joined the Lingnan faculty recently and was a bachelor then. Baker had been assigned to the Wesley House, on Ma Kong Ding, which was "not being used by the Methodists," and he lived there "with some students who might subsequently become ordinands [candidates for ordination]." Writing to his parents in England, Baker described his dining companion (who had been brought up as Methodist) as Episcopalian, "though [he] doesn't do very much about it." Nevertheless, he thought him "rather a good egg—very different from the average American and with more of that gentle Eastern (American) voice and outlook that I always think must have been characteristic of [President Woodrow] Wilson and [US Ambassador to the UK] Walter Page."[14]

---

13. E. W. Meisenhelder, *The Dragon Smiles* (New York: Pageant Press, 1968), pp. 12–13; Farris, *Enclave to Urbanity*, p. 205; "Committee on Public Safety," 26 July 1948, Box 120, TLUA–HYL.
14. "List of Staff, Lingnan University," 12 October 1936, Folder Miscellaneous—Lingnan University 1/3, Box 66, Collection No. 1192, Cadbury & Cadbury Papers, Haverford College Library; Gilbert Baker, *Flowing Ways: Our*

The college teaching staff (in the spring of 1938, my father's second year at Lingnan) totaled eighty, of whom sixty-one were Chinese and nineteen were foreign.[15] While the Chinese professors were provided for by the predominantly Chinese Board of Directors, most of the foreign teachers, including my father, were financially supported by the Board of Trustees in New York (the American Foundation). As the head of the New York office, Olin Wannamaker, once explained the relationship between the two boards, "The Chinese Directors have sent us every year a list of those members of the American faculty whose continuance in service they desired . . . Appointment or re-appointment by our own Board of Trustees has always been based upon the receipt of such request from the Chinese Board of Directors." This, on paper at least, was how the two boards were supposed to work.[16] Other foreign teachers came from one or another Christian mission. For example, Gilbert Baker, who taught History and Christian Religion, was sponsored by the Church Missionary Society. Due to the Depression, the number of foreign faculty supported by the American trustees had been "greatly reduced": it had been as many as twenty-eight in 1928.[17]

My father's department, Western Languages and Literature, was part of the College of Arts and Sciences. In 1936–1937 it had a staff of five. Its head was a Chinese American, Baldwin Lee 李寶榮 (1901–1996), who held a PhD from Columbia's Teachers College (1928). Unlike the other members of the department, Lee had not been hired by the American Foundation, but for complex reasons it paid his salary (HK$2,500). The other four members of the department's faculty, all with an annual salary of HK$1,800, were assistant professor Pauline Aiken (Yale PhD, 1934), instructor Helen C. Banta (Ohio Wesleyan BA, 1934), instructor Patty (Hynes) Wallace (University of Minnesota BA, 1935), and my father, who though hired as an assistant professor had been promoted on arrival to associate professor (thus passing over Pauline Aiken, even though she had seniority on the job). Three of the five were women.[18] The department offered a full range of courses from Freshman English to Poems of the Romantic Movement. (Despite its name, the department offered few Western language and literature courses other than English.) My father's teaching responsibilities (in the spring of 1938) were Freshman English (with 17 students), Nineteenth-Century Novel (4), Literary Criticism (3), Shakespeare (6), and Thesis (2).[19]

The initial reaction to my father's arrival in the department was quite favorable, though Pauline Aiken might have had reason to think otherwise. Chairman Baldwin Lee thanked the American trustees profusely: "I feel that we owe you much for sending to us this year so outstanding a man as Dr. Rhoads. He has already proved himself a genuine asset. This semester, in addition to carrying a full normal load, he is aiding us in caring for the large number of exchange students by conducting a reading course in European Drama for several of them." Provost Henry echoed the assessment. In January 1937 he

Life in China (Dorking, Surrey: Joan Baker, 1996), p. 57; Gilbert Baker to his parents, Lingnan University, 28 September and 2 November 1936, Folder 15, and 10 October 1938, Folder 18, Box 5, RG 8, China Records Project, Miscellaneous Personal Papers Collection, Special Collections, YDSL.

15. "List of Teaching Assignments, Lingnan University, Semester II, 1937–38," Box 143, TLUA–HYL.
16. ODW to HGR, New York, 8 February 1945, Box 101, TLUA–HYL.
17. ODW to William E. Hocking, New York City, 16 July 1935, Box 64, TLUA–HYL; Baker, *Flowing Ways*, pp. 57, 61.
18. Baldwin Lee to ODW, Canton, 19 October 1936, Box 69, and "Field Budget 1936–1937: Salaries, Allowances, etc.," 13 May 1936, Box 148, TLUA–HYL; Lingnan University Catalog, 1936–1937, pp. 86–90, in Folder 3251, Box 181, China College Files—Lingnan University, RG 11, United Board Archives, YDSL.
19. "Courses Offered in the College of Arts and Sciences—1937–1938," in Corbett, *Lingnan University*, pp. 193–197; "List of Teaching Assignments, Lingnan University, Semester II, 1937–38," Box 153, TLUA–HYL.

Figure 3.3: Lingnan's College of Arts and Sciences faculty on steps of Grant Hall, March 1937. From Folder 657, Box 59, RG 14, Special Collections, YDSL. #1 = Dean C. Y Hui 許滇陽; #2 = Sinn Yuk Ching; #3 = Patty Wallace; #4 = Baldwin Lee; #5 = Arthur Knipp; #6 = Frederic Chang; #7 = Clinton Laird; #8 = William Hoffmann; #9 = Gilbert Baker; #10 = Henry Frank. My father is not in the photo.

wrote Olin Wannamaker, "You would be highly pleased . . . if you could see how finely Rhoads is fitting in. You made no mistake in persuading him to throw in his lot here."[20] In the meantime, my father had been given a Chinese name, one that approximated in Cantonese the pronunciation of "Howard Rhoads": 路考活 Lo Hau Wut. It was doubly appropriate that his Chinese surname not only sounded like "Rhoads" in Cantonese but also meant "road" or "roads."

In the course of his first year at Lingnan, my father would have had many occasions to visit the office of James Henry, the provost and resident director of the American Foundation, and there to meet Henry's long-time personal secretary, Mrs. Chan Ngan Chi Kit. The two quickly fell in love. It seems likely that it was this developing relationship with my father that precipitated my mother's divorce from Chan Cheuk Ming in late February 1937. A month later, my father presented her with a copy of the Temple Shakespeare edition of *The Tragedy of Romeo and Juliet*; it came with a laconic dedication: "Chi Kit, 4-1-37, HGR."[21] The divorce and her relationship with my father reportedly caused a scandal in my mother's family, though the precise nature of the scandal is unclear. Was it the divorce itself? Or the love affair with a foreigner? Or both?

---

20. Baldwin Lee to ODW, Canton, 19 October 1936, Box 69, and James M. Henry to ODW, Canton, 7 January 1937, Box 70, TLUA–HYL.
21. In my personal collection.

In any case, soon thereafter my father and mother were married in a "simple Chinese ceremony." Only then, at the beginning of May, did my father inform his and my mother's boss, James Henry, stating "that since her divorce a couple of months ago, she has been at outs with her family, etc., and that he had to marry her in order to protect her." Provost Henry was absolutely dumbfounded. As he confided to Wannamaker, "I told him his action was irregular; that I should have been consulted. His reply was that he felt he had to do it—not in the ordinary sense of 'had to'—and was quite prepared to resign if I felt he ought to!" When Henry questioned whether the Chinese wedding my father and mother had had "was legal in American law," they were married again, on 18 June 1937, which is the date they later gave for their marriage when they registered my birth with the American consulate six and a half months later. (Perhaps they had "had to" get married after all.) My mother was then twenty-seven; my father, thirty-six. She called him Howard, he called her Kit. Their second wedding was held at Provost Henry's home on campus and conducted by forestry professor Donald D. Stevenson (1903–1993), an ordained Presbyterian minister.[22] It is unclear if any of my mother's family attended either of the wedding ceremonies. There are no photographs.

One immediate consequence of their marriage was that my mother lost the secretarial job at the American Foundation that she had held for the past four years. According to botany professor William E. Hoffmann (1896–1989), "Dr. Henry said he would like to keep Mrs. Rhoads but that it would be impossible to have the wife of a staff member as a secretary." Another consequence was that my father's salary, now that he was a married man, was increased by one-third. Thus, the American Foundation's proposed budget for 1938–1939 shows that his salary had jumped from HK$1,800 to HK$2,400.[23]

A mixed marriage such as my parents' was unusual for the time and the place; there seems to have been only one other among the teaching staff at Lingnan then or later. Two years earlier, in September 1935, Ruth McCullough (1908–1966), then an English instructor, was married to Mack Kwok Chun 麥國珍, a 1931 Lingnan graduate in the employ of the British firm Imperial Chemicals Co. (She had taught at Lingnan since 1931; it was her departure in 1936 that created the vacancy in the department that my father filled. She was to teach at Lingnan again in 1947–1949.) Among Western expatriates in China intermarriage was generally frowned upon; in prewar Hong Kong there was definitely, in historian Philip Snow's words, a "deep-seated prejudice" against it. The academic environment, however, may have been more accommodating. According to Provost Henry, the university's president, Chung Wing Kwong, had been "extremely happy" about Ruth Mack's marriage and "thinks it a forward step toward international good-will." Indeed, in a radio address in 1936, President Chung foresaw "a day when there are no longer racial lines between black, white, yellow, red, and brown." The provost himself, though not opposed, sounded less enthusiastic.[24] Nevertheless, my father's colleagues at Lingnan seem to have acccptcd his marriage to my mother. So, too, in time did my mother's family.

22. James M. Henry to ODW, Canton, 4 May 1937, and "Canton Wedding," *South China Morning Post* (Hong Kong), 28 June 1937, clipping, Box 71, TLUA –HYL; "Certificate of Marriage" for HGR and CKR, American Consular Service, Canton, 18 June 1937, in my personal collection.

23. William E. Hoffmann to "Inky" [Ingeborg B. Stolee], Canton, 10 August 1937, Folder 158, Box 24, RG 175, Sarah Refo Mason Papers, YDSL; James M. Henry to ODW, Canton, 4 May 1937, Box 71, and "Final Draft of Proposed Field Budget for Year 1938–1939," 23 May 1938, Box 148, TLUA–HYL.

24. James M. Henry, Canton, to ODW, 10 September 1935, Box 65, TLUA–HYL; Phillip Snow, *The Fall of Hong Kong: Britain, China, and the Japanese Occupation* (New Haven: Yale University Press, 2003), p. 294; Wang, *Managing God's Higher Learning*, p. 8.

Soon after their second or "American" wedding in mid-June 1937, my father and mother left Guangzhou—possibly by train on the newly completed Guangzhou–Hankou railroad—to "spend their honeymoon in the north." Their most likely destination was Beijing (then known as Beiping), the as yet unspoiled old imperial capital, which at that time was widely regarded (at least by foreigners like the Lingnan exchange student Edmund W. Meisenhelder III [1915–2002]) as China's "most fascinating city." My father's colleague, Patty Wallace, took advantage of the new rail connections to visit Beijing that same summer. According to her husband, the zoologist Franklin Wallace, "Peking, in those days, was absolutely impressive with the great walls and gates, and so on . . . We spent a week seeing the sights."[25]

If my parents did go to Beijing, their visit might well have coincided with the outbreak of the Sino-Japanese War. On 7 July 1937, Japanese troops stationed outside the city skirmished with nearby Chinese soldiers. Unbeknownst then to most people, this "Marco Polo Bridge Incident" soon escalated into a full-scale (if undeclared) war, as first Japan poured soldiers into North China and then a month later Chiang Kai-shek, obliged now by the Xi'an Incident of the previous December to take a more forceful stance against Japanese aggression, opened a second front in Shanghai.[26] The optimism of the Nanjing decade had come to an end.

As a result, by the time the fall semester of 1937 began at Lingnan, China was at war. During the first year of the war, South China was spared an invasion, as most of the fighting took place on the North China Plain and in the Yangtze River valley. Guangzhou, however, was not spared bombardment by Japanese naval warplanes operating from bases in Taiwan and aircraft carriers off the China coast.[27] Thus, in late November 1937, an observer at Lingnan wrote, "Since Aug. 31, Canton has been air raided 102 times. Sometimes more than 30 planes come at one time, as [if] they were a group of birds." A couple of months later, William W. Cadbury (1877–1959), a long-time professor at the medical school, reported, "Since Nov. 24th [1937] there has not been a day without an alarm, once or more times, often three or four. Altogether more than 200 air raids have been staged in or near Canton."[28] These early air raids were probably directed at military targets, described by historian Hans van de Ven as "railroads, bridges, and railroad stations," and did limited damage in the city itself. Thus, Gilbert Baker, at almost the same time as Dr. Cadbury, wrote, "Things are still quite quiet here and the crowds in the streets are practically back to normal. There has been no bombing of the city since November 24, and that was the only occasion since September." And when the British writers W. H. Auden and Christopher Isherwood visited Guangzhou at the beginning of March 1938, "We saw few signs of air-raid damage. For several months now, the Japanese had dropped no bombs on the centre of the city—attacking only the railway-stations, the flying-field, and the suburbs."[29]

25. "Canton Wedding," *South China Morning Post*, 28 June 1937, p. 3; Meisenhelder, *The Dragon Smiles*, p. 159; Wallace, "Midwest China Oral History Interviews," pp. 14–15.

26. Meisenhelder, *The Dragon Smiles*, p. 169; Jay Taylor, *The Generalissimo: Chiang Kai-shek and the Struggle for Modern China* (Cambridge, MA: Harvard University Press, 2011), pp. 145–148; Coble, *China's War Reporters*, pp. 19–24.

27. Macri, *Clash of Empires in South China*, pp. 64–66.

28. Yuk Chau Ng to Ingeborg B. Stolee, [Canton], 24 November 1937, Folder 158, Box 24, RG 175, Sarah Refo Mason Papers, YDSL; William W. Cadbury to ODW, Canton, 23 January 1938, Box 73, TLUA–HYL.

29. Hans van de Ven, "Bombing, Japanese Pan-Asianism, and Chinese Nationalism," in *The International History of East Asia, 1900–1968: Trade, Ideology, and the Quest for Order*, ed. Antony Best (London and New York: Routledge, 2010),

Soon afterward, however, the Japanese, in a desperate though ultimately unsuccessful effort "to break the Nationalist will to fight and so bring the war to an end," switched to a "campaign of urban terror bombing" and began to bomb and strafe the city day and night and to target residential areas. In addition to bombs, the Japanese planes dropped leaflets calling on the local population to join Japan in common opposition to Chiang Kai-shek and the Communists.[30] In Guangzhou the terror bombing seems to have reached a crescendo from 28 May to 15 June 1938, when the city was bombed on an almost daily basis, twice or three times a day. The targets now included the power plant and waterworks in Sai Tsuen, the railroad terminals at Wong Sha and Tai Sha Tou, the two railroads, the Pearl River Bridge, the government offices around Central Park, the main north/south business street (Wing Hon Road 永漢路, now Beijing Road 北京路), Tin Tze Wharf, and the upscale Tung Shan residential district. Cumulatively, according to Chinese anti–air raid officials, from September 1937 to October 1938, 2,630 Japanese bombs were dropped on Guangzhou, killing 1,453 people and wounding 2,926, in addition to demolishing 2,004 buildings. Despite all that, the Pearl River Bridge did not fall; during air raids, the central section of the drawbridge was raised "so as to give a smaller target for bombs." And the two local railroads (the Guangzhou–Hankou and Canton–Kowloon lines) continued to operate. As the missionary Dr. Frank Oldt observed, "On both roads there are large work gangs with materials for repair and as soon as a place is torn up it is repaired in a few hours and trains proceed." In early June 1938, the news agency Reuters reported that "large sections of the city are now almost completely deserted." Perhaps as many as half of the city's one-million-plus residents had fled to their native villages or to Hong Kong.[31]

The Anglo-French settlement of Shameen, however, was off-limits to both the Japanese and the refugees. Although it was only a quarter of a mile from the much-bombed Wong Sha terminus of the Guangzhou–Hankou Railroad, Shameen itself was never bombed, because Britain and France were not yet at war with Japan. Thus it became (in the words of Shuhsi Hsu) "the only oasis of safety in a desert of desolation." Though barred from the island, thousands of refugees, nevertheless, daily flocked each day to the waterfront "to obtain the protection which its proximity to Shameen affords." Meanwhile, the foreign residents of the settlement, according to one of them, "gathered on rooftops to watch the raid[s]."[32]

Lingnan too, because of its distance from the most prominent military targets and because of its foreign connection, was largely spared the Japanese aerial bombardment. But not entirely. As the American Director in New York, Olin Wannamaker, reported, "Three bombs, which were most probably aimed at the suburban residence of Governor Wu [Tiecheng 吳鐵城], of Kwangtung Province, fell on June 8 at the western part of our grounds, in land used for agricultural purposes. Some of the residences of our faculty

pp. 103–105; Gilbert Baker to his parents, Holy Trinity College, [Canton], 27 December 1937, Folder 17, Box 5, RG 8, China Records Project, Miscellaneous Personal Papers Collection, YDSL; W. H. Auden and Christopher Isherwood, *Journey to a War*, rev. ed. (London: Faber & Faber, 1973), p. 25.

30. Van de Ven, "Bombing, Japanese Pan-Asianism, and Chinese Nationalism," pp. 105–106; Gilbert Baker, Canton, 17 January 1938, Folder 18, Box 5, RG 8, China Records Project, Miscellaneous Personal Paper Collections, YDSL.

31. Shuhsi Hsu, *Three Weeks of Canton Bombings* (Shanghai: Kelly & Walsh, 1939), pp. 1–30; Zhang Genfu, *Kangzhan shiqi de renkou qianyi—jian lun dui xibu kaifa de yingxiang* [Population migration in the resistance period and its effect on the development of the western regions] (Beijing: Guangming ribao chubanshe, 2006), p. 177; Oldt, "His Story," pp. 1,013, 1,022, 1,029, Dr. Frank Oldt Papers, HC-48, United Theological Seminary.

32. Hsu, *Three Weeks of Canton Bombing*, pp. 11–13; Richard P. Dobson, *China Cycle* (London: Macmillan & Co., 1946), pp. 52–59, 73–74.

Figure 3.4: Japanese bombardment of Guangzhou, 1937–1938. From Folder 1, Box 305, RG 8, Special Collections, YDSL.

members, including certain Americans, were only a relatively short distance from the area struck by the bombs. Fortunately, no buildings were damaged and the only casualty was one Chinese woman." Nevertheless, the following day the university authorities chartered a train to evacuate 150 to 200 students to Hong Kong. As the train made its way over the Chinese section of the Canton–Kowloon Railroad, it was bombed twice by the Japanese. The locomotive was hit and disabled, but the passenger coaches were not. The students were "forced to seek refuge in soaking paddy fields" beside the railroad tracks.[33]

As historian Parks Coble notes, the "aerial bombardment of civilian populations was . . . a relatively new phenomenon" at this time, one that provoked much opposition and generated widespread sympathy for its victims.[34] In Guangzhou, some of the Lingnan faculty members (notably chemist Clinton N. Laird [1880–1959], medical doctor William Cadbury, historians Henry C. Brownell [1887–1970] and Gilbert Baker) joined with local missionaries and the Guangzhou YMCA to form the Canton Committee for Justice to China. Its aim, as Gilbert Baker recalls, "was to influence public opinion, particularly in the U.S.A. and Great Britain, and to urge their governments to take some action to restrain Japan in this undeclared war." To this end, beginning in October 1937 and continuing to at least June 1938, it published a series of eight pamphlets or newsletters. While the committee did not demand a military response, it did call for, as two of its five objectives, an

---

33. ODW to Alfred H. Holt, New York City, 15 June 1938, Box 74, TLUA–HYL; Hsu, *Three Weeks of Canton Bombings*, pp. 17, 22–24.
34. Coble, *China's War Reporters*, p. 64.

"Economic Boycott of Japan by Western Powers" and "Aid to China in the purchase and transportation of means of defense." The Guangzhou YMCA, jointly headed by Edward H. Lockwood (1887–1957) and Y. L. Lee, coordinated the committee's activities.[35]

Meanwhile, so long as there was no Japanese invasion, Lingnan University tried to operate as normally as it could throughout the 1937–1938 school year, though with a depleted student body. According to Gilbert Baker, "At Lingnan University, where I taught courses on history and religion, we held classes in sand-bagged basement rooms for some months. All departments were asked to adapt their lectures to the war situation. . . . So we [in the religion program] planned a course on the Meaning of Adversity for Men of Faith in all ages." On the other hand, the Primary School was closed down, the Middle School relocated to Hong Kong, and the American student exchange program discontinued.[36]

The Western Languages and Literatures Department, however, was in turmoil. By the time the 1937–1938 school year began, Baldwin Lee had resigned and Pauline Aiken, unable to tolerate the Japanese air raid alerts, had departed. My father now took over as department head. Though Baldwin Lee previously had praised him as "outstanding," my father was not universally admired among his colleagues. Patty Wallace, who had shared an office with him, was scathing in a confidential letter she wrote to Provost Henry as she and her husband Franklin were leaving China: "Although he may have admirable qualities in some directions—it would be hard to imagine anyone with less interest and enthusiasm for his work, with less diligence and sense of any responsibility toward his position—than he has. And I do not feel that this is a temporary lassitude due to strains upon his nervous system this year. I think you realize that the pose Dr. R. affects is that of the tired cynic. . . . I think the department would be better with no head at all than with the alternative." The provost himself, while acknowledging that "Rhoads is apparently a good teacher," had some doubts about his qualifications as department head.[37] Nevertheless, the job fell to my father, though only in his second year, because he was now the senior professor in the department. The only other candidate might have been Julia (Mitchell) Kunkle (1878–1973), who held a PhD from Columbia (1915), but she taught only part-time at Lingnan; the rest of the time she was at the Canton Union Theological College at Paak Hok Tung, where her husband, J. Stewart Kunkle, was the president. As it turned out, Patty Wallace may well have been correct: my father did not distinguish himself as an administrator.

My parents, once married, were assigned a house in the Model Village near the Hoffmanns.[38] My mother, though pregnant, was absorbed into the social life of the university, which included being responsible once a semester for the weekly Friday staff tea. Thus, in her first year as a faculty spouse, she was scheduled to host the staff tea on 17 December 1937 and again on 22 April 1938. William Cadbury's diary entry for 22

35. Baker, *Flowing Ways*, p. 89; issues No. 2–6 and 8 of the committee's newsletter are in Folder Letters of WWC, 1937–1940, Box 1, and Folder Canton Comm. for Justice to China, Box 3, Collection No. 1160, William Warder Cadbury Papers, 1877–1951, Quaker Collection, Haverford College Library, Haverford, PA.

36. Baker, *Flowing Ways*, p. 78; Henry C. Brownell to Carl and Josephine, Canton, 20 October 1937, Folder 34, Box 1, Brownell Papers, University of Vermont Library; ODW, "Memorandum on Conditions at the University," 9 November 1937, and "Memorandum on the Situation and the Needs of the University," 3 February 1938, Folder 3238, Box 179, China College Files—Lingnan University, RG 11, United Board Archives, YDSL.

37. James M. Henry to ODW, Canton, 4 May 1937, and Patty H. Wallace to Henry, Nearing Singapore, 21 June 1937, enclosed in Henry to ODW, Canton, 29 July 1937, Box 71, TLUA–HYL. Henry's notation on Wallace's letter: "Please destroy after reading."

38. William E. Hoffmann to Ingeborg B. Stolee, Canton, 10 August 1937, Folder 158, Box 24, RG 175, Sarah Refo Mason Papers, YDSL.

Figure 3.5: The Lingnan family with visiting trustee, Harold B. Hoskins, April 1938 (detail). From Folder 645, Box 58, RG 14, Special Collections, YDSL. #1 = Trustee Harold Hoskins; #2 = President Y. L. Lee; #3 = American Director Olin D. Wannamaker; #4 = Dean Chu Yau Kwong; #5 = Provost James Henry; #6 = Frederic Chang; #7 = Henry Frank; #8 = Henry Brownell; #9 = Jane Brownell; #10 = my father; #11 = my mother.

April 1938 reads as follows: "No air raid today. Tea served at Dr. & Mrs. Rhoads." Gilbert Baker, who was British, found the staff tea to be something of "an ordeal." As he wrote his parents, "It is usually a stand up affair and according to American custom you don't eat one thing at a time but all at once!! That is, you fill up your plate with sandwiches and cakes and peanuts and balance a cup of lemon tea on it and then eat at leisure."[39]

Adding to my parents' travails, on 7 January 1938, exactly six months after the Marco Polo Bridge Incident and the outbreak of the Sino-Japanese War, I was born in Lingnan's infirmary, with the university's attending physician, Chan Yuen Kok 陳元覺 (1903–1942), a graduate of Peking Union Medical College, overseeing the delivery.[40] I was given the Chinese name Lo Hong Lok 路康樂, meaning "healthy and happy"; it was, of course, also the name of the village where Lingnan was located. I have no idea why I was given my English names, Edward John Michael. Nine months later, on 9 October 1938, I was

---

39. "Staff tea list," Folder Documents relating to the social lives of WWC & CJC, Box 1, and William W. Cadbury's diary, Entry of 22 April 1938, Box 50, both in Collection No. 1192, Cadbury & Cadbury Papers, Haverford College Library; Gilbert Baker to his parents, Lingnan, 2 November 1936, Folder 15, Box 5, RG 8, China Records Project, Miscellaneous Personal Papers Collection, YDSL.

40. ER's "Report of Birth," Canton, 13 June 1938, in my personal collection; on Dr. Chan Yuen Kok, see "Lingnan University Faculty and Staff List, 1939," p. 3, Folder Miscellaneous—Lingnan University 1/3, Box 66, Collection No. 1192, Cadbury & Cadbury Papers, Haverford College Library.

Figure 3.6: Two new mothers (mine on the right), Guangzhou, 1938.

baptized by Gilbert Baker, the Anglican missionary who had come to Lingnan a few months before my father (and who was to become later on [1966–1980] the Bishop of Hong Kong and Macau). My "sponsors" were, in addition to Baker, our neighbors in the Model Village, Professor William Hoffmann and his wife Winifred (1898–1986).[41]

Three days after my baptism, the Japanese military, having already intensified its aerial bombing of Guangzhou, opened up a third front in the war—in South China. On 12 October, the Japanese Twenty-First Army came ashore at Bias Bay, northeast of Hong Kong, and within ten days had marched into Guangzhou.[42] Unlike Wuhan, the tri-city area in central China that the Japanese captured at the same time but only after a bitter struggle lasting four months, Guangzhou on 21 October was "evacuated en masse in about 24 hours." General Yu Hanmou 余漢謀, who had succeeded Chen Jitang as the province's military leader, had simply abandoned the city without a fight, perhaps as part of Chiang Kai-shek's grand strategy of trading space for time. Both General Yu and Governor Wu Tiecheng were widely criticized; with puns on their names, Yu Hanmou was ridiculed as

41. ER's Baptism Certificate, in my personal collection; Gilbert Baker to his parents, Lingnan University, 10 October 1938, Folder 18, Box 5, RG 8, China Records Project, Miscellaneous Personal Papers Collection, YDSL.

42. Catharine Jones Cadbury to Friends at Home, Canton, 19 October 1938, Folder 1938, Box 17, Collection No. 1192, Cadbury & Cadbury Papers, Haverford College Library; Tobe Ryōichi, "The Japanese Eleventh Army in Central China, 1938–1941," in *The Battle for China: Essays on the Military History of the Sino-Japanese War of 1937–1945*, ed. Mark Peattie, Edward J. Drea, and Hans van de Ven (Stanford: Stanford University Press, 2011), pp. 213–214.

Figure 3.7: Japanese troops entering Guangzhou, 21 October 1938. Image courtesy of Ko Tim Keung.

Figure 3.8: The burning of Sai Kwan as seen from Shameen, as Nationalist troops retreat from the city, October 1938. From Folder 1, Box 305, RG 8, Special Collections, YDSL.

having "lacked a plan" (*wu mou* 無謀) and Wu Tiecheng as having "lost a city" (*shi cheng* 失城).[43] The Nationalists retreated up the North River to northern Guangdong.

As another part of Chiang Kai-shek's grand strategy—that of scorched earth—"Canton went out in a blaze of glory," in the words of British American Tobacco agent Richard P. Dobson. "The Shakee Bund, the row of shops immediately facing the island of Shameen, was deliberately fired . . . The climax came with the explosion of an ammunition dump at Wongsha station, which broke most of the windows on Shameen and knocked a number of houses off their foundations." According to journalist Hallett Abend, who visited the city in the spring of 1939, "It is the fashion in China to blame the Japanese for the almost utter destruction of this once great and prosperous city of Canton . . . But the greatest havoc and loss, fully ten times that occasioned by Japanese aerial raids, was caused by the Chinese dynamiting and setting fire to the city at the time they evacuated."[44] Yet again the Pearl River Bridge somehow survived more or less intact.

At Lingnan, which was three weeks into the new school year and under a new president (Y. L. Lee), classes were suspended immediately on news of the invasion, and the students were told to go home. At the same time, on the urgent advice of the American consul, Provost James Henry sent the wives and children of the Western staff—among them my mother and her ten-month-old baby—off to Hong Kong just before the Pearl River was closed to shipping. This was the first time our family had to flee our home; it would happen three more times over the next dozen years. On arriving in Hong Kong on 13 October, my mother and I, along with at least one other American staff member (Alice Joy [MacDonald] Campbell), found temporary refuge at the Luk Kwok Hotel on the waterfront in the Wan Chai district of Hong Kong Island. Like Shameen, British Hong Kong was not yet a target of the Japanese invasion. Most of the Chinese faculty, too, fled to Hong Kong, joining the half-million Chinese refugees who had sought shelter there from war.[45] Among these other refugees were my mother's father and his two families as well as her sister Chi Kin and her family.[46]

Acting on a suggestion from the predominantly Chinese Board of Directors, the Board of Trustees in New York immediately reclaimed possession of the Lingnan campus in order to prevent its seizure by the invaders, for the United States too was not yet at war with Japan. Provost Henry reported that he was having a dozen American flags made to fly over the university.[47] Consequently, even as they rapidly took over the rest of Guangzhou city, the Japanese left the campus alone (as it did Shameen as well). Lingnan could thus

43. Irving N. Linnell, telegrams to the Secretary of State et al., Canton, 26 and 29 October 1938, Folder Canton 1938, 110.2-875, Box 1, UD 2286: China, US Consulate, Canton, Classified General Records, 1937–1948, RG 84, Records of the Foreign Service Posts of the Department of State, USNA–CP; Macri, *Clash of Empires in South China*, pp. 90–102, 144; and Zuo Shuangwen, *Hua'nan kangzhan shigao* [A draft history of the War of Resistance in South China] (Guangzhou: Guangdong gaodeng jiaoyu chubanshe, 2004), p. 63. On Yu Hanmou, see Howard L. Boorman and Richard C. Howard, eds., *Biographical Dictionary of Republican China* (New York: Columbia University Press, 1967–1971), 4. 61–62.

44. Zuo Shuangwen, *Hua'nan kangzhan shigao*, pp. 58–60; Dobson, *China Cycle*, p. 87; Hallett Abend, *Chaos in Asia* (New York: Ives Washburn, 1939), p. 124; Gilbert Baker to his parents, Lingnan University, 24 October 1938, Folder 18, Box 5, RG 8, China Records Project, Miscellaneous Personal Papers Collection, YDSL. On Chiang's scorched earth policy, see Van de Ven, *China at War*, pp. 105–108.

45. William E. Hoffmann to Ingeborg Stolee and Mr. and Mrs. Franklin Wallace, Canton, 18 October 1938, Folder 158, Box 24, RG 175, Sarah Refo Mason Papers, YDSL; James M. Henry to ODW, Canton, 17 October 1938, and Y. L. Lee to ODW, Hong Kong, 10 November 1938, Box 75, TLUA–HYL.

46. Ngan Ki Ping, personal communication, "Gei Changshun de beiwanglu" 給昌順的備忘錄 [Memorandum to (Ngan) Cheong Shun] (Part II), 22 April 2016; Luo Ren, "Huan wo fan tanfu de ziyou," 16 January 2016.

47. James M. Henry to ODW, Canton, 17 October 1938, and Y. L. Lee to ODW, Hong Kong, 10 November 1938, Box 75, TLUA–HYL.

have continued to operate in occupied China. This is what Yenching and St. John's both did.[48] Lingnan, however, did otherwise. While it maintained a physical presence at its Guangzhou campus, it moved its academic activities to British Hong Kong.

Provost James Henry and most of the Western faculty, along with a few of the Chinese staff, remained behind to look after the Hong Lok campus and to prevent vandalism. According to Corbett's official history, "Historian [Henry] Brownell took charge of cows and pigs, water buffaloes and goats. Mathematician [Wilfred E.] MacDonald [1881–1943] ran the garden store where supplies of fruit, vegetables, milk and butter were sold. [Arthur R.] Knipp [1887–1974], physicist, and [Henry] Frank, chemist, took charge of the power plant, keeping the campus supplied with light and water." The Lingnan staff also set up on the campus one of Guangzhou's five relief centers. In mid-November 1938, Provost Henry reported, "We have 6,500 regular refugees," with an additional "300 wretches at our North Gate begging for admission." Despite enormous difficulties, the Western faculty members and their spouses managed to keep the refugee camp going for over a year. They did not close it down until the end of January 1940.[49]

My father, however, was not among the Western faculty who stayed behind in Guangzhou. Instead, Provost Henry had decided that he would be "more useful to us in Hongkong than here [in Guangzhou]." My father thus was able to rejoin my mother and me at the Luk Kwok Hotel after a separation of only about ten days.[50] He, along with three other colleagues from the Western Languages Department, were sent to Hong Kong in order to join the Chinese faculty to restart the university. For with the approval of the Chinese national Ministry of Education and the Guangdong provincial government, President Y. L. Lee had entered into negotiations with Hong Kong University to borrow some of its facilities. The result was that on 14 November, about a month after classes were suspended in Guangzhou, Lingnan University was able to resume operations in Hong Kong. Student enrollment numbered 482, which was only 20 percent fewer than before, because most Lingnan students had homes or relatives in Hong Kong.[51] At first, the Western Languages Department accounted for nearly all of the Western faculty in Hong Kong. The following year (1939–1940), in response to pleas from President Lee to strengthen the teaching staff, several more of the Western professors in Guangzhou, including Brownell (History), Frank (Chemistry), and Knipp (Physics), were transferred to Hong Kong. Provost Henry remained behind.[52]

Hong Kong at this time, as a newly arrived British police officer recalled a half-century later, was "a beautiful backwater on the coast of South China, far removed from the pulsating concrete jungle of today." It lacked the sophistication and dynamism of

48. On Yenching, see Sophia Lee, "Yenching University and the Japanese Occupation, 1937–1941," in *New Perspectives on Yenching University, 1916–1952*, ed. Arthur Lewis Rosenbaum (Chicago: Imprint Publications, 2012), pp. 107–150; on St. John's, see Mary Lamberton, *St. John's University, Shanghai, 1879–1951* (New York: United Board for Christian Colleges in China, 1955), pp. 177–184.

49. Corbett, *Lingnan University*, pp. 133–135; Y. L. Lee to ODW, Hong Kong, 10 November 1938, and James M. Henry to Harold B. Hoskins, Canton, 18 November 1938, Box 75, and W. E. MacDonald to ODW, Canton, 19 February 1940, Box 79, TLUA–HYL.

50. James M. Henry to ODW, Canton, 17 October 1938, Box 75, TLUA–HYL; "Americans Quit Canton," *New York Times*, 23 October 1938, p. 30.

51. Y. L. Lee to ODW, Hong Kong, 10 November 1938, Box 75, TLUA–HYL; "Lingnan Classes," *South China Morning Post*, 18 November 1938, p. 8; see also Bernard Hong-kay Luk, "War, Schools, China, Hong Kong: 1937–49," in *Beyond Suffering: Recounting War in Modern China*, ed. James Flath and Norman Smith (Vancouver: UBC Press), pp. 36–58.

52. James M. Henry to ODW, [Hong Kong?], 9 January 1939, and Action of Board of Directors, 14 April 1939, enclosed in Y. L. Lee to Henry, [Hong Kong], 17 April 1939, Box 76, TLUA–HYL.

contemporary Shanghai ("The Paris of the Orient"). Nevertheless, the view across the harbor from mainland Kowloon, particularly in the early evening, was as enchanting then as it is now. As described by a long-time Chinese resident, "Hong Kong Island presented a spectacle of innumerable lights cascading down from the foreign residences on the lofty Peak, through the mid-levels where the rich Chinese lived, past the foothills where the middle and lower classes dwelt, to the business district along the curving shore."[53] After the Japanese overran Guangzhou and adjacent areas of Guangdong Province, Hong Kong over the following three years came to play a role much like that of the foreign concessions in Shanghai: a "solitary [or isolated] island" (*gudao* 孤島), that is, an oasis of freedom and resistance surrounded by hostile Japanese. It was also a vital conduit—for arms, money, and personnel—from the outside world to the Chinese Nationalist regime ensconced in the interior. Though a British colony, Hong Kong was overwhelmingly—something like 98 percent—Chinese in population.

Hong Kong University, located on southwestern Hong Kong Island, had agreed to share its facilities with Lingnan, which was allowed the use of fourteen classrooms "all evenings in the week from 5:30 to 9:30." As a refugee institution, Lingnan was thus transformed essentially into a night school. Its students, however, were permitted to use the HKU library, and its administrators—principally President Y. L. Lee and the Dean of the College of Arts and Sciences, Chu Yau Kwong 朱有光 (1902–1975)—were allotted an office on the second floor of HKU's Main Building. In addition to collaborating with Hong Kong University, Lingnan rented a piece of farmland in Hong Kong's New Territories for the instructional use of its College of Agriculture.[54] In the fall of 1940, however, under pressure from the Guangdong provincial government, the College of Agriculture left Hong Kong and relocated to Ping Shek 坪石, in northern Guangdong near the Hunan border.[55]

Thus, during the three years from 1938 to 1941, Lingnan University was administered from and operated in two different locations (actually, three locations, following the removal of the School of Agriculture to Ping Shek). While President Lee and almost all of the Chinese faculty were in Hong Kong, working out of Hong Kong University, Provost Henry and some of the Western staff were in Japanese-occupied Guangzhou, keeping the old campus open. Though based in Guangzhou, Henry made frequent trips to Hong Kong to confer with his Chinese colleagues, and he continued, as the resident director of the American Foundation, to oversee the assignment of the Western personnel.

Despite such unsettled conditions, Lingnan was "filled beyond capacity." According to history professor Henry Brownell, writing in November 1941, "Few South China students now want to go to the occupied territory of the North and they cannot without great expense reach the interior." For them Lingnan University in Hong Kong was about their only choice. These refugee students, however, often found that the Hong Kong University students with whom they now shared a campus did not necessarily share their hostility toward Japan. Eileen Chang 張愛玲 was an HKU student from 1939 to 1941. In her novella, *Lust, Caution*, the chief character reminisces, "Hong Kong University had lent a

---

53. George Wright-Nooth, with Mark Adkin, *Prisoner of the Turnip Heads: The Fall of Hong Kong and Imprisonment by the Japanese* (London: Cassell, 1996), p. 28; Li Shu-fan, *Hong Kong Surgeon* (New York: E. P. Dutton & Co., 1964), p. 90.

54. Y. L. Lee to ODW, Hong Kong, 10 November 1938, Box 75, TLUA–HYL; "Lingnan Classes," *South China Morning Post*, 18 November 1938, p. 8; Corbett, *Lingnan University*, pp. 135–136; Peter Cunich, *A History of the University of Hong Kong, Volume 1, 1911–1945* (Hong Kong: Hong Kong University Press, 2012), pp. 392–393.

55. Corbett, *Lingnan University*, pp. 136–137.

few of its classrooms to the Cantonese [i.e., Lingnan] students, but lectures were always jam-packed, uncomfortably reminding them of their refugee status. The disappointing apathy of average Hong Kong people toward China's sense of national emergency filled the [Lingnan] classmates with a strong, indignant sense of exile."[56] This widespread political apathy among the local Hong Kong Chinese was due, in part, to the unwillingness of the colony's British rulers to mobilize them against the Japanese threat.

In Hong Kong, after a short spell at the Luk Kwok Hotel, my father moved us into an apartment in the Causeway Bay section of Hong Kong Island. A staff list for the university, dated October 1939, gives our new address as 9 Tin Hau Temple Road, 2/F. (Tin Hau Temple Road is a long winding road; No. 9 is at its southern end, near the present-day Tin Hau MTR station.) This was where we were still living, according to my cousin Luo Ren, at the time of the Japanese attack on Hong Kong two years later.[57]

Having joined Lingnan in 1936 on an initial three-year contract, my father was up for reappointment in 1939. In this regard, Provost Henry wrote, in late January 1939, "If the University is returning to Canton, I should certainly not recommend Dr. Rhoads for reappointment. If it is continuing in Hongkong however, there can be no objection to retaining him another year if he should wish to stay." Henry gave no reasons for such a halfhearted endorsement. He later wrote that "Rhoads is easily one of the best qualified men we have ever had & I hope we can keep him," but that he was not suited to be head of a department. Evidently, this view was shared by President Lee and Dean Chu. In the end they agreed to give my father a five-year reappointment, with a furlough (or sabbatical) to be taken in 1942–1943; during his furlough year, when he would be away from the campus, the university administrators intended to look for his replacement as department head.[58]

Meanwhile, between May 1940 and January 1941, my father suffered a series of mysterious and debilitating illnesses. They ranged from "a swollen & lame knee" (May) to possibly rheumatic fever, which confined him to bed for six weeks (July), and to "a dilated heart" (September). When he had recovered to some extent, in mid-November, he arranged to meet "his 2 classes at home, each meeting twice a week for 2 hours so as to make up lost time." It was not until mid-January 1941 that Henry Brownell was able to report, "Rhoads has been coming to the University 3 times a week and feels no serious effects." In the same time period, in addition to his other ailments, my father had a tooth extraction and a tonsil operation.[59] Despite these afflictions, we as a family were able to spend the summer of 1940 back on the Lingnan campus in Guangzhou.[60]

---

56. Henry C. Brownell to Aunt Laura, Hong Kong, 21 November 1941, Folder 35, Box 1, Brownell Papers, University of Vermont Library; Eileen Chang, *Lust, Caution*, trans. Julia Lovell (New York: Anchor Books, 2007), p. 20.

57. "Lingnan University Faculty and Staff List, 1939," Folder Miscellaneous—Lingnan University 1/3, Box 66, Collection No. 1192, Cadbury & Cadbury Papers, Haverford College Library; "Lingnan University Staff List, 1940–41 (Correct up to January 1, 1941)," Box 82, TLUA–HYL; Luo Ren, "Huan wo fan tanfu de ziyou," 16 January 2016.

58. James M. Henry to ODW, [Hong Kong?], 26 January 1939, Box 76; Henry [to ODW], [Hong Kong?], 4 February 1940, Box 79; "Vacancy in Department of English," 20 January 1941, and Henry to ODW, Macao, 28 March 1941, Box 82; Y. L. Lee to ODW, Hong Kong, 4 April 1941, Box 83; and Henry to ODW, Hong Kong, 24 July 1941, Box 84, TLUA–HYL.

59. H. C. Brownell to ODW, Hong Kong, 16 May, 8 June, 8 July, and 5 August 1940, Box 80; 16 November and 17 December 1940, Box 81; and 16 January 1941, Box 82; and James M. Henry to ODW, Hong Kong, 24 September 1940, Box 81, TLUA–HYL.

60. H. C. Brownell to ODW, Hong Kong, 5 August 1940, Box 80; and Charlotte Gower to ODW, Hong Kong, 23 September 1940, Box 81, TLUA–HYL; Mazie Laird to Catharine Jones Cadbury, [Canton], 1 August [1940], Folder Last names L (except Lambe), Box 32, Collection No. 1192, Cadbury & Cadbury Papers, Haverford College Library.

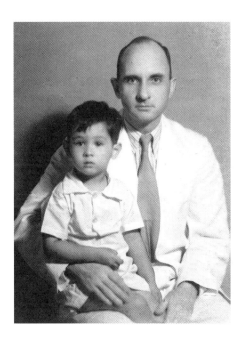

Figure 3.9: My father and me, Hong Kong, ca. 1940–1941.

My mother, in the meantime, had gone back to work at Lingnan. Before she met my father, she had been James Henry's personal secretary, but she had lost her job on marrying my father. By the spring of 1940, however, she was once again employed in the Lingnan University office, now located in the Main Building of Hong Kong University, where she took dictation and typed letters for both President Y. L. Lee and Dean Y. K. Chu. Their letters, beginning in April 1940 and continuing to at least mid-October 1941, carry her typist tags, YLL/CKR and YKC/CKR, respectively. She was also responsible for compiling the statistics for the annual reports required to maintain Lingnan's accreditation by the Regents of the University of the State of New York.[61] Perhaps because she was now working for the university's Chinese administrators rather than for Provost Henry and the American Foundation, her employment seemed no longer to be a concern. Outside of work, my mother continued her association with the Canton Women's International Club, which had also relocated to Hong Kong. She was, according to Brownell, its Corresponding Secretary. My father, as her guest, attended the club's March 1941 meeting, which was held at the European YMCA in Kowloon and featured a program of international music.[62]

Interestingly, also employed at the Lingnan University office as a clerk, at least in the fall semester of 1939, was my mother's younger half-sister Ngan Chi Tsing 顏志清. According to the staff directory, "Ngaan [*sic*] Chi Tsing" was twenty-three years old, a native of Nanhai County of Guangdong, a graduate of the Holy Spirit School (an English-language middle school staffed by Maryknoll Sisters from the United States), and living at 173 Lockhart Road, G/F, in the Wan Chai section of Hong Kong Island. The eighth child of Ngan Heung Cho, she was the first by his concubine, Wong Sam Mui. The Lockhart Road address may have been that of her mother, who maintained a residence separate

61. James M. Henry to ODW, Hong Kong, 10 March and 28 March 1940, Box 79; Y. K. Chu to ODW, Hong Kong, 11 April 1940, Y. L. Lee to Paul Monroe, Hong Kong, 22 April 1940, and Henry C. Brownell to ODW, Hong Kong, 16 May 1940, Box 80, TLUA–HYL.

62. Henry C. Brownell to ODW, Hong Kong, 16 January 1941, Box 82, TLUA–HYL; "Women's Club Meets," *South China Morning Post*, 24 March 1941, p. 5.

from my grandfather's third wife, Sam Gwu.[63] The Japanese invasion, following on the Depression, had wiped out the Chinese silk industry, including the Wing Tai Loong company. My grandfather, like many other Chinese refugees in Hong Kong, may have been left unemployed. At one point, his wife, Sam Gwu, while living at Sham Shui Po in Kowloon, operated a "punching machine" that punched "metal disks out of thin metal plates"; at another point, having moved to Wan Chai, she sold used stamps to collectors out of a storefront and lived in the back.[64]

To help her with caring for a two-year-old child and allow her to resume working, my mother would have needed the services of an "amah" or nanny. It was then common practice among even middle-class Chinese and expatriate families to employ one or more live-in servants to help with the whole gamut of household chores. Wenzell Brown (1912–1981), my father's colleague in the Western Languages Department, in his thinly fictionalized account of the fall of Hong Kong and its aftermath, describes my father (or, rather, Martin Pearson, the character based on my father) as having two servants, a fifteen-year-old girl named Ah Bau and an older, resourceful woman named Ah Jing or Ah Jung.[65]

Figure 3.10: Ngan Heung Cho and his wife, Sam Gwu, and their family at Tiger Balm Garden, Hong Kong, ca. 1941. Photo courtesy of Ngan Ki Ping (who is the second child from the right).

63. "Lingnan University Faculty and Staff List, 1939," in Folder Miscellaneous—Lingnan University 1/3, Box 66, Collection No. 1192, Cadbury & Cadbury Papers, Haverford College Library; Ngan Ki Ping, personal communications, 8 November 2014, and "Gei Changshun de beiwanglu" (Part II), 22 April 2016.

64. Lilian Li, China's *Silk Trade: Traditional Industry in the Modern World, 1842–1937* (Cambridge, MA: Council on East Asian Studies, Harvard University, 1981), pp. 5–6; "Siye juzi Cen Guohua zhi nü Cen Yufang huiyi fuqin shengping"; Ngan Ki Ping, personal communication, "Part One of Tentative notes in response to various e-mails . . . ," 8 November 2014.

65. Wenzell Brown, *Hong Kong Aftermath* (New York: Smith & Durrell, 1943), pp. 39–40.

Figure 3.11: Our "amah," Ah Hoh, n.d.

This older servant may have been, in real life, Ah Hoh. Née Look Woon Hoh, Ah Hoh (1903?–1995?) seems to have been one of the independent-minded women from silk-producing Shunde County who refused to marry and instead organized themselves into sisterhoods. Such marriage-resisting spinsters flourished within this circumscribed area of the Pearl River Delta (and nowhere else in China) during the nineteenth and early twentieth centuries. Initially they supported themselves locally in the various phases of silk production, but when the Chinese silk industry declined in the late 1920s and 1930s they migrated from the delta to nearby cities like Guangzhou and Hong Kong, where they found work as domestic servants.[66] This may have been the case with Ah Hoh. At Lingnan she had kept house for the family of chemistry professor Henry S. Frank (1902–1990) through the 1930s and had helped raise the Franks' three children, Alice, Austin, and Marian. Henry Frank and family, however, had left on furlough for the United States in the fall of 1939, and when he returned the following fall he had had to leave his wife and children behind. It was perhaps after the departure of the Franks for the United States in 1939 that Ah Hoh came to work for our family. Austin Frank, however, is of the opinion that she did not come work for us until after his father's internment by the Japanese at the beginning of 1942. In either case, Ah Hoh joined the Rhoads family in Hong Kong and was to remain with us long afterward. She lived with us and was treated as almost a member of the family. According to Austin Frank, she was known to the children she looked after as Hoh Tseh (Elder Sister Hoh).[67]

What had prevented Henry Frank's family from returning to Hong Kong with him at the start of the 1940–1941 academic year was the worsening diplomatic relations between Japan and the West and the threat of war. In June 1940, as a precaution against a Japanese attack, the British authorities in Hong Kong had suddenly ordered the evacuation of all British women and children to Australia. The US Department of State followed suit

---

66. Marjorie Topley, "Marriage Resistance in Rural Kwangtung," in *Women in Chinese Society*, ed. Margery Wolf and Roxane Witke (Stanford: Stanford University Press, 1975), pp. 67–88; Andrea Sankar, "Spinster Sisterhoods— Jing Yih Sifu: Spinster-Domestic, Nun," in *Lives: Chinese Working Women*, ed. Mary Sheridan and Janet W. Salaff (Bloomington: Indiana University Press, 1984), pp. 51–70.
67. Austin Frank, personal communications, 7 and 18 July 2013.

in October with a somewhat less dire warning; it "suggested," but did not order, that American women and children likewise evacuate.[68] Women and children already abroad, like the Franks, were discouraged from returning to China. Under such circumstances, my father must have thought about getting his wife and child out of possible harm's way. Where, however, could we have gone? Because of my father I was, from birth, an American citizen and thus eligible to go the United States. My mother, however, was not, and under the Chinese Exclusion laws in effect at this time, it would have been extremely difficult, if not impossible, for her to go to the US or even to the Philippines, which was then an American possession. An alternative was to leave Hong Kong for those parts of the interior of China that were not under Japanese occupation. My father, along with a departmental colleague, apparently did consider this option, and later "felt rather regretful that they did not take this step."[69] So we remained in Hong Kong.

Tensions continued to build. On 14 November 1941, James Henry, before leaving Hong Kong and returning to Guangzhou, wrote, "For the life of me I do not see how trouble is going to be avoided and for my part it seems to be that whatever is going to happen will come in the next 4 weeks."[70] His premonition was to come true one week earlier than he imagined.

68. Snow, *Fall of Hong Kong*, p. 42; US State Department directive, 24 October 1940, Box 81, TLUA–HYL.
69. ODW to Harold B. Hoskins, New York, 26 September 1942, Box 91, TLUA–HYL.
70. James M. Henry to ODW, Hong Kong, 14 November 1941, Box 86, TLUA–HYL.

4

The Fall of Hong Kong (1941–1943)

Hong Kong's "isolation" from the war that had been going on in China for four and a half years ended abruptly at the beginning of December 1941, when the Japanese launched an audacious, simultaneous attack on various American, British, and Dutch territories in the Pacific. Thus, on 8 December 1941 (7 December in the US)—hours after the bombing of the American naval facilities at Pearl Harbor—the Japanese Twenty-Third Army invaded Hong Kong from its land border with China. After Japanese planes had immobilized the colony's token air force on the very first day, Japanese troops advanced quickly across the rural New Territories and within four days had captured urban Kowloon. The British were forced to retreat to Hong Kong Island, which then came under heavy aerial bombardment and artillery shelling. On the night of the 18th, after the British had twice brusquely rejected a demand to surrender, the battle-hardened Japanese troops crossed the harbor, landing at North Point, and engaged the defenders in vicious battles. A week later, on the afternoon of Christmas Day, the British capitulated.[1] On the 28th the Japanese army celebrated their victory with a parade through the streets of downtown Hong Kong.

Chaos and terror reigned on Hong Kong Island, where my parents and I were then living, throughout this three-week period and afterward. During the first ten days, before the Japanese landed on the island, there had been air raids and bombardments, directed primarily at military targets, which however were scattered everywhere. A British police officer later recounted that "being bombed, shelled or mortared is an extremely frightening experience. You have absolutely no control over the situation. Nothing seems to offer adequate protection; the awful explosions, the unbelievable noise, the violent shock waves and the sickening apprehension as to where the next one will land, can combine to produce terror and inertia in all but the most courageous individuals."[2]

Over the next ten days, after the landing on the north shore of the island, there was street-to-street fighting, with hapless civilians caught in the middle. Zaza Suffiad was a Hong Kong University student living with her parents and siblings in an apartment on Tin Hau Temple Road in Causeway Bay, the same neighborhood as ours. She describes the scene on 19 December, the day after the landing, as she and her family made their way to her grandmother's house on Leighton Hill Road, next to the racecourse in Happy Valley:

---

1. Tony Banham, *Not the Slightest Chance: The Defence of Hong Kong, 1941* (Vancouver: UBC Press, 2003); see also Kwong Chi Man and Tsoi Yiu Lun, *Eastern Fortress: A Military History of Hong Kong, 1840–1970* (Hong Kong: Hong Kong University Press, 2014), ch. 8.
2. Wright-Nooth, *Prisoner of the Turnip Heads*, pp. 54–55.

Figure 4.1: Japanese victory parade, Wan Chai, Hong Kong Island, 28 December 1941. Image courtesy of Ko Tim Keung.

In our hurry to get there, we stepped over many dead bodies. People were shot in the street, in cars and trucks, and even in ambulances. It was a terrifying sight. Reaching our grandmother's house, we met cousins and friends who had also gathered there thinking it was safer ground. Unfortunately, that was not to be. That very night, there suddenly came loud banging on the door. Three Japanese soldiers entered, armed with guns and bayonets. In the darkness—the electricity was out—they shone their flashlights at our faces and hands. When they saw a wrist watch, they snatched it. They were also looking for women. When a soldier approached my oldest sister, who was sitting on the floor holding her two-year-old baby, she quickly pinched the baby and he started to cry. That was enough of a distraction that the soldier turned his attention elsewhere. They pulled three of the women upstairs and raped them.[3]

After the British had surrendered on the 25th, until the Japanese restored some semblance of order and held their victory parade on the 28th, some of the Japanese troops engaged in unruly behavior that, to some observers and historians, was reminiscent of the Rape of Nanjing.[4] As they invaded people's homes and plundered, raped, and killed at will, some local Chinese, taking advantage of the disorder, looted abandoned shops and private homes. Food prices shot up. Bodies of dead British soldiers lay unattended everywhere. It was dangerous to be out and about.[5]

---

3. Zaza Hsieh, "My War Years in Hong Kong, China and India," in *Dispersal and Renewal: Hong Kong University during the War Years*, ed. Clifford Matthews and Oswald Cheung (Hong Kong: Hong Kong University Press, 1998), p. 40.
4. See Snow, *Fall of Hong Kong*, pp. 81–82, and Li, *Hong Kong Surgeon*, pp. 108–111.
5. Brown, *Hong Kong Aftermath*, ch. 1–2; Norman Briggs, *Taken in Hong Kong, December 8, 1941: Memoirs of Norman Briggs, World War II Prisoner of War*, comp. Carol Briggs Waite (Baltimore: PublishAmerica, 2006), Section II.

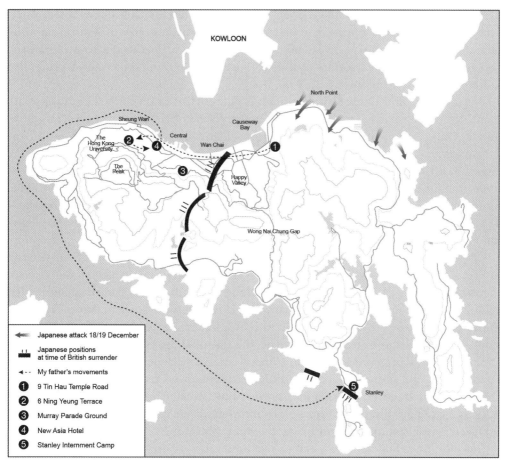

Map 4.1: Hong Kong Island, December 1941–January 1942. Map by Ada Au-Yeung.

Causeway Bay, where we and the Suffiads were living, was near the Japanese beach-head at North Point and in the path of their advance up toward the Wong Nai Chung Gap; along with Happy Valley, it was also where "poorly disciplined Japanese rear-area troops" may have been doing the plundering and raping.[6] At some point amid all this turmoil, my parents, with their soon-to-be four-year-old son in tow, fled their flat on Tin Hau Temple Road and joined three other members of Lingnan's Western Languages Department (Wenzell Brown, Carlton L. Castle [1916–1989], and Ernest J. Kelley [1897–1979]) in seeking refuge with their senior colleague, chemistry professor Henry Frank. (The fifth member of the department, John C. Guthrie [1916–2007], had enlisted in the Hong Kong Volunteer Defence Corps and joined the armed resistance.) Frank, who had returned from the US without his family, had rented a two-room apartment at 6 Ning Yeung Terrace, near Hong Kong University, which was on the opposite side of the island from the fighting.[7] According to journalist Emily Hahn, "On that side of the island we didn't have any shells except a stray one that came hurtling now and then across the Peak.

---

6.   Chi Man Kwong, personal communication, 20 July 2020.
7.   "Lingnan University Staff List, 1940–41 (Correct up to January 1, 1941)," Box 82, and Y. L. Lee to ODW, Kukong, 27 January 1942, Box 87, TLUA–HYL; Brown, *Hong Kong Aftermath*, pp. 37–41.

Planes were bombing Mount Davis nearby, but they left us pretty well alone."[8] Meanwhile, according to Wenzell Brown's fictionalized account, Japanese troops had broken into our home at Causeway Bay, threatened the younger of our two servants with rape, and had taken away an odd assortment of items, including "a razor, a picture of a dog, [my mother's] bracelets and some jade."[9]

In the week after the British surrender, my parents and I remained at Frank's apartment. In Brown's book, I make a cameo appearance as "Joe Pearson," who "was never quiet." Once, "when the Chinese landlord told us that Japanese officers were in the apartment below . . . [w]e were ordered not to make a sound," so as not to attract the attention of the Japanese. "Mrs. Pearson tried to hold Joe who was not old enough to understand. She talked to him softly in Cantonese. Joe squirmed and banged and tried to free himself." Fortunately, after half an hour, the Japanese left the apartment downstairs. The crisis passed: I had not betrayed our presence. Brown and Castle ("Clayron") soon left Frank's place; we stayed.[10]

Japan's justification for its military actions had been to liberate the oppressed peoples of East and Southeast Asia from the yoke of Western imperialism; its slogan was "Asia for the Asians." During the three-week war in Hong Kong, its planes had dropped leaflets calling on the local Chinese—and Indians too—to reject their British overlords and rally to the Japanese side. These appeals met with indifferent success. Most Chinese residents stood on the sidelines, neither coming to the aid of the British nor welcoming their "rescuers." In those parts of mainland China it already occupied, including Guangzhou, Japan had set up indigenous, collaborationist regimes, such as that of Wang Jingwei. Oddly enough, however, the Japanese, having thus dramatically ended ninety-nine years of British colonial rule, never returned Hong Kong to the Chinese. Instead, they simply replaced British colonial rule with Japanese military rule.[11]

As the United States, Britain, and the Netherlands were now openly at war with Japan, their nationals in Hong Kong were soon rounded up and incarcerated. Enemy combatants (including John Guthrie, the English teacher at Lingnan) were sent to prisoner-of-war camps at Sham Shui Po and elsewhere; civilians, like my father, were dealt with separately. On 4 January 1942, ten days after the surrender, the Japanese gendarmerie (Kempeitai) published an order directing all "enemy civilians" (principally British, American, and Dutch) to assemble the following morning at the Murray Parade Ground in the central business district of Hong Kong Island (now the site of the Cheung Kong Centre). They were not told the purpose of the assembly, and afterward they were not allowed to return home to fetch their belongings. Instead, those who showed up, numbering about one thousand, were led off to several hotels along the waterfront near the present-day Macau ferry terminal in Sheung Wan district.[12] Among them was Wenzell Brown: "We marched, down the main streets of the city [principally, Des Voeux Road Central]. Chinese coolies gazed at us, sombre-eyed. The Japanese guards made a show of

---

8.   Emily Hahn, *China to Me: A Partial Autobiography* (Garden City, NY: Doubleday, Doral & Company, 1944), p. 273.
9.   Brown, *Hong Kong Aftermath*, pp. 39–40. Of Brown's book, published soon after the events, Tony Banham, *Not the Slightest Chance*, p. 392, says the following: "this book does more to capture the atmosphere of wartime Hong Kong than any other. Well worth reading to understand what the experience must have been like." Brown became, in the 1950s and 1960s, a prolific pulp fiction writer.
10. Brown, *Hong Kong Aftermath*, pp. 40–41.
11. John M. Carroll, *A Concise History of Hong Kong* (Lanham, MD: Rowman & Littlefield, 2007), p. 121.
12. Geoffrey Charles Emerson, *Hong Kong Internment, 1942 to 1945: Life in the Japanese Civilian Camps at Stanley* (Hong Kong: Hong Kong University Press, 2008), p. 36.

their authority and prodded us with their sticks." Brown eventually ended up opposite a Wing On department store at what he in his book calls the South Asia Hotel but was most likely the New Asia Hotel, at 206–210 Des Voeux Road Central.[13]

Not all enemy aliens showed up at the Murray Parade Ground on 5 January, however. My father, for one, did not. Instead, the head of Hong Kong University had been "able to arrange with the Japanese military authorities for the campus to be reserved as a temporary internment camp for University staff, other British nationals and some of the expatriate staff of Lingnan University." Thus, our family had stayed put with Henry Frank. But it turned out to be just "a short reprieve."[14] Several days later, according to Brown, my father—together with Henry Frank ("Dobson") and Ernest Kelley ("Murphy")—showed up at the waterfront hotel, "staggering under the weight of heavy suitcases" and evidently accompanied by my mother and Ah Hoh.[15] Other families, including the Brownells and the Lairds among the Lingnan contingent, managed to remain at liberty even longer— until the beginning of February—and so avoided being sent to the waterfront hotels altogether.[16] My mother and I, however, were not subject to internment, as we were not considered "enemy aliens." If Austin Frank is correct, it was at this time, after his father had been interned, that Ah Hoh came to work for us.

Though Brown described the four-story New Asia Hotel as "a waterfront brothel before the war" and "a tenth-rate dirty little Chinese hotel," it seems to have been, in fact, a fairly respectable establishment, part of a small hotel chain with branches in Guangzhou and Shanghai.[17] Nevertheless, conditions for the 350 men, women, and children who found themselves confined there in January 1942 were pretty awful. Six people were jammed into a room with only one bed and no lights; according to Brown, "it was almost impossible for all six to get into the room at the same time." Bathing and toilet facilities were scarce and primitive: "A solitary bathtub . . . was soon filled high with filth and rubble. There was no water and no opportunity for bathing. One toilet seat served the ninety-odd people on our floor." They were fed "spoiled food." They "were never permitted to go out for air or exercise." Many came down with dysentery. Historian Geoffrey Emerson concurs that the internees at the hotels experienced "appallingly overcrowded, filthy conditions with very poor food."[18] According to Brown, "Dr. Pearson [his name for my father] sat hour after hour on the edge of Dobson's [i.e., Henry Frank's] bed, staring

13. Brown, *Hong Kong Aftermath*, pp. 53–54, 69; but elsewhere, in "'Tell America What They Have Done to Us . . .'," *Saturday Review*, 9 January 1943, p. 6, he calls the place where he was taken the New Asia Hotel. For the address of the hotel, see "G.R. [George Rex] Licensing Sessions," *South China Morning Post*, 17 October 1932, p. 4.

14. Cunich, *History of the University of Hong Kong*, vol. 1, p. 403; Jean Gittins, *Stanley: Behind Barbed Wire* (Hong Kong: Hong Kong University Press, 1982), p. 32.

15. Brown, *Hong Kong Aftermath*, p. 64. Austin Frank, personal communication, 7 July 2013, tells a wonderful story about Ah Hoh at the time of his father's internment. "Ah Hoh accompanied my father to the hotel to which he had to report and before entering he handed her his gold pocket watch. This was a lovely engraved hunting-case Elgin, a watch which had been given to his maternal grandfather by his wife at the time of their fiftieth wedding anniversary in the 1870s. My father asked her to keep it for him if she could, but said if she became desperate she should sell it to take care of herself. Then, when he returned to the [Lingnan] campus in 1946 she handed it back to him. . . . I now have the watch."

16. C. N. Laird [to Family], [Rio de Janeiro], 6 August 1942, and Laird [to no name] Washington, 6 May 1943, Folder 155, Box 23, RG 175, Sarah Refo Mason Papers, YDSL.

17. Brown, *Hong Kong Aftermath*, p. 54; Wenzell Brown, "I Was a Prisoner of the Japs [Part 1]," *Liberty* magazine, 10 October 1942, p. 18; "New Canton Hotel," *South China Morning Post*, 28 June 1929, p. 13; "A New Chinese Hotel [in Shanghai]," *South China Morning Post*, 23 August 1932, p. 16.

18. Brown, *Hong Kong Aftermath*, pp. 54–83; Geoffrey Charles Emerson, "Behind Japanese Barbed Wire: Stanley Internment Camp, Hong Kong, 1942–1945," *Journal of the Hong Kong Branch of the Royal Asiatic Society* 17 (1977): 31.

into space. We knew that he was thinking of his wife and son, yet his attitude of dejection soon got on our nerves."[19]

Finally, beginning about 21 January the internees were released from their several waterfront hotels and taken to an internment camp on the south side of Hong Kong Island. "Many were dazed by the first sunlight they had seen for more than three weeks," Brown wrote. For the moment, however, they were relieved. "No matter where we went," they reckoned, "it could not be worse than the filthy brothels from which we had come." As they left their hotels, they "were paraded through the main streets again in order that the Chinese might witness the fall of the white man." An old ferry boat took them around the island to Stanley.[20]

The internment camp, which covered about one square mile, was located on the neck of a small, hilly peninsula between Stanley Village (now the site of the tourist-friendly Stanley Market) and Stanley Fort, and had beautiful views of the sea, the sky, and offshore islands. The camp occupied the grounds of St. Stephen's College (an Anglican preparatory school) and portions of Stanley Prison (though not the prison itself). The internees by early February 1942 numbered close to 2,800. Most (2,400) were British; 325 were American, and 42 were Dutch "and perhaps as many Canadians." They included about 1,300 men, 1,000 women, and 400 children. Among the Americans, besides my father, were eight of his Lingnan colleagues, three of their wives, and two teenage daughters.[21]

Meanwhile, with the US now at war with Japan, the Lingnan campus in Guangzhou had lost its diplomatic immunity and was taken over by the Japanese, as was the Anglo-French settlement of Shameen. The Americans who had remained at the campus, including Provost James Henry, were interned separately in Guangzhou, where for more than a year they were subject to a loose form of house arrest. According to Greg Leck, who has compiled a voluminous study of all the internment camps in China, "Canton camp was probably the best in China in terms of food, housing, and treatment."[22]

The Hong Kong internees arrived at Stanley less than a month after the fighting ended. St. Stephen's College had been the scene of last-ditch resistance by the British and of a brutal retaliatory massacre of wounded soldiers and attending nurses by the Japanese. "Everywhere was littered with the debris of war," British police officer George Wright-Nooth recorded in his diary. Some of the dead still lay about; others had been hastily buried in shallow graves. The building where Wright-Nooth initially lodged "had a shell hole through the roof, all windows were smashed and the walls scarred by bullets or shrapnel. The water pipes had burst, the drains were blocked and overflowing, blood was splattered everywhere." It was up to the inmates themselves to fix the place up.[23]

---

19. Brown, *Hong Kong Aftermath*, p. 77.
20. Brown, *Hong Kong Aftermath*, pp. 85, 87.
21. Emerson, "Behind Japanese Barbed Wire," p. 31; Emerson, *Hong Kong Internment*, p. 59; "Staff members of Lingnan University," 17 January 1942, Box 87, TLUA–HYL. The Lingnan internees at Stanley, aside from my father, were Wenzell Brown, Henry Brownell (with wife Jane and daughter Betty Jane), Carlton Castle, Henry Frank, Charlotte Gower, Ernest Kelley, Arthur Knipp (with wife Rene and daughter Margaret), and Clinton Laird (with wife Mary Soles).
22. Greg Leck, *Captives of Empire: The Japanese Internment of Allied Civilians in China, 1941–1945* ([Bangor, PA]: Shandy Press, 2006), pp. 434–437, 528–529. The Lingnan internees in Guangzhou were William Cadbury (and wife Catharine), J. Linsley Gressitt (with wife Margaret and baby Sylvia), James Henry, William Hoffmann, and Wilfred MacDonald (and wife Mabel). Mathematics professor MacDonald died of cancer just before he could be repatriated in 1943, and Mrs. Hoffmann was separately interned in Manila and not released until the end of the war.
23. Wright-Nooth, *Prisoner of the Turnip Heads*, pp. 87–88.

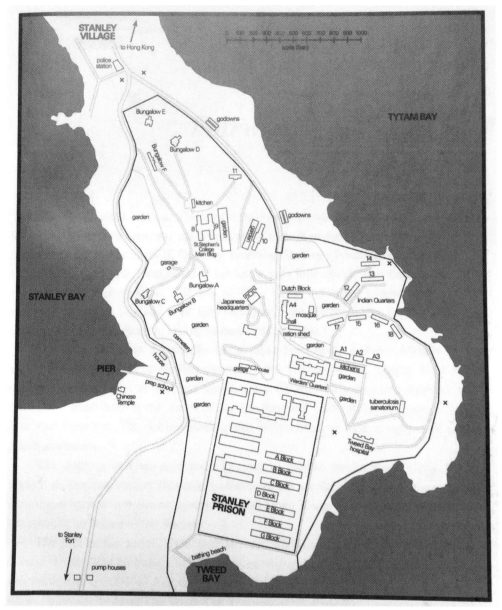

Map 4.2: The Stanley Civilian Internment Camp. From Geoffrey Emerson, *Hong Kong Internment*; used with permission. A1, A2, and A3 = The American Block; x = guard stations.

Figure 4.2: Representatives of the American internees and Japanese officials, Stanley internment camp, June 1942. From *New York Herald Tribune*, 17 August 1942. Alvah W. Bourne, the chair, is fifth from the right; Henry Frank is third from the left.

Once they were taken into the barbed-wire enclosure, they were largely left alone. According to historian Emerson, "the Japanese had little to do with them. A few necessities, namely a minimal amount of food, were provided, but the internees were left to run the Camp themselves." Each of the three principal national groups—the British, the Americans, and the Dutch—formed a self-governing council, whose elected chief officer was authorized to deal with the officials in charge of the camp.[24] Henry Frank, the Lingnan chemistry professor, was a member of the American council.

Each of the three national communities tended to live together and apart from the others. They each found their own housing in the camp. The Americans occupied the second floor of the former Prison Officers' Club and three nearby three-story blocks of flats, which were known to the internees as the American Quarters or the American Block and which previously had housed the European warders of the prison. Historian Geoffrey Emerson writes, "each flat [in the American Quarters] had several rooms, living and dining areas, bedrooms, kitchen and Western-style toilet. These had been designed for one family, but during internment an average of thirty internees lived in each flat." Each room in a flat thus held four to six internees.[25] According to information passed on by "a Chinese lad" to the wife of the American YMCA secretary in Free China, my father shared a room with three Lingnan colleagues—Henry Frank, Ernest Kelley, and Carlton Castle—and possibly with Wenzell Brown and one other person as well. Their flat was on the ground floor of one of the three buildings in the American Block. "Very few

24. Emerson, "Behind Japanese Barbed Wire," p. 33; Brown, *Hong Kong Aftermath*, pp. 129–130; Allman, *Shanghai Lawyer*, p. 7.
25. Emerson, *Hong Kong Internment*, p. 45.

Figure 4.3: The "American Block" at Stanley, 2010.

[internees] had beds," Clinton Laird later wrote. "Some had cots, and many rolled up in blankets on the floor."[26]

Europeans and Americans with wives and children—like the Brownells, the Knipps, and the Lairds among the Lingnan contingent—were interned as families and lived together as families. My father may have tried to have my mother—and, thus, me too—join him in the camp. The reason might have been, as Dr. Li Shu-fan said of another woman in a similar situation, that she "would find greater safety and freedom from [Japanese] molestation in the camp" and also that "she would not have to worry about the necessities of life, for with the closing of business houses and the suspension of shipping it would be hard to earn a living [on the outside]."[27] However, according to Carlton Castle, writing from the American Block at the end of January 1942, "All Chinese and Eurasian people have been asked to leave the camp. That means that Mrs. Rhoads will not be able to join hcr husband as he had hoped to have her do."[28] A few Eurasians and Chinese did remain in the camp, but my mother and I were not among them. Instead, though living in Hong Kong until mid- or late March, we were on the outside, staying (with Ah Hoh) not in our

26. Muriel Lockwood to Priscilla, Ruth, and Brownell Family, Kukong, 10 March 1942, Folder 35, Box 1, Brownell Papers, University of Vermont Library; Brown, *Hong Kong Aftermath*, p. 114. C. N. Laird [to family], [Rio de Janeiro], 6 August 1942, Folder 155, Box 23, RG 175, Sarah Refo Mason Papers, YDSL.

27. Li, *Hong Kong Surgeon*, p. 141.

28. C. L. Castle to Mr. Chan, Hong Kong, 30 January 1942, Folder Last names A–C (except Cadbury), Box 43, Collection No. 1192, Cadbury & Cadbury Papers, Haverford College Library.

old flat on Tin Hau Temple Road but rather in Henry Frank's abandoned apartment near Hong Kong University.[29]

Unlike the internees in Guangzhou, those at Stanley were not allowed to send or receive letters. As a result, they were largely cut off from news of the external world. As Presbyterian missionary M. S. Ady recalled afterward, "One of the chief troubles all of the time [in Stanley] was that we were so isolated, almost hermetically sealed. There was no communication from the outside except for the little news smuggled in." Lingnan chemistry professor Clinton Laird likewise wrote after his release from captivity, "I doubt if anyone can appreciate how completely out of touch we were at Stanley with the outside world, how impossible it was to write or receive letters. Dr. Rhoads got some messages from his wife through the grapevine, and I had a very short letter from Dr. Henry [interned in Guangzhou] through the [Japanese] military, and that was all in months."[30]

As Laird mentioned, my parents, though physically separated, were able by some means to communicate with each other. One way was with the help of local foreigners who were not interned because they were citizens of neutral nations, such as George Stacy Kennedy-Skipton, a Hong Kong civil servant of Irish descent. Kennedy-Skipton was a friend of Henry B. Refo (1898–1993), an American Presbyterian missionary who had taught at Lingnan in the 1920s and whose wife, Sarah Flaniken (1895–1956), had been one of my mother's teachers at True Light Middle School. When Henry Refo entered the Stanley internment camp in early February 1942, he wrote to Kennedy-Skipton, enclosing a long wish list of daily-use items that the internees lacked. This letter also included a note from my father to my mother, together with a request that Kennedy-Skipton "get her on the phone" and "tell her that her husband will be sending letters to her in care of the D.M.S. from time to time and for her to go there say twice a week to get them. She may leave letters for him with them also."[31] The Director of Medical Services to whom Refo referred was Dr. Selwyn Selwyn-Clarke, who, though British, was not interned until 1943.

Another local foreigner who helped my parents and other internees exchange information with the world outside the camp was Edgar Laufer, a German Jewish refugee employed by China Light and Power in Hong Kong. In late January 1942, Laufer visited my father's colleague Carleton Castle and helped him smuggle out a long letter, which my mother, acting as an intermediary in this case, was then to deliver to a "Mr. Chan," its intended recipient. In this letter Castle mentioned that my mother had been able to similarly pass a note to my father.[32] On yet another occasion, a former student of Wenzell Brown showed up on the other side of the camp's barbed-wire fence bearing a couple of

29. H. B. Refo [to George Kennedy-Skipton], [Stanley], no date, in File HKRS 158-3-12, Mr. G. S. Kennedy-Skipton—Committee of Enquiry, 8 March 1943 to 28 May 1947, Public Records Office, Hong Kong.

30. M. S. Ady, "Hongkong," A Report Prepared for Conference with Repatriated Missionaries, First Presbyterian Church, New York City, 31 August–1 September 1942, Folder 17, Box 62, RG 82, Secretaries' Files: China Mission, Presbyterian Board of Foreign Missions, Presbyterian Historical Society; Clinton N. Laird to ODW, [Rio de Janeiro], 5 August 1942, Box 90, TLUA–HYL.

31. Sarah Alice Refo to Family and Friends, Aboard the *Gripsholm*, 1 August 1942, Folder 172, Box 26, RG 175, Sarah Refo Mason Papers, YDSL; H. B. Refo [to George Kennedy-Skipton], [Stanley], no date, in File HKRS 158-3-12, Mr. G. S. Kennedy-Skipton—Committee of Enquiry, 8 March 1943 to 28 May 1947, Public Records Office, Hong Kong. On Kennedy-Skipton, see Philip G. Cracknell, "The Strange Case of Mr. Kennedy-Skipton" (November 2014), battleforhongkong.blogspot.co.uk (last accessed 11 July 2020).

32. C. L. Castle to Mr. Chan, Hong Kong, 30 January 1942, Folder Last names A–C (except Cadbury), Box 43, Collection No. 1192, Cadbury & Cadbury Papers, Haverford College Library.

messages. One of them was from my mother to my father ("Pearson" in Brown's telling), saying, "She and the boy had left the city in an attempt to get to the interior."[33]

The Americans, as a whole, were generally better off than the other two national groups in the camp. According to Jean (Hotung) Gittins, a Eurasian native of Hong Kong living among the British contingent, "The Americans . . . stood out as the most favoured nation: throughout their short internment they enjoyed many privileges in food and accommodation which were denied the rest of the camp." An American internee concurred: "We lived in luxury in comparison with the British."[34] The reason for this, according to Wenzell Brown, was that the chief representative of the Americans, a man he called "Jack Bayne," had deliberately "padded the number of Americans coming into the camp and, by so doing, secured more than a fair allotment of space [and food] for our group." "Jack Bayne" was, in real life, William P. Hunt, whom Emily Hahn identified as "the American shipping man and dashing buccaneer." Others did not speak so admiringly of Hunt. He was later transferred by the Japanese to Shanghai and was succeeded as chief representative of the Americans by Alvah W. Bourne Jr., a Standard Oil executive.[35] The Americans had also managed to bring into camp from Hong Kong's American Club a very good library, which was housed in what had been the Prison Officers' Club. The books were made available only to the Americans.[36]

"If living conditions presented a grim picture," writes Gittins, "food in the camp was infinitely worse." "The biggest problem throughout internment," historian Emerson agrees, "concerned food. There simply was never enough, and what there was, was very poor. . . . Food was delivered daily to Camp by a ration truck and distributed to the various kitchens in camp. . . . The meals usually consisted of rice and a stew poured on top, made from whatever meat (usually water-buffalo meat), fish and/or vegetables were provided." Each national group of internees was expected to cook their own food, which the Americans prepared in "a community mess hall" located in what had been a fourteen-car garage across the road from the American Block.[37] According to information that one of the Lingnan internees, Carlton Castle, managed to smuggle out, "They get two meals a day, rice with but little vegetable & sometimes a little fish. Castle says they are hungry all of the time." As journalist and internee Gwen Dew wrote, "It was a sad and dreary sight to see the ragged internees line up each day [at 10 and 5] with their tin pails and cans for food which was unsatisfying and disagreeable anyway, eating just to stay alive." Also, Clinton Laird noted, "No dishes, or tableware were provided so plates and spoons were at a premium and tin cans were used for a great variety of things."[38]

Except for their chief representatives, the internees rarely had to deal directly with the Japanese. When they did cross paths with a Japanese, there were specific instructions on how to behave. According to Wenzell Brown, "The hat must be removed from the

33. Brown, *Hong Kong Aftermath*, p. 245.
34. Gittins, *Stanley: Behind Barbed Wire*, p. 117; M. S. Ady, "Hongkong," Folder 17, Box 62, RG 82, Secretaries' Files: China Mission, Presbyterian Board of Foreign Missions, Presbyterian Historical Society.
35. Brown, *Hong Kong Aftermath*, p. 114; Briggs, *Taken in Hong Kong*, pp. 155–159, calls him "The Brain"; Hahn, *China to Me*, p. 278.
36. David Bellis, "78 Years Ago: Hong Kong's Wartime Diaries," for 28 August 1942, Barbara Anslow's Diary, https://gwulo.com/78-years-ago (accessed 28 August 2020).
37. Gittins, *Stanley: Behind Barbed Wire*, p. 55; Emerson, "Behind Japanese Barbed Wire," p. 34; Allman, *Shanghai Lawyer*, p. 7.
38. E. H. Lockwood to Mrs. James Henry, Kukong, 31 March 1942, Box 88, TLUA–HYL; Gwen Dew, *Prisoner of the Japs* (New York: Alfred A. Knopf, 1943), p. 238; C. N. Laird [to Family], [Rio de Janeiro], 6 August 1942, Folder 155, Box 23, RG 175, Sarah Refo Mason Papers, YDSL.

head; hands must not be in the pockets; there must be no smoking; we must bow. Above all, it was stated, we must at no time look down upon a Japanese soldier." Violators were slapped in the face or otherwise punished. Following the successful escape of several internees in late March 1942, a twice-daily roll call, at 8 a.m. and 10 p.m., was instituted.[39]

In addition to constant hunger, life in the camp was marked by monotony and perhaps a sense of hopelessness. According to Emily Hahn, the American journalist who had managed to stay out of Stanley because she had once been married to a Chinese but who nevertheless managed to keep in touch with some of the internees, "The Stanley people were being starved and herded like cattle, but they had no responsibility, nothing to do except to line up and wait for boiled water and food, after they had cleaned their rooms and picked up their blankets." According to Brown, "In the early evenings, the internees sat outside their quarters, gossiping, sometimes reading to each other the few books that they possessed. Others strolled up and down the roads and hailed one another as they walked. The camp was like a small town, save that the inhabitants were incredibly ragged and half-starved." It was, surprisingly, also a noisy place. Barbara (Redwood) Anslow, a British internee, recalls that "people were always coming and going, we led a very outdoor life. In the evenings there was intermittent conversation between the occupants of every room, and in the corridors and the queues for the bathroom."[40]

Carlton Castle, in the letter smuggled out of the camp in late January, gave a detailed account of the internees' daily routine. They rose at 8; dressed, washed, walked around the grounds between 8 and 10; ate their first meal at 10 and afterwards cleaned up the kitchen; worked (e.g., sawing wood, burying garbage) between 11 and 2 or 3; had tea at 3 ("this is quite a simple affair consisting of one of the two slices of bread we are allowed as a ration and a plain cup of tea"); rested or studied between 3 and 5; ate their second meal at 5; socialized between 5 and 8 ("we walk around and exchange rumours with fellow enternees [*sic*]"); and recreated between 8 and 10 ("the four of us usually play bridge").[41]

My father, according to Brown, spent much of the time during his internment worrying about his health. "Pearson was a hypochondriac." He was constantly counting his pulse, taking his temperature, and checking his reflexes. "The walls of his room were soon covered with charts, as they had been at the [waterfront] hotel." (There may, however, have been some basis for my father's alleged hypochondria, because he had been quite ill from May 1940 to January 1941.) Also, according to Brown, my father "alternated periods of moody silence with the singing of little tunes [and nonsense rhymes]." Furthermore, "Pearson rarely left the room, although on occasions he took a slow, poking jaunt about the camp. He carried with him a stick made from the branch of a tree . . . He was always dressed in his one suit—a bright green tweed with a design of red triangles in it. . . . Actually the suit was of excellent quality; there was not the slightest sign of fading throughout a seven-month period. Pearson, however, lost forty pounds and soon the green suit billowed about him in waves."[42]

Mercifully for the Americans, their internment at Stanley was relatively brief. As a result of negotiations between Japan and the United States (with Switzerland and the

39. Brown, *Hong Kong Aftermath*, pp. 166–168; Emerson, *Hong Kong Internment*, pp. 158–159.
40. Hahn, *China to Me*, p. 340; Brown, *Hong Kong Aftermath*, p. 243; Barbara Anslow, *Tin Hats and Rice: A Diary of Life as a Hong Kong Prisoner of War, 1941–1945* (Hong Kong: Blacksmith Books, 2018), p. 324.
41. C. L. Castle to Mr. Chan, Hong Kong, 30 January 1942, Folder Last names A–C (except Cadbury), Box 43, Collection No. 1192, Cadbury & Cadbury Papers, Haverford College Library.
42. Brown, *Hong Kong Aftermath*, pp. 152–156.

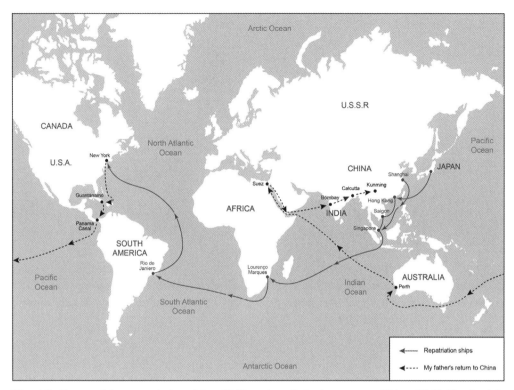

Map 4.3: Route of the repatriation ships, 1942, and my father's return to China, 1943. Map by Ada Au-Yeung.

International Red Cross as intermediaries), it was agreed that there would be an exchange of diplomatic personnel and enemy civilians. Japanese who had been detained in the US after the outbreak of war (among them Ambassador Nomura Kichisaburō) were allowed on 19 June 1942 to leave New York aboard the Swedish liner, the *Gripsholm*, bound for Lourenço Marques, Portuguese East Africa (now Maputo, Mozambique), which was neutral in the war. At roughly the same time, a Japanese passenger ship, the *Asama Maru*, departed Japan with 432 repatriates (including Joseph Grew, the American ambassador to Japan) and headed for Hong Kong. Both vessels were clearly marked, and traveled with their lights blazing, so that they would not be mistaken for troop ships. Arriving off Stanley Peninsula on 29 June, the *Asama Maru* picked up 377 (mostly American) internees, including my father and all his Lingnan colleagues in the camp. Max Hill, an American journalist already aboard, described the new arrivals as "mostly skin and bones." The ship left Hong Kong the next day.[43] During the couple of weeks prior to their departure, the rest of the camp had bid the Americans farewell with a concert and a dance. A day or two before they left, the elected leaders of the American community got all dressed up and had their photograph taken with the two Japanese camp officials.[44] (See Figure 4.2.)

---

43. Max Hill, *Exchange Ship* (New York and Toronto: Farrar & Rinehart, 1942), p. 174; Emerson, *Hong Kong Internment*, pp. 64–67; Leck, *Captives of Empire*, pp. 285, 287.
44. Anslow, *Tin Hats and Rice*, pp. 95, 99; Brown, *Hong Kong Aftermath*, p. 270.

Figure 4.4: Japanese passenger ship, *Asama Maru*, 1936. Photo by Walter E. Frost. Image courtesy of the City of Vancouver Archives.

The *Asama Maru* took on another 200 or so repatriates in Saigon, French Indo-China (now Ho Chi Minh City, Vietnam), before sailing to Japanese-occupied Singapore, where it met up with an Italian liner, the *Conte Verde*, bearing about 600 American internees from Shanghai. Thereafter, as a passenger aboard the *Asama Maru* recalled, "after a stop off the Malay coast 50 miles from Singapore, a sight of the crater of Krakatoa and views of Sumatra and Java as we passed through the Sunda Strait we saw no further land and no boats except the *Conte Verde* . . . until we reached Lourenco Marques." According to Max Hill, "We pitched, tossed and rolled for two weeks, seeing nothing but our companion ship, the *Conte Verde*, and the sky and the rough blue waters and whitecaps of the Indian Ocean." When the two ships arrived at Lourenço Marques on 22 July, the *Gripsholm* was already in port. The American and Japanese repatriates traded places the following day.[45]

It was only when the more than 1,500 Americans had boarded the *Gripsholm* that they were free from Japanese captivity. "We had been lifted . . . into a floating hotel where we could have movies, entertainments, dances, bars, magazines and newspapers only two months old, swimming pools and, above all, freedom of speech." "At last people could speak up without hesitation, interviews could be held, questionnaires could be answered, radio news could be heard." And memoirs could be written. The food, too, was far better, more varied and more plentiful. "We made gluttons of ourselves with oatmeal or Cream of Wheat, bacon or ham and eggs and toast and jam and coffee for breakfast, and luncheons and dinners always were ample and well cooked."[46]

During their six-day layover in Lourenço Marques, the American repatriates were each advanced $50 by the US government. Most of them, still quite bedraggled from

45. Hill, *Exchange Ship*, pp. 230–231; William C. Kerr to Dear Friends, On board Repatriation Ship MS *Gripsholm*, 21 August 1942, Box 1 (Old Box 1), Arthur Greenwood Robinson Papers on the Yung Wing Mission and YMCA Work in North China, Houghton Library, Harvard University, Cambridge, MA.
46. Hill, *Exchange Ship*, pp. 260, 278; William G. Kerr to Dear Friends, On board Repatriation Ship M.S. *Gripsholm*, 21 August 1942, Box 1 (Old Box 1), Arthur Greenwood Robinson Papers, Houghton Library, Harvard University.

Figure 4.5: The transfer of repatriates, as those on the *Asama Maru* prepare to board the *Gripsholm*, Lourenço Marques, 24 July 1942. From *New York Herald Tribune*, 17 August 1942.

Figure 4.6: Newly-freed American internees, relaxing aboard the *Gripsholm*, August 1942. From *New York Herald Tribune*, 17 August 1942.

Figure 4.7: Swedish repatriation ship, *Gripsholm*, in American waters, ca. 1942. Image courtesy of The Maritime Museum and Aquarium, Gothenburg.

their internment, "went into town and fixed themselves with new outfits." Presumably my father could now shed the "bright green tweed" that he had been wearing for months and change into some new clean clothes. The repatriates also "had a chance to see what the Portuguese have made of East Africa and could explore the neighboring veldt" and look at "the giant hippos in a nearby river."[47]

The *Gripsholm* departed Lourenço Marques on 28 July. "Our voyage from the wintry winds around the Cape of Good Hope into spring farther north in the South Atlantic was as calm and quiet as the sea itself." "The next land we saw [on 10 August] was Rio de Janeiro, that amazing city of skyscrapers almost surrounding the lofty peak on which towers the impressive figure of the Christ." At Rio the thirty-one Latin American diplomats and their families who had also been interned by the Japanese disembarked; at the same time "a number of officials of the State Department, and other departments of the [US] government, including the F.B.I.," came on board, their job to debrief and/or interrogate the passengers. Departing Brazil, "the *Gripsholm* swung out to the mid-Atlantic, to avoid German submarines which were active along the Brazilian Coast and the Caribbean Sea," but otherwise "the voyage home from Rio almost resembled a pleasure tour, thanks to the smoothness of the sea."[48]

Finally, on 25 August 1942, two months after leaving Hong Kong, the internees reached New York Harbor and tied up in Jersey City, New Jersey. There they were subjected to further interrogation by various government agencies on the lookout for spies and others whose loyalty or "nationality status" was suspect. It took four days to complete the immigration process and clear the ship. Of the 1,500 passengers, about 148 (or 10 percent) were sent to nearby Ellis Island for further investigation. They included "about twenty missionaries who are held because of 'pacifist' activities aboard ship."[49] Once off the ship, my father went to Philadelphia to stay with his cousin, Anna Davis, and her husband Alexander L. Pugh Jr. (1904–1989). Meanwhile, the US State Department requested reimbursement of $525 for the voyage on the *Gripsholm*, plus another $50 for the money advanced by the government in Lourenço Marques, for each of the (adult) repatriates, which in the case of the Lingnan personnel the American trustees paid.[50]

A year later, in September 1943, another hundred or so Canadian internees at Stanley, together with thirty Americans and Canadians who had been interned in Guangzhou (including Provost James Henry and the other Lingnan personnel), were similarly repatriated aboard the *Teia Maru* and the *Gripsholm*, with the exchange taking place this time at Goa rather than Lourenço Marques.[51] The rest of the internees at Stanley, numbering more than two thousand and most of them British, remained behind for two more years, until the war ended in 1945. John Guthrie, the Lingnan English teacher who had joined

47. Briggs, *Taken in Hong Kong*, p. 228; William G. Kerr to Dear Friends, On board Repatriation Ship M.S. *Gripsholm*, 21 August 1942, Box 1 (Old Box 1), Arthur Greenwood Robinson Papers, Houghton Library, Harvard University; John B. Powell, *My Twenty-Five Years in China* (New York: Macmillan Company, 1945), p. 412.
48. Hill, *Exchange Ship*, p. 278; William G. Kerr to Dear Friends, On board Repatriation Ship MS *Gripsholm*, 21 August 1942, Box 1 (Old Box 1), Arthur Greenwood Robinson Papers, Houghton Library, Harvard University; Powell, *My Twenty-Five Years in China*, pp. 414–416.
49. "More Than 150 On *Gripsholm* Held for Inquiry," *New York Herald Tribune*, 28 August 1942, news clipping in Folder 2, Box 32, Subseries 2B, MRL 12, Foreign Missions Conference of North America Records, Burke Library, Union Theological Seminary, Columbia University, New York. On pacifist, or allegedly pro-Japanese, activities among missionaries aboard the *Gripsholm*, see Briggs, *Taken in Hong Kong*, pp. 235–236.
50. ODW to Albert L. Scott, New York, 19 June 1942, Box 89, TLUA–HYL.
51. Emerson, *Hong Kong Internment*, p. 69; Leck, *Captives of Empire*, pp. 295–304.

the Hong Kong Volunteer Defense Corps and been treated as a prisoner of war, was also not released until then.

In the meantime, the Lingnan campus in Guangzhou had been taken over by "Guangdong University" 廣東大學, which the pro-Japanese provincial government had established. Before departing for America, Provost Henry had "ordered three of our Chinese staff to stay on and cooperate with the puppets in every way, as this seemed the surest way . . . to ensure a minimum of destruction." This three-person campus group may have been identical to the one that President Lee had previously appointed in October 1938 "to 'stay through' to help the American Foundation." Two of the three men charged with keeping an eye on the campus were Hoh Shai Kwong 何世光 (1904–1983) of the Chemistry Department and Tong Fuk Cheung, the Chinese secretary of the American Foundation (and my mother's former colleague).[52] Both would be accused after the Communist revolution of having collaborated with the Japanese and/or the Americans.

Difficult as conditions in the Stanley internment camp were, life for people on the outside, like my mother and me, was hardly any better. As Dr. Li Shu-fan had suggested, at least within the camps the Japanese provided a minimum amount of food and safety. On the outside, with soaring prices and shuttered stores, food was expensive and hard to come by. Banks were closed, accounts frozen, and spending money not readily obtainable. Alongside marauding soldiers, lawless bands of Chinese roamed the streets and looted private homes. When Wenzell Brown's former student brought a message from my mother to my father, he told Brown, "The city . . . was a hell-hole. Hundreds were starving in the streets each day. The Japanese were trying to empty Hong Kong. No food was given out save to those who worked for the Japanese."[53] Women and children, in particular, were actively encouraged to leave the city; exit permits, known as "return to one's native place certificates" (*huixiang zheng* 回鄉證), were readily granted. Within a year the population of Hong Kong had fallen by one-third, from one and a half million to one million (and by the end of the war it had been reduced by another third).[54] Those who had fled to Hong Kong from the Japanese in 1938 now made their way back to their homes or native places in the interior. My grandfather Ngan Heung Cho and his family joined this exodus. His concubine Wong Sam Mui and her children went to the ancestral Ngan Bin Village, while his wife Sam Gwu and her children settled for Guangzhou. Also returning to the bombed-out city were my mother's sister Chi Kin and her family.[55]

In recognition of his social standing in Guangzhou, the Japanese offered my aged grandfather, now close to seventy years old and unemployed, a position as a local headman in the *baojia* 保甲 mutual-security system. Though the position was well-compensated, he turned it down in favor of a low-wage job on Shameen Island with an unidentified commercial firm belonging to a neutral foreign country. And so his family scraped by. In the evenings, Ngan Heung Cho devoted himself to compiling a Cantonese dictionary based

52. Y. L. Lee, "Resume of Events during the Period October 12 to 18, 1938," in Lee to ODW, Hong Kong, 10 November 1938, Box 75, TLUA–HYL; Harry A. Bork to Fred Osborn, Chungking, 29 October 1945, reproduced and circulated in a memorandum from ODW to Harold B. Hoskins, New York City, 16 November 1945, in Folder Last names L, Box 25, Collection No. 1192, Cadbury & Cadbury Papers, Haverford College Library.

53. Brown, *Hong Kong Aftermath*, p. 245; James M. Henry to ODW, Canton, 29 March 1942, Box 143, TLUA–HYL.

54. Gao Tianqiang [Ko Tim Keung] and Tang Zhuomin, eds., *Xianggang Rizhan shiqi* [Hong Kong during the Japanese occupation] (Hong Kong: Sanlian shudian, 1995), pp. 96–97; see also Li Guanghe, "Kangzhan shiqi Rizhan Xianggang de 'guixiang' yundong shuping" [A commentary on the "return to the native place" movement during the Japanese occupation of Hong Kong], *Minguo dang'an*, no. 2 (2010): 109–114.

55. Ngan Ki Ping, "Gei Changshun de beiwanglu" (Part II), 22 April 2016, and personal communication, 1 August 2016.

on the Roman alphabet (that is, a dictionary of Chinese characters as pronounced in Cantonese and phonetically rendered according to the Roman alphabet, beginning with Auk 屋 and ending with Yut 軏). According to my Uncle Ki Ping, there are two manuscript copies of this ninety-one-page lexicon. His copy clearly states, "This book was compiled at the time the Japanese invaders [*Rikou*日寇] were in Guangzhou city."[56] It is doubtful that this lexicon served any utilitarian purpose. Nevertheless, its compilation says something about the range of my grandfather's intellectual interests as well as his persistence and hard work. He was certainly living up to the spirit of Yan Hui, the Confucian disciple who was the putative ancestor of the Ngan/Yan lineage.

My mother and I, together with our amah Ah Hoh, likewise joined the exodus from Hong Kong. We left even as my father was still languishing in the Stanley internment camp. According to a letter dated 29 March 1942 from Provost James Henry, himself interned in Guangzhou, "Mrs. Rhoads and the baby were to leave for the interior . . . I was told a week ago."[57] As previously noted, my father had been made aware of our departure via Wenzell Brown's student. It is possible that we left Hong Kong at about the same time as my grandfather and my aunt Chi Kin, and perhaps traveled in their company.

Unlike them, however, our ultimate destination in "the interior" was not occupied Guangzhou but northern Guangdong. The Japanese had captured Guangzhou and Hong Kong but lacked the manpower to extend their control much beyond those two cities and portions of the Pearl River Delta. As a result, the retreating Chinese military forces had been able to regroup and consolidate in the northern part of Guangdong Province, with Qujiang (now better known as Shaoguan) as the wartime capital of the province and the headquarters of the Seventh War Zone under the command of General Yu Hanmou. (Much criticized for having abandoned Guangzhou to the Japanese, Yu nevertheless stood in Chiang Kai-shek's good graces and had escaped punishment.) A number of schools, including Lingnan, had also relocated to the area. Northern Guangdong became part of what was popularly called "Free China" or, alternatively, "the Great Rear Area" (*Dahoufang* 大後方). Thus, rather than heading home, some of the Chinese who left Hong Kong made their way instead to Qujiang. Students, in particular, received Chinese government funding for their journey as well as for their studies, and they were exempt from military conscription.[58]

Based on retrospective accounts of Lingnan and Hong Kong University students, there were three main escape routes from Hong Kong to Qujiang.[59] One was by sea to Guangzhouwan and then by land to Guilin and Hengyang. This circuitous route was the one taken, for example, by Anna Chan 陳香梅 (1923–2018, the future Mrs. Claire Chennault), then a second-year student at Lingnan at Hong Kong. In May 1942, after they had received exit permits, she and her sisters first went by ferry to Macau, which as a Portuguese colony was neutral in the war and was never occupied by the Japanese. Then they took another boat to Guangzhouwan (now Zhanjiang), on the southwestern coast near French Indo-China. Because Guangzhouwan, a "leased territory," was nominally

---

56. Ngan Ki Ping, "Zi yuan," p. 1. I have a photocopy of this lexicon, courtesy of my uncle.

57. James M. Henry to ODW, Canton, 29 March 1942, Box 143, TLUA–HYL.

58. Diana Lary, *Chinese People at War*, p. 39; Brian Yu, *The Arches of the Years* (Toronto: Joint Centre for Asia Pacific Studies, 1999), pp. 73, 81–82.

59. For the reminiscences of Lingnan students, see *Dacun suiyue—Kangzhan shiqi Lingnan zai Yuebei* [The Tai Tsuen years—Lingnan in northern Guangdong during the War of Resistance] (North York, Ontario: "Dacun suiyue" chubanzu, 1998); for those of HKU students, faculty, and staff, see Clifford Matthews and Oswald Cheung, eds., *Dispersal and Renewal*.

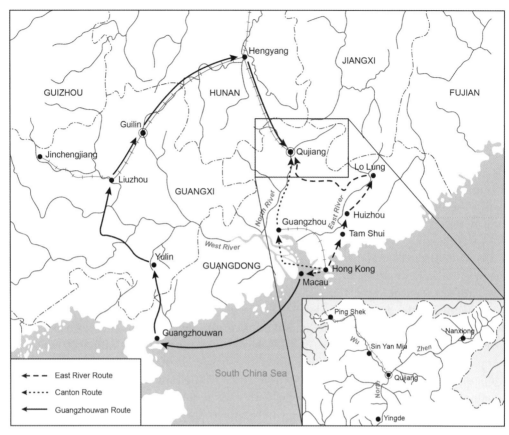

Map 4.4: Escape routes from Hong Kong to Qujiang, 1942. Map by Ada Au-Yeung.

under the control of the Vichy French, it too was not occupied by the Japanese (at least not until February 1943). On the outskirts of Guangzhouwan lay Free China. Anna Chan and her sisters were next carried in sedan chairs—other refugees walked—to Yulin in Guangxi Province. They then went—perhaps by truck and boat, as others did—to Liuzhou, where they caught a train on the Hunan–Guangxi line to Guilin and onward to Hengyang, in Hunan. Finally, in Hengyang they could switch to the Guangzhou–Hankou line and head south to Qujiang, which during the war was the southern terminus of the railroad.[60]

The second main escape route was overland via Huizhou; this was the one taken by Rayson Huang 黃麗松, then a senior at Hong Kong University, and his younger brother Raymond in the summer of 1942. The two men took a bus to Sha Tou Kok 沙頭角, on the northeastern border of Hong Kong's New Territories, and then a boat across Mirs Bay to a village on the opposite shore. There they were met by a paid guide, who took them on foot across a bandit-infested "no-man's-land" to the small town of Tam Shui 淡水. Once in Tam Shui, where a unit of the Chinese Nationalist army was stationed, they had reached

---

60. Anna Chennault, *A Thousand Springs: The Autobiography of a Marriage* (New York: Paul S. Ericksson, 1962), pp. 90–94; Chen Xiangmei, *Chen Xiangmei quanji* [The complete works of Anna Chennault] (Shijiazhuang: Hebei renmin chubanshe, 2000), 4: 58–68. On Guangzhouwan as a transit point to Free China, see Chuning Xie, "China's Casablanca: Refugees, Outlaws, and Smugglers in France's Guangzhouwan Enclave," in *1943: China at the Crossroads*, ed. Joseph W. Esherick and Matthew T. Combs (Ithaca: East Asia Program, Cornell University, 2015), pp. 391–425.

Free China. From there they took a small riverboat to the regional hub of Huizhou and then another riverboat up the East River to the town of Lo Lung 老隆. Finally, at Lo Lung, where there was a motor road, they caught a charcoal-burning truck that four or five days later deposited them at Qujiang, where a Hong Kong Government Relief Office was located.[61] The highway from Lo Lung to Qujiang may have been one of those built during the warlord regime of Chen Jitang.

Besides the Guangzhouwan and the East River routes, there was, according to Muriel Lockwood (1899–1991), wife of YMCA secretary Edward Lockwood, a third escape route from Hong Kong to Qujiang, "the Canton route." For Qujiang was only about 150 miles due north of Guangzhou, and Japanese control extended less than half that distance. The railroad from Guangzhou to Qujiang had been torn up by the retreating Nationalists, but it was still possible to reach the wartime capital by the North River or by motor road.[62]

It is not clear which route my mother, Ah Hoh, and I took to get from Hong Kong to Qujiang. James Henry himself gave two different locations as way stations on our escape. In a diary entry, dated 5 April 1942, he wrote, "Mrs. Rhoads and the infant Rhoads have proceeded into the interior via Kwang Chow Wan"; a week earlier, however he had written that we "were to leave for the interior via Kongmoon."[63] Jiangmen (Kongmoon) is in the Pearl River Delta, nowhere near Huizhou and the East River. This suggests that we might have taken "the Canton route." If so, perhaps we went from Hong Kong to Guangzhou in the company of my mother's father and her sister Chi Kin and their families and then, leaving them behind in Guangzhou, made our separate way northward to Qujiang. Indeed, this was what my cousin Luo Wen, Chi Kin's son, did a year later, in 1943, when at age thirteen he was taken by relatives or friends from Guangzhou to Qujiang to attend high school in Free China. His parents had intended to join him in Qujiang, but soon afterward "the road from Guangzhou to northern Guangdong was shut down." As a result, they and their other two children went to Macau instead. The teenager Luo Wen was to spend the rest of the war by himself in northern Guangdong.[64]

According to historian Peter Cunich, escapees from Hong Kong "faced weeks on the road and a host of dangers. The refugees were only able to take with them what possessions they could carry in their suitcases or wear on their backs." Some "had to walk long distances; where inns were available for overnight stops, they were usually infested with mosquitoes, bed-bugs and other vermin."[65] Traveling largely on her own, burdened by a young child but ably assisted by Ah Hoh, my mother somehow managed to make it to Qujiang. On 3 April, Edward Lockwood, at Qujiang, reported that among the Lingnan staff "arriving here" was "the wife of the English professor Mrs. country Street," adding that "I may not have spelled this name properly. She brought the four year old son with her." Though Lockwood had garbled my father's name—Street for Rhoads—he clearly was referring to my mother and me.[66] If we had set out from Hong Kong in mid- or late

61. Rayson Huang, *A Lifetime in Academia: An Autobiography* (Hong Kong: Hong Kong University Press, 2000), pp. 21–24. This East River route was also an important military supply line to Free China from Hong Kong; see Macri, *Clash of Empires in South China*, pp. 62 (map), 109.

62. Muriel Lockwood to Brownell Family, Kukong, 10 March 1942, Folder 35, Box 1, Brownell Papers, University of Vermont Library; Macri, *Clash of Empires in South China*, pp. 194 (map), 294.

63. James M. Henry to ODW, Canton, 29 March 1942, Box 143, and Henry, "Memorandum, April 4–May 6, 1942," Box 88, TLUA–HYL.

64. Luo Wen, copy of emails to Fan Huaici and Li Junyan, 22 April and 19 May 2013, courtesy of Yi Luo.

65. Cunich, *History of the University of Hong Kong*, vol. 1, pp. 413–414.

66. Edward H. Lockwood, [Kukong], to William W. Cadbury, 3 April 1942, Folder Last names L, Box 25, Collection No. 1192, Cadbury & Cadbury Papers, Haverford College Library.

March, as James Henry earlier intimated, it had taken us a couple of weeks to get to Qujiang. Having already fled from Guangzhou to Hong Kong, we were now refugees yet again; so, of course, was my father, when he was repatriated to the US.

Qujiang (Kukong in Cantonese) had been a backwater place before the war. Located at the confluence of the Wu and Zhen rivers to form the North River, about 145 miles north of Guangzhou, it was (and still is) the regional hub of northern Guangdong. It was also situated on the Guangzhou–Hankou railroad, whose completion in 1936 was, as noted previously, hailed as a notable triumph for Chiang Kai-shek and the Nationalists. However, two years after the railroad was completed, the Chinese had ripped out the Guangzhou end of the line in order to stymie the Japanese, leaving Qujiang as its southernmost station.

As the wartime capital of the province, Qujiang, like Chongqing at the national level, had been transformed, with government agencies of all types and their attendant officials relocating there. Owing to the flood of refugees from Guangzhou and Hong Kong, the city boomed, with its population swelliing nearly ten times, from 30,000 to 280,000.[67] "Two long streets running through the peninsula formed by two rivers, it has spread onto both opposite shores," a Western visitor wrote in 1943. According to another account, "There are two good bridges, a concrete one over the east river [the Zhen] and a new wooden one over the west [the Wu]. There are also several pontoon bridges, so the rivers are not nearly so much of a nuisance as the Yangtze at Chungking . . . All along the pontoon bridge and down the river banks are sampans, sometimes doing a bit of ferrying business but more often just moored to the bank. These boats are homes by day and hotels by night." Yet another Western visitor observed that the city "had the full flavor of Cantonese ways, with its people clattering through their colonnaded streets on wooden clogs, dressed in shiny black pajamas, bickering fiercely in their quacking dialect." Science historian Joseph Needham, passing through in early 1944, found it "a particularly pleasant city . . . with flowery gardens and streets arcaded in the southern style against the sun."[68]

Among the government offices that relocated to Qujiang was the Maritime Customs Service. Founded in 1854, the Customs was a foreign-staffed agency of the Chinese government, with stations in ports all along the China coast and on major inland waterways. From the earliest days its overall head, the Inspector General, had been a Westerner, as were most of the commissioners in charge of the local customs stations. When the Pacific War broke out at the end of 1941, Japan replaced the British Inspector General with one of their own and put the system under Wang Jingwei's collaborationist regime. In response, Chiang Kai-shek's government in Chongqing immediately set about creating from scratch an alternative Customs Service under a new British Inspector General (C. H. B. Joly) for those parts of the China interior that it controlled.[69] So it was that a customs station was

---

67. Edward H. Lockwood, Report on the wartime work of the Kukong YMCA, 1945, p. 3, Folder 82, Box 13, RG 175, Sarah Refo Mason Papers, YDSL.

68. "Excerpts from a letter by the Assoc. Boards from William P. Fenn re a trip of inspection to the Christian colleges in southeastern China," June 1943, Box 94, TLUA–HYL; [Duncan Wood], "Duncan's Travels," 24 December 1942, Unit Letter No. 38, Folder Friends Ambulance Unit, Reports—Unit Letters, #1–38, General Files 1942—Foreign Service—Country China (FAU Reports #d) to Doukhobors, AFSC Archives, Philadelphia; Graham Peck, *Two Kinds of Time* (Boston: Houghton Mifflin Company, 1950), p. 558; Joseph Needham and Dorothy Needham, eds., *Science Outpost: Papers of the Sino-British Science Co-operation Office* (British Council Scientific Office in China), 1942–1946 (London: Pilot Press, 1948), p. 223.

69. Robert Bickers, "The Chinese Maritime Customs at War, 1941–45," *Journal of Imperial and Commonwealth History* 36 (2008): 295–311.

established in early 1942 at Qujiang. It was headed by Edgar Bathurst (1901–1972), a twenty-year British veteran of the Maritime Customs, and two Chinese subordinates. A Western visitor described Bathurst as "a suave, Civil-servant type of man."[70]

According to historian Catherine Ladds, "despite the fact that the majority of people who had dealings with the Customs were Chinese, most official business was conducted in English until the 1930s." This remained the case, at least in Free China, into the 1940s. As a result, there was a demand in the Customs Service for office workers who were fluent in both English and Chinese—a demand that was increasingly met by Chinese "lady-typists."[71] Thus, in early April, as he was setting up his office, Commissioner Bathurst reported that he had "engaged temporarily as of 6th April a woman stenographer typist who had escaped from Hongkong, a Mrs. Lo Ngan Chi Kit (路顏志潔). I have found her a very capable stenographer typist indeed; she is most useful in the office and is making herself essential." My mother had managed to find this job almost immediately upon our arrival in Qujiang. It was, according to Lingnan president Y. L. Lee, "a nice job" but one that "keeps her quite busy." Hired originally on a temporary basis, she was soon "made a Service-Listed Typist." In early 1943, when Bathurst was ill and away from the office for about a month, she met with him at the hospital and helped him deal with all the important correspondence; he once again praised her as "an extremely capable stenographer."[72]

For the next year or so, from April 1942 to June 1943, my mother, Ah Hoh, and I lived somewhere in Qujiang. The location of the Customs House, where my mother was employed, is unclear. I had thought that it might have been located in the city center, perhaps on the middle section of Fengdu Road 風度路, the main avenue that runs down the length of the narrow peninsula between the two rivers, where Lockwood's YMCA office was located. But Commissioner Bathurst's correspondence indicates otherwise. Instead, he described the Customs office as "only a very cold drafty wooden bungalow, not too well built" and located "in an inaccessible position . . . on no road whatsoever, having been entirely surrounded by recently erected wooden huts."[73]

As to where we lived: According to Bathurst, due to the influx of refugees from Hong Kong, housing in Qujiang was in very short supply and very expensive. He himself, "in spite of every assistance from many people," had been unable to find a house to rent and was forced to move into a houseboat moored along one of the city's two rivers.[74] We may have been more fortunate than Bathurst. Perhaps with the help of the Lockwoods and Y. L. Lee, we may have found lodging in the eastern suburb, near the bridge over the

---

70. Sun Xiufu, comp., *Zhongguo jindai haiguan gaoji zhiyuan nianbiao* [Chronological table of high-ranked staff of the Maritime Service in modern China] (Beijing: Zhongguo haiguan chubanshe, 2004), p. 273; on Bathurst, see the Database of Chinese Maritime Customs Staff website at the University of Bristol, www.bristol.ac.uk/history/customs/resources/servicelists/databases.html (accessed 20 January 2014), and [Duncan Wood], "Duncan's Travels," 24 December 1942, Unit Letter No. 38, Folder Friends Ambulance Unit, Reports—Unit Letters #1–38, General Files 1942—Foreign Service—Country China (FAU Reports #d) to Doukhobors, AFSC Archives.

71. Catherine Ladds, *Empire Careers: Working for the Chinese Customs Service, 1854–1949* (Manchester: Manchester University Press, 2013), pp. 86, 87.

72. E. Bathurst to C. H. B. Joly, Kukong, 13 April 1942, Joly to Bathurst, Chungking, 13 August 1942, and Bathurst to Joly, Kukong, 9 February 1943, Kukong Semi-Official Correspondence, 1942–1943, 679(1)/32498, Maritime Customs Service Archives, Second Historical Archives of China (on microfilm); Y. L. Lee to ODW, Kukong, 8 April 1942, Box 88, and 20 June 1942, Box 89, TLUA–HYL.

73. E. Bathurst to C. H. B. Joly, Kukong, 9 January 1943 and 9 February 1943, Kukong Semi-Official Correspondence, 1942–1943, 679(1)/32498, Maritime Customs Service Archives, Second Historical Archives of China.

74. E. Bathurst to C. H. B. Joly, Kukong, 2 April 1942, Kukong Semi-Official Correspondence, 1942–1943, 679(1)/32498, Maritime Customs Service Archives, Second Historical Archives of China.

Zhen River and near the train station, where Lockwood and his family lived (and where
the Friends Ambulance Unit was headquartered).[75] While my mother was at work in the
city, I would have been in the care of Ah Hoh. In their presence and in the absence of
my father and other native English-speakers, I grew up speaking Cantonese as my first
language.

As the provincial capital and the headquarters of the Seventh War Zone, Qujiang
had been since 1938 a target of Japanese air raids. This was part of a concerted campaign
of terror bombing. According to Hagiwara Mitsuru, "In the three years following the
onset of stalemate on the ground [1939–1941], the Japanese conducted repeated heavy
and discriminate bombing of Chinese cities in an attempt to terrorize Chinese urban
populations and thus break down the resistance of the Chinese population as a whole."[76]
The strategy wreaked havoc but ultimately failed to force the Chinese government to
capitulate. Edward Lockwood, in his personal correspondence, described one particularly devastating bombardment in Qujiang in August 1940: "There is now no pretence
[*sic*] of firing at military objectives. . . . Three days ago 11 Jap bombing planes flew over
the city and dropped about forty bombs on the heart of the city destroying about 70 buildings, giving serious injury to more than fifty and death to about forty persons."[77]

As a result, a Western visitor observed in late 1942, "The town is very air-raid conscious and has posts on which balls are displayed to warn the people of the approach of
enemy aricraft [*sic*]. From these posts, too, are [*sic*; a?] sort of muezzin [Muslim prayer
call] is sounded to tell you how many planes are in the air and where they are last seen."
There were, Lockwood explained, three alarms. "The second alarm tells us the planes
are approaching the city and are not far away. The third alarm comes when the planes
are so close that the sound of the motors can be heard." Once the alarms were sounded,
usually in the early morning, the people were instructed to evacuate the city and head
for the hills on the far side of either river. There they stayed until 2:30 or 3:00 in the
afternoon, when the danger was over and "shops are opened and homes resume their
usual activity."[78] Thus, Edgar Bathurst, the Customs Commissioner, on arriving in the city
in March 1942, found that "apparently work is only carried on in Kukong for three hours
a day from 3 p.m. to 6 p.m. as the majority of people take to the hills during the morning
for fear of air-raids. After 6 p.m. there is little light to carry on work as the electric power
is weak and kerosene is costly." He went on to add, however, that, unlike the rest of the
city, "the Customs staff carries on a full working day from 8 a.m. to 5 p.m."[79]

According to Rayson Huang, who had arrived at Qujiang in 1942 about the same
time as we did, the city "had on occasions been heavily bombed. Fortunately for us, these

75. Muriel Lockwood Refo, "Midwest China Oral History Interviews," pp. 26–28; [Duncan Wood], "Duncan's Travels,"
     24 December 1942, Unit Letter No. 38, Folder Friends Ambulance Unit, Reports—Unit Letters #1–38, General
     Files 1942—Foreign Service—Country China (FAU Reports #d) to Doukhobors, AFSC Archives.
76. Hagiwara Mitsuru, "The Japanese Air Campaigns in China, 1937–1945," in Peattie, Drea, and Van de Ven, eds.,
     Battle for China, p. 248.
77. Edward H. Lockwood to Joe Kidd, Kukong, 22 August 1940, Edward H. Lockwood Papers, 1937–1944, Manuscripts
     Division, William L. Clements Library, University of Michigan, Ann Arbor.
78. [Duncan Wood], "Duncan's Travels," 24 December 1942, Unit Letter No. 38, Folder Friends Ambulance Unit,
     Reports—Unit Letters #1–38, General Files 1942—Foreign Service—Country China (FAU Reports #d) to
     Doukhobors, AFSC Archives; Edward H. Lockwood to Joe Kidd, Kukong, 22 August and 9 September 1940, Edward
     H. Lockwood Papers, University of Michigan Library.
79. E. Bathurst to C. H. B. Joly, Kukong, 2 April 1942, Kukong Semi-Official Correspondence, 1942–1943, 679(1)/32498,
     Maritime Customs Service Archives, Second Historical Archives of China.

raids were no more although there was still a false air raid alarm from time to time."[80] In fact, however, the air raids had not stopped, though they may have become much less frequent. On 11 January 1943, Y. L. Lee reported on a particularly destructive raid: "Indeed it was indiscriminating bombing by the Japanese bombers in the last few days. I do not know exactly how many people were killed: some say two hundred, some say more. The number of houses burnt down must be above the number of two thousand. . . . The enemy came again day before yesterday: six big bombers flying right over our University campus before they flew south to bomb Kukong."[81] Living in the suburbs, as we probably were, we may have been relatively safe from the Japanese bombardment. Nevertheless, as Lockwood pointed out, "You have a helpless felling [sic; feeling] when you are out in the open and know that planes may soon be overhead. The danger is not only from the bombs but [also] from the anti-aircraft gun shells. A piece of shrapnel hitting in the wrong place can do a good deal of damage."[82]

It was also to this part of Free China that Lingnan University relocated from Hong Kong. President Y. L. Lee had long been under pressure from the Guangdong provincial government to move the university away from the British colony. It was in response to this pressure that Lingnan's College of Agriculture had left Hong Kong in 1940 for Ping Shek on the Hunan border. When Hong Kong fell to the Japanese, classes at both Lingnan and Hong Kong University stopped immediately. Whereas HKU remained closed for the duration of the war, Lingnan University was able to reopen in northern Guangdong, where General Yu Hanmou, the top military official, offered to sell a large piece of land to the university at a nominal price. This property was located in Qujiang County, about twenty miles north of the county seat, at Tai Tsuen 大村 ("Big Village"), which the Lingnan people promptly renamed Ling Tai Tsuen 嶺大村 ("Lingnan University Village"). "Here," according to university historian Corbett, "amid fine old camphor trees were sixty or more mat sheds and other temporary buildings which had been used as a training camp for high officers of the Kwangtung army."[83] This became the new campus for Lingnan's College of Arts and the Lingnan Middle School. Though overshadowed by Kunming and Chengdu, Qujiang, too, was a center of academic life in wartime China. In addition to Lingnan, other colleges that found refuge in northern Guangdong included National Sun Yat-sen University (in Ping Shek), Soochow University, and Canton Union Theological College (both in Tai Tsuen).

President Y. L. Lee, who had arrived at Qujiang via the East River route, set about in the spring and summer of 1942 to get the campus up and running. With all the Western faculty members interned in Hong Kong and Guangzhou, he sent out a call to his Chinese faculty members, who had scattered to the four winds, to return to Lingnan. In early April he informed Olin Wannamaker that "more than eight professors have come into Free China. We are doing our best to take good care of them. . . . I have requested all other Chinese professors to come in." (Among the Chinese professors who heeded his call was Sinn Yuk Ching 冼玉清 [1895–1965], in Chinese literature; she had come to Qujiang by way of Guangzhouwan.) Together with Sz-to Wai 司徒衛 (1889–1961), the energetic

80. Huang, *Lifetime in Academia*, p. 24.
81. Y. L. Lee to ODW, Kukong, 11 January 1943, Box 93, TLUA–HYL; Sha Dongxun, comp., *Guangdong kang-Ri zhanzheng jishi* [A chronology of the anti-Japanese war of resistance in Guangdong] (Guangzhou: Guangzhou chubanshe, 2004), pp. 434, 436.
82. Edward H. Lockwood to Joe Kidd, Kukong, 22 August 1940, Edward H. Lockwood Papers, University of Michigan Library.
83. Corbett, *Lingnan University*, p. 140.

principal of the Middle School, President Lee had the existing mat-sheds repaired and new ones constructed. "For those [faculty members] who came with families a small house was built." The result was, according to Sz-to Wai, that "if you stand on top of the hill, you will see fifty or sixty buildings, some half-hidden under big camphor-trees, some exposed on the mountain-side, with pink walls and purple roofs." Some of the buildings carried names from the Hong Lok campus, such as Swasey Hall and Grant Hall.[84] By September 1942, Lingnan was able to reopen for classes at its Tai Tsuen campus, with about three hundred students in attendance. Previously, when Guangzhou fell to the Japanese, Lingnan students had found refuge at Hong Kong University; now, in a reversal of roles, some of the students at Lingnan were refugees from HKU, including Rayson Huang's younger brother, Raymond.[85] Anna Chan, too, continued her education at Lingnan's Tai Tsuen campus.

As President Lee worked to get Lingnan started up, he turned again to my mother for help. The three main faculties of Lingnan University were strung out along the Wu (or west) tributary of the North River and the Guangzhou–Hankou railroad: the College of Agriculture at Ping Shek, the College of Arts and Sciences at Tai Tsuen, and the College of Medicine at Qujiang (at a hospital run by British Methodist missionaries). For ease of communication with the outside world, President Lee's administrative office was located in Qujiang, where he shared space with Edward Lockwood's YMCA. Though my mother had a full-time job with the Maritime Customs, she nevertheless found time to help with some of President Lee's English correspondence, as she had done earlier in Hong Kong, serving as (in my father's words) "a sort of unofficial secretary to President Lee." Thus, two of Lee's typed letters to the American trustees, in June and July 1942, carry the identifying typist tag "YLL/CKR."[86]

As the reopening of the university approached in the fall of 1942, my mother was asked "to rejoin the Lingnan staff." On 1 September, President Lee wrote, "I have just bought a new typewriter, $5,000, for the Univ. and I am trying it out now. Mrs. Rhoads has been helping in the last few months and I hope not to bother her any more. She has been very busy with her own job [at the Customs]." Nevertheless, by late October his letters to the New York office were regularly carrying the "YLL/CKR" tag. According to Wannamaker, my mother was now working at two jobs: "serving as secretary to President Lee in the evening, after completing her regular work in connection with some government office during the day."[87]

Meanwhile, my father had also made arrangements to send money to my mother from America. While still interned at Stanley, he had managed to get a message out via Lockwood at Qujiang, asking his college friend and personal attorney in Philadelphia, John Wendell Cooper, to transfer some funds to my mother from my father's bank account in the US. Overcoming several bureaucratic obstacles, Cooper was able on 1 May 1942 to transmit, via the Bank of China and Lockwood, a sum of US$300, which Olin Wannamaker deemed sufficient to "support Mrs. Rhoads and the child for a period

84. Y. L. Lee to ODW, Kukong, 8 April 1942, Box 88, and Sz-to Wai, "Lingnan Is Born Again in Free China," [1943], p. 6, Box 143, TLUA–HYL; Zhuang Fuwu, "Xian Yuqing jiaoshou nianpu" [Chronological biography of Professor Y. C. Sinn], *Lingnan wenshi*, 1994, No. 4.
85. Sz-to Wai, "Lingnan Is Born Again," [1943], p. 7, Box 143, TLUA–HYL; Huang, *Lifetime in Academia*, p. 24.
86. Y. L. Lee to ODW, Kukong, 20 June 1942, Box 89, and 29 July 1942, Box 90, and HGR to ODW, Bala Cynwyd, 19 September 1942, Box 91, TLUA–HYL.
87. Y. L. Lee to ODW, Kukong, 1 September 1942, Box 91, HGR to ODW, Bala Cynwyd, 19 September 1942, Box 91, ODW to William A. Riley, New York, 18 January 1943, Box 93, TLUA–HYL.

ranging between three and five months."[88] It is likely that my father, after his repatriation to the US, continued to send us funds.

Thus, my mother, while living in Qujiang, had three sources of income: from the Customs Service, from Lingnan University, and from my father. It is unknown how much money she made from her jobs at the Customs and at Lingnan, but whatever it was it undoubtedly was not sufficient to keep pace with inflation. Customs Commissioner Edgar Bathurst, in his reports for 1942–1943, repeatedly complained about the impact of rising prices on the fixed salaries of his employees. In early May 1942, he noted that the price of rice had doubled in the two months since he took up his post; in early January 1943, he wrote that "the prices of commodities are still increasing rapidly and the staff is being badly hit, especially the lower employees who are absolutely unable to live or even exist on a wage [in Chinese National Currency, or CN] of $248.00 a month." Furthermore, as he pointed out in February 1943, "it does not seem that one is able to purchase any Rice (except sweepings), Salt, etc., through the usual shops, all of which display signs showing Government prices whereas enquiry seems to indicate there are no stocks to sell. It is therefore difficult for the public and/or staff to purchase except from the black market." He later prepared a chart comparing the price of rice (both "Superior" and "Inferior") at Qujiang on 15 September 1942 and on 15 May 1943. During those eight short months, the price of Superior rice had risen from CN$481.17 per 100 kg to $2,966.30 and of Inferior rice from $352.74 to $826.75 (the official price) and $2,645.60 (on the black market).[89] Under such conditions, it is easy to understand why my mother might have required three sources of income to support her family in Qujiang.

---

88. See the exchange of correspondence between ODW and Cooper between 13 April and 2 May 1942, Boxes 88 and 89, TLUA–HYL.

89. E. Bathurst to C. H. B. Joly, Kukong, 2 May 1942, 7 January 1943, and 23 February 1943, and Bathurst to Frederick W. Maze, Kukong, 18 May 1943, Kukong Semi-Official Correspondence, 1942–1943, 679(1)/32498, Maritime Customs Service Archives, Second Historical Archives of China.

5

The Family Reunited in Free China (1943–1944)

When the Lingnan internees in Hong Kong arrived back in the United States in late August 1942, Olin Wannamaker at the New York office of the American trustees strove to find jobs for them and so "relieve our budget." Chemistry professor Clinton Laird, for example, went to work for the Board of Economic Warfare in Washington, while historian Henry Brownell taught successively, from 1943 to 1946, at Macalester College, Drew University, and Rhode Island State College (now the University of Rhode Island). Others, like Wenzell Brown, were discontinued.[1]

For my father, Wannamaker wrote to the University of Pennsylvania, but without success.[2] In any case, my father was single-mindedly intent on getting back to China and to his family as quickly as possible. From his temporary abode in the Philadelphia suburb of Bala Cynwyd, home of his cousin Anna Pugh, he badgered Wannamaker for assistance. Wannamaker, however, was not keen on sending him back. My father's difficult personality and poor administrative skills had been much criticized. Provost James Henry, while still interned in Guangzhou, wrote of him, "he is so mordant and bitter at times and is not a good administrator at all." Though my father had received a five-year reappointment prior to the fall of Hong Kong, it had been hoped that he could be gracefully eased out as department head (if not as a faculty member). According to Wannamaker, chemistry professor Henry Frank, who had shared quarters with my father at Stanley, "definitely advises against a long-term engagement of Rhoads." For the information of the trustees, Wannamaker described my father as follows: "One of the best trained men we have. In that respect hard to replace. But has been sharply criticized for lack of enthusiasm, self-centered attitude, and lack of stimulating influence on younger teachers and students." His recommendation to the trustees as to what to do with him was to keep him on in a "temporary arrangement," but for no longer than three months.[3]

1. ODW to Y. L. Lee, New York, Box 91, TLUA–HYL; C. N. Laird [to no name], Washington, 6 May 1943, Folder 155, Box 23, RG 175, Sarah Refo Mason Papers, YDSL; Henry C. Brownell's questionnaire for China Christian College Faculty Members, Fall 1947, Folder 3256, Box 182, China College Files – Lingnan University, RG 11, United Board Archives, YDSL.
2. ODW to Secretary, Employment Office, University of Pennsylvania, New York, 24 July 1942, and John M. Fogg Jr., to ODW, Philadelphia, 28 July 1942, Box 90, TLUA–HYL.
3. James M. Henry to ODW, Canton, 18 August 1942, Box 90, ODW to Henry, New York, 18 September 1942, and "Explanation of Suggested Budgets for American Personnel to Be Submitted to Executive and Finance Committees on 9/15/42 for Action," 8 September 1942, Box 91, TLUA–HYL. Henry's correspondence with ODW, while he was interned in Guangzhou, was conducted via Edward Lockwood in Qujiang.

At the same time, however, as he remarked to the head of the trustees, Wannamaker recognized that "we are under some degree of obligation to cooperate with Dr. Rhoads in rejoining his wife and child, since the family was separated while he was remaining in our service."[4] Moreover, President Y. L. Lee at Qujiang was begging the trustees to send to his newly-reopened campus some of the old Lingnan faculty members, mentioning specifically Henry Frank and Henry Brownell. But whether for professional or family reasons, neither man was available. When pressed for an opinion about my father, President Lee, noting that he was "typing this letter myself" (i.e., my mother did not type it), replied non-committally, "From the University point of view any American professor that the Trustees can send out at this time of our struggle for a better faculty, will be more than welcome."[5] Unlike Frank and Brownell, my father was willing and available.

So anxious was my father to get back to China that within a month of his return to the United States, he offered to pay his own way, drawing on his savings and perhaps his inheritance from his mother: "If you can get me out to Free China I am prepared to bear my own traveling expenses, and also to teach in the University, if necessary, on a bare subsistence wage." Wannamaker took him up on his desperate offer, but with several conditions. As Wannamaker explained to the president of the Board of Trustees, "We can make the appointment of Dr. Rhoads definitely for one year and take all necessary pains to avoid becoming even morally committed to him for an indefinite period." Furthermore, "We should stipulate exemption from responsibility on our part for the cost of his return to America." In other words, the trustees would take him on for no more than one year, and they would pay for neither his trip out to China nor his return. His salary would be $100 a month for twelve months, which was what his annual base salary of $1,200 had been in Hong Kong.[6] My father went along with these conditions.

While Wannamaker had agreed to help my father "get back to Free China," he doubted that "we could obtain a passport for him or means of transportation."[7] The United States, after all, was at war and unlikely to pay much heed to the plight of one unimportant civilian. Nevertheless, he proceeded to assist my father by turning to Joe J. Mickle and the Foreign Missions Conference of North America, a cooperative body of 123 Protestant mission boards and agencies with which the Lingnan trustees were affiliated, though they were not formal members. At the Foreign Missions Conference, Mickle headed the Committee on Passports and Transportation, which coordinated the dispatch of missionaries abroad. He and the committee had recently prepared for its member boards a set of "General Recommendations Concerning Procedure to be Followed in Securing Transportation."[8]

Guided by these recommendations from Mickle's committee, Wannamaker helped my father get over several logistical hurdles, one after another. First, he wrote to my father's draft board in Bryn Mawr requesting an exemption from military service so that he could "leave the United States in the near future and return to his duties in China":

---

4.   ODW to Harold Hoskins, New York, 26 September 1942, Box 91, TLUA–HYL.

5.   Y. L. Lee to ODW, [Kukong?], 29 October 1942, Box 91, TLUA–HYL.

6.   HGR to ODW, Bala Cynwyd, 25 September 1942, and ODW to Harold Hoskins, New York, 26 September 1942, Box 91, ODW to HGR, New York, 11 December 1942, Box 92, and "Revised Draft of Field Personnel Budget for 1941–1942," 26 May 1941, Box 149, TLUA–HYL.

7.   ODW to James M. Henry, New York, 18 September 1942, Box 91, TLUA–HYL.

8.   Committee on Passports and Transportation, "General Recommendations Concerning Procedure to be Followed in Securing Transportation," 22 October 1942, Folder 19, Box 7, RG 27, Foreign Missions Conference of North America Records, Presbyterian Historical Society, Philadelphia.

"The reason why we attach great importance to the possibility of having Dr. Rhoads released and permitted to return to his work in China is that he is the only member of the American faculty of the University to whom we can at the present time hope to send back to that work." Perhaps because my father was then forty-two years old, the exemption was granted almost immediately.[9] Next, Wannamaker wrote on behalf of my father to the Passport Division of the US State Department requesting a new passport—his old one had been surrendered on the *Gripsholm*. The reason he gave was probably the same as that given to the draft board. The application was approved on 2 November, though the passport itself would be not issued until transportation had been arranged.[10] Then, as part of "the long torment of injections requiring approximately six weeks," Wannamaker arranged for my father to get his yellow fever inoculation in New York, for it was unavailable in Philadelphia. The series of injections were completed in mid-December.[11]

Finally, when all but transportation had been arranged, Wannamaker notified Mickle and his committee that my father was ready to travel. He was informed that "for a civilian" like my father, air transport was "out of the question," but sea transport was a possibility. By 11 December, Wannamaker was confident enough that this had been arranged that he sent a Western Union telegram to President Y. L. Lee in Qujiang, "RHOADS PROBABLY SAILING SOON."[12] At the last moment, however, my father ran afoul of some unexpected (and unspecified) "treasury regulation." By the time the problem was resolved, the ship had left without him. As he wrote Wannamaker, "I regret very much and was much exasperated by the turn of events which kept me from the earlier sailing."[13] All he could do was wait for another ship.

Unfortunately, my father's hopes of quickly finding another ship were stymied by the Allies' North African campaign. In their first large-scale offensive of the war, American troops along with British Commonwealth forces had landed in French North Africa (now Morocco, Algeria, and Tunisia) in early November 1942 to battle the Germans and Italians. As a result, as Joe Mickle explained in late January 1943, "The Army authorities in Washington hold out very little prospect of being able to grant us transportation until the campaign in North Africa is ended. Practically all available shipping is being used for the North African campaign and very few boats are going elsewhere."[14]

The North African campaign was not to end until mid-May, with a morale-boosting victory for the Allies that paved the way for them to invade Italy by way of Sicily. However, the Germans and Italians were already on the defensive in early March. It was then that my father finally got a piece of good news: on 1 March, Wannamaker passed along to him some confidential information from Mickle's committee: "Within a period of thirty to forty-five days, a ship will be leaving for South Africa and Egypt," and my father had been nominated as one of four persons bound for India. My father was told that the steamship

9.   ODW to Local Draft Board #4, New York, 3 October 1942, and HGR to ODW, Bala Cynwyd, 10 October 1942, Box 91, TLUA–HYL.

10. ODW to HGR, New York, 14 October 1942, Box 91, and R. B. Shipley to HGR, Washington, 2 November 1942, Box 92, TLUA–HYL. Ruth Shipley was Chief of the Passport Division.

11. ODW to James M. Henry, New York, 13 November 1942, and HGR to ODW, Bala Cynwyd, 4 December 1942, Box 92, TLUA–HYL.

12. ODW to Joe J. Mickle, New York, 8 December 1942, Margaret Brewer to HGR, New York, 16 December 1942, ODW to Y. L. Lee, New York, Western Union, 11 December 1942, Box 92, TLUA–HYL. Brewer was ODW's secretary.

13. HGR to ODW, Bala Cynwyd, 19 December 1942, Box 92, and ODW to Y. L. Lee, New York, 18 January 1943, Box 93, TLUA–HYL.

14. Joe J. Mickle, "Confidential Report Concerning Present Transportation Prospects," 29 January 1943, Box 93, TLUA–HYL.

fare from the US to India would be between $500 and $800 and that the airfare from India into China would be another $360, all of which he had previously agreed to pay out of his own pocket. (These sums came close to his annual salary.) The luggage limitation was "one small trunk," which greatly disheartened my father: "Mrs. Rhoads and my boy," he wrote Wannamaker, "are getting more and more in need of clothing and shoes." Nevertheless, on 17 March he was finally issued his passport, along with various necessary visas. He was reminded to keep the time and place of embarkation a secret, "even to close relatives."[15]

The next day, on the eve of his departure, my father made several formal requests of the American trustees. As recorded by Wannamaker, one was that "in the event that Mr. Rhoads should be lost, he requests that we give all possible assistance to Mrs. Rhoads to enable her to get ultimately to the United States"; another was that "if he should be lost, and she also should become a victim of the war or be lost in any way to their son, he wishes us to help in [every] possible way in getting the boy, Edward John [Michael] Rhoads, to the United States to be put in the care of his cousins the Pughs. He is depending upon Mr. Pugh to assist in this in every possible way." This was, in effect, my father's last will. On 19 March, almost exactly six months after his return to the United States aboard the *Gripsholm*, my father left New York on a reverse journey aboard the M/S *Fernplant*, a Norwegian cargo ship whose very name, Wannamaker emphasized to his staff members, was a military secret that "must never be mentioned outside this office."[16]

But contrary to what Mickle had told Wannamaker, my father's ship was headed for Egypt not by way of South Africa but rather by way of Australia. (See Map 4.3.) On the first part of the journey, from New York to the Panama Canal via Guantánamo Bay, Cuba, the *Fernplant* traveled in convoy with about twenty other ships. During the voyage, according to Anna Pugh (based on a letter from my father), the convoy "had two alarms but all the ships got there safely." From then on, the Norwegian ship was on its own as it sailed across the Pacific and Indian Oceans. "On board ship," she told Wannamaker, "he says that everything is comfortable, food is good and his ship mates congenial." The letter to Anna Pugh, dated 4 May, was evidently posted in Fremantle, Western Australia. At this time, he told her, he was two-thirds of the way to his destination (Egypt), which he expected to reach within a month. Indeed, he arrived in Suez via Aden on 29 May, ten days ahead of schedule.[17]

My father and those of his fellow passengers who were bound for India immediately boarded another (unnamed) vessel, which "was not so comfortable as the first." Leaving on 1 June, they sailed down the Red Sea, stopping at Port Sudan on the 6th and Djibouti on the 14th, then crossed the Arabian Sea, arriving in Bombay (now Mumbai) on 23 June, "three months and four days after leaving New York." All in all, as he wrote Wannamaker from India, "it seems a bit strange to say that the trip was uneventful—yet it was exactly that. Except for one day on the Red Sea, when we sighted and sank (with our guns) a

---

15. Committee on Passports and Transportation to FMC Board Members, New York, 6 November 1942, and Joe J. Mickle, 27 February 1943, Folder 19, Box 7, RG 27, Foreign Missions Conference of North America Records, Presbyterian Historical Society; ODW to HGR, New York, 1 March and 8 March 1943, and HGR to ODW, Bala Cynwyd, 9 March 1943, Box 93, TLUA–HYL.

16. ODW, "Memorandum of Details Mentioned by Dr. Howard G. Rhoads," 18 March 1943, Box 93, TLUA–HYL. The underscoring is in the original.

17. Anna E. D. Pugh to ODW, Bala Cynwyd, 8 May [?] 1943, and ODW to Y. L. Lee, New York, 1 June 1943, Box 94, and Pugh to ODW, 9 July 1943, Box 95, TLUA–HYL; on the voyage record of the *Fernplant*, see warsailors.com/singleships/fernplant.html (accessed 26 October 2015).

drifting mine, nothing out of the ordinary happened." From Bombay, on the west coast of India, he traveled—almost certainly by train—to Calcutta (now Kolkata), on the east coast.[18] According to an American doctor who had made this 1,200-mile trip across India eight months earlier, "the scenery was not remarkable—the land is flat like our middle west—endlessly flat, it seemed to me—and everywhere rice paddies or corn fields—mostly rice paddies separated from one another by little hedges. The population seemed sparse—little thatched straw houses of peasants occasionally being seen, and some clay or red tile one-story houses."[19]

With the Japanese in control of the entire coastline of China and also of British Burma (now Myanmar), the only way to get into Free China from India was by air. My father waited in Calcutta for three weeks before he caught a flight on a "C. N. A. C. freight plane" leaving from the Dum Dum Aerodrome for Kunming on 19 July. "This will be less comfortable, I suppose, than a passenger plane, but all my luggage will accompany me, and that is with a great deal of discomfort." The China National Aviation Corporation was a subsidiary of Pan American Airways, with its wartime operational headquarters in Calcutta. Together with the Air Transport Command of the US Army Air Force, it was responsible for ferrying freight and passengers between India and China. My father's plane fare was 900 rupees, or about US$273, not including the cost of his excess luggage. This was roughly in line with what Wannamaker had told him to expect.[20]

According to others who made the journey from Calcutta to Kunming at about the same time as my father, the flight was in two legs. The first, from Calcutta to the Dinjan airfield in northeastern Assam, was relatively uneventful. It flew "over cultivated fields and low forest-clad hills," then "a broad valley and the mighty Bramaputra [*sic*] river," as a member of the Friends Ambulance Unit on his way to China described his journey. The second leg of the flight, by contrast, was quite perilous, for it involved flying over "the Hump," the eastern end of the Himalayas. "Leaving [Dinjan], we flew toward a mountain barrier, rising steadily until lost in the clouds, rocking and lurching violently." According to the Lingnan graduate Anna Chan, the future wife of US General Claire Chennault, whose Flying Tigers often operated in the area, "the weather over the towering peaks of the highest mountain range on earth was viciously unpredictable. Violent wind and snow-storms struck the laboring transports without warning. Thick, impenetrable fog could close in quickly, blotting out the ice-covered peaks that soared into the sky more than twenty-thousand feet. Japanese fighter pilots added to the danger, prowling the Hump and slowing down unarmed transports."[21]

Kunming, the capital of Yunnan Province, was the gateway to China from the outside world. Its airport then was "one of the busiest on the globe." The operational headquarters of Chennault's Fourteenth Air Force, it had a large American presence. According to Graham Peck (1914–1968), a staff member of the US Office of War Information who had passed through the city earlier in 1943, "for miles around the crowded airfield, the

18. Anna E. D. Pugh to ODW, Bala Cynwyd, 9 July 1943, and HGR to ODW, Calcutta, 18 July 1943, Box 95, TLUA–HYL.

19. Ernest Evans to Family, Calcutta, 25 October 1942, Folder Friends Ambulance Unit Letters and Cables, General Files 1942—Foreign Service—Country China (FAU Reports #d) to Doukhobors, AFSC Archives.

20. HGR to ODW, Calcutta, 18 July 1943, Box 95, and Kukong, 16 October 1943, Box 96, TLUA–HYL; HGR's passport, no. 13903 (in my sister's collection), p. 10. The rupee-dollar exchange rate of 3.30 to 1 is in William M. Leary Jr., *The Dragon's Wings: The China National Aviation Corporation and the Development of Commercial Aviation in China* (Athens: University of Georgia Press, 1976), p. 169.

21. John F. Rich to Family, Kutsing, 2 April 1943, Folder China—John Rich Correspondence, Foreign Service 1943—Country China, AFSC Archives; Chennault, *A Thousand Springs*, p. 28.

landscape was dotted with new barracks and supply dumps. The dusty roads were crawl-ing with American soldiers and army vehicles."[22] On 20 July, immediately on arrival, my father went to the American consulate to register as a US citizen. Nine days later he was issued a visa by the Yunnan office of the Chinese Ministry of Foreign Affairs permitting him to travel onward to Qujiang.[23] During his brief stay in Kunming, he may have had an opportunity to spend some time with Gilbert Baker, his former colleague at Lingnan who had baptized me. After the Japanese attack on Guangzhou, the Anglican bishop of Hong Kong, Ronald O. Hall, had sent Baker to help start up "a student church in Kunming, which would serve the universities which were being set up [there]." Baker and his new wife, Martha (Sherman) Baker (1911–1976), were to spend most of the rest of the war years in Kunming.[24]

Leaving Kunming, my father managed, so he wrote Wannamaker, to get "a lift on a British Military Mission truck and then in a US army jeep as far as the rail head." The route he followed probably took him from Kunming east along (in Graham Peck's words) "a narrow, two-lane dirt and gravel highway leading deviously over the mountains" to Guiyang, the capital of Guizhou Province, then south on another mountain road down into Guangxi Province. According to members of the Friends Ambulance Unit, Guizhou was "wild and mountainous and barren," but once they reached Guangxi, "we felt our-selves in a different land . . . the roads are lined with trees . . . The country continued to be mountainous, but the vegetation seemed richer and the grass greener." It would have taken my father, by YMCA secretary Edward Lockwood's calculations, about six to ten days by truck to get from Kunming to the railhead mentioned by my father. This railhead was Jinchengjiang (now Hechi) in Guangxi.[25]

At Jinchengjiang, according to Lockwood, a four-day trip along three different railway lines would have awaited my father. First, a train on the Guizhou–Guangxi line going southeast to Liuzhou, traveling "through mountainous country . . . passing small plains in which sugar and sweet potatoes were growing well." Then a second train on the Hunan–Guangxi line going northeast via Guilin to Hengyang, "ambling through a very pleasant country of rolling grassy hills and wide, well-cultivated plains." And, finally, a third train on the Guangzhou–Hankou line going south to Qujiang. (The second and third legs of this journey were, of course, part of the Guangzhouwan escape route that refugees had taken from Hong Kong to Qujiang. See Map 4.4.) According to the Friends Ambulance Unit people, "the track is broad gauge throughout and the rolling stock is well cared for and up to date; it includes many engines and carriages belonging to north China companies such as the Lung-hai, which are now in exile down here."[26] My father

22. Theodore H. White and Annalee Jacoby, *Thunder Out of China* (New York: William Sloane Associates, 1946), pp. 160–161; Peck, *Two Kinds of Time*, p. 439.

23. HGR's passport, pp. 6, 18.

24. Baker, *Flowing Ways*, p. 115.

25. HGR to ODW, Kukong, 16 October 1943, Box 96, TLUA–HYL; Peck, *Two Kinds of Time*, pp. 444–445; [Duncan Wood], "Duncan's Travels," 24 December 1942, Unit Letter No. 38, Folder Friends Ambulance Unit, Reports—Unit Letters #1–38, General Files 1942—Foreign Service—Country China (FAU Reports #d) to Doukhobors, AFSC Archives; Edward H. Lockwood, Report on the wartime activities of the Kukong YMCA, 1945, p. 9, Folder 82, Box 13, RG 175, Sarah Refo Mason Papers, YDSL.

26. [Duncan Wood], "Duncan's Travels," 24 December 1942, Unit Letter No. 38, Folder Friends Ambulance Unit, Reports—Unit Letters, #1–38, General Files 1942—Foreign Service—Country China (FAU Reports #d) to Doukhobors, AFSC Archives; Zhang Yucai, comp., *Zhongguo tiedao jianshe shilue, 1876–1949* [A history of the con-struction of China's railroads, 1876–1949] (Beijing: Zhongguo tiedao chubanshe, 1997), pp. 275–285, 320–325, and 329–332.

finally reached his destination, Qujiang, on 17 August 1943, two months after arriving in Kunming, almost five months to the day after he left New York, and over a year and a half since he last saw his family in Hong Kong.[27] My mother, I'm sure, was delighted and relieved to see him, but to me he was a virtual stranger. If I recall correctly, I may have hidden under a bed to avoid meeting him again.

My father arrived just in time for the beginning of Lingnan's second academic year at Qujiang. Being part of the College of Arts, the English Department was located on the Tai Tsuen campus near the Sin Yan Miu 仙人廟 (now Meicun 梅村) train station, about twenty miles north of Qujiang city. (See Map 4.4 inset.) According to President Lee, "The Fairy's Temple [Sin Yan Miu] is on the westside of the railway track and our University site is on the eastside of the railway track, just about fifteen minutes' walk from the station."[28] Earlier, at the beginning of June, around the time my father reached Suez on his way back to China, my mother had quit her job with the Maritime Customs and, with me and our amah Ah Hoh, had moved upriver from Qujiang, where we had been living for the past year, to Tai Tsuen to await his arrival.[29] Visiting in January 1944, Muriel Lockwood described the campus, and our accommodations there, as follows: "The buildings are grouped on a hillside, partly under big camphor trees & partly on the open hill. They are mostly temporary structures of bamboo with mud plastered on the outside. The Rhoads have a little cottage which I fear is pretty cold in winter & hot in summer." Fortunately for us, the winter of 1943–1944 (at least as of the end of January) was "unusually warm, no rain as yet."[30]

The setting at Tai Tsuen was, by all accounts, idyllic. In the words of President Lee, "our site is at the edge of several hills and behind two villages. Beyond the villages are rice fields. The highest peak among our hills is, I think, about five hundred feet. The foot of one of the hills is all covered with old camphor trees forming a long forest." Sz-to Wai, the Middle School headmaster, who was also an accomplished painter, rhapsodized about the scenery: "huge camphor trees, cool weather, thirty kinds of birds, lovely wild flowers, and spreading rice-fields, the whole atmosphere artistic."[31] William P. Fenn, following a visit to the campus on behalf of the Associated Boards for Christian Colleges in China, wrote: "The site is a grove of beautiful old camphor trees overlooking paddy fields. Roads and paths wind and twist charmingly in the shade of these trees." Ronald Hall, the refugee Anglican bishop of Hong Kong, on one of his frequent visits to Tai Tsuen, commented that "the hillside when I was there was ablaze with golden yellow azaleas."[32] According to President Lee, "many people think that our campus is the most beautiful of all the war-time university campuses." Certainly, science historian Joseph Needham, visiting in 1944, concurred: "Lingnan University occupied one of the most beautiful temporary campuses

---

27. Y. L. Lee to ODW, Kukong, 24 August 1943, Box 95, TLUA–HYL.
28. Y. L. Lee to ODW, Kukong, 11 December 1942, Box 92, TLUA–HYL.
29. Chinese Maritime Customs Staff database, for "Lo Ngan Chi Kit"; Y. L. Lee to Henry Brownell, Kukong, 15 June 1943, Box 94, TLUA–HYL.
30. Parts of a letter from Mrs. E. H. Lockwood to Catharine Jones Cadbury and others, Kukong, 31 January 1944, Folder Last Names L (except Lambe), Box 32, Collection No. 1192, Cadbury & Cadbury Papers, Haverford College Library.
31. Y. L. Lee to ODW, Kukong, 11 December 1942, Box 92, and Sz-to Wai, "Lingnan Is Born Again," [1943], p. 5, Box 143, TLUA–HYL.
32. "Excerpts from a letter by the Assoc. Boards from Dr. William P. Fenn re a trip of inspection to the Christian colleges in southeastern China," June 1943, Box 94, TLUA–HYL; David M. Paton, *R. O.: The Life and Times of Bishop Hall of Hong Kong* ([Hong Kong]: The Diocese of Hong Kong and Macao, and The Hong Kong Diocesan Association, 1985), p. 118.

Figure 5.1: Overview of Lingnan's campus at Tai Tsuen, looking east toward the Yao Mountains, ca. 1943. From Folder 5802, Box 405, RG 11, Special Collections, YDSL. The university library is atop the hill at center; faculty residences and the camphor forest are at the left; the village of Tai Tsuen is at the right.

in China, some distance from the railway, in a magnificent grove of camphor trees, with wooden buildings, with porches and verandas of pleasant design."[33]

Bucolic as the setting may have been, it was also very primitive. There was no electricity and no running water. As one visitor noted, "all the water used has to be carried up from the stream at the foot of the hill. The lighting problem seems one of the most serious." Oil lamps were relied upon. "For meals," as Zaza Suffiad, then teaching at the Middle School, recalls, "we ate mainly rice and beans with vegetables and tofu . . . A fried egg was a luxury, and we had to pay extra for it. . . . Some evenings, we walked with

---

33. Y. L. Lee, President's Report for the Year 1942–1943 to Members of the Board of Directors, Kukong, 23 August 1943, Box 95, TLUA–HYL; Needham and Needham, *Science Outpost*, p. 225.

Figure 5.2: "Distant view of buildings and camphor trees at Lingnan University," April 1944. Photo by Joseph Needham. Image courtesy of the Needham Research Institute, Cambridge. This photo may have been taken from atop the hill by the library.

lanterns down to the village centre where a few shops stayed open to sell Chinese desserts. We would order a few dishes and just sit and talk."[34]

Moreover, the surrounding region, if not Tai Tsuen itself, was not spared the threat of Japanese air raids. Though largely stalemated, the war continued, and so did the now sporadic aerial bombardment. Writing on 23 September 1943, President Lee reported that "within the last two days the Japanese have dropped quite a number of bombs in Kukong and I was in the midst of the bombing yesterday, but it was not so severe as it was in last January. Most of the bombs were rather small." Customs Commissioner Edgar Bathurst confirmed that "once more daily air-raid alarms have commenced."[35] Three months later, at the end of December, Bathurst reported more raids on Qujiang: "Alarms are, as usual, almost a daily occurrence but we are now seeing more planes. We have had three actual raids this month, the last one, by 16 planes, killing more than 300 people." Joseph Needham recorded yet another air raid alert on 18 April 1944, just as he was about to travel from Qujiang to Tai Tsuen.[36] These bombing runs over Tai Tsuen and Qujiang

---

34. Excerpts from a letter from Professor Arthur W. March to James M. Henry, [Kukong?], 28 February 1944, Folder Last Names K-M, Box 45, Collection No. 1192, Cadbury & Cadbury Papers, Haverford College Library; Hsieh, "My War Years in Hong Kong, China and India," p. 43; Situ Yu and Xu Zhijun, "Lingdacun shenghuo de pianduan huiyi" [Fragmentary recollections of life at Ling Tai Tsuen], *Dacun suiyue*, p. 125.

35. Y. L. Lee to ODW, Kukong, 23 September 1943, Box 95, TLUA–HYL; E. Bathurst to L. K. Little, Kukong, 1 October 1943, Kukong Semi-Official Correspondence, 1943–1946, 679(1)/32499, Maritime Customs Archives, Second Historical Archives of China; Sha Dongxun, *Guangdong kang-Ri zhanzheng jishi*, pp. 497, 498, 500.

36. E. Bathurst to L. K. Little, Kukong, 30 December 1943, Kukong Semi-Official Correspondence, 1943–1946, 679(1)/32499, Maritime Customs Archives, Second Historical Archives of China; Joseph Needham, Travel

were part of the Japanese response to the US Fourteenth Air Force operating from their newly constructed airfields in Nanxiong and Suichuan, in northern Guangdong and southern Jiangxi respectively. As Bathurst explained, if the Japanese were "frustrated" (by, say, the weather) in bombing the American airbases, they would drop their bombs "on towns in their way on the return journey [to their home base in Guangzhou]." Fortunately, as President Lee had noted in an earlier letter, "most of our buildings [at Tai Tsuen] are covered up by camphor trees . . . We have . . . quite a number of places where students and faculty members can take shelter in five minutes' walk."[37]

Enrollment at Lingnan in the 1943–1944 school year, according to geographer George B. Cressey, who visited the campus in February 1944, numbered 510, including 43 women. (Another set of statistics, for both the middle school and the college, gives 598 as the total enrollment, including 183 women.) "At the last entrance examinations there were 2500 applicants, of whom 154 were accepted. Lingnan students appear unusually bright, and were very responsive to the writers [*sic*] lectures. Most of them are from Hongkong and Canton." As for the university's "working equipment," however, Cressey found it to be "far below standard. The library has a set of the Encyclopedia Britannica, but the few other books are gifts or loans from alumni and missionary friends." Needham, who had come on behalf of the Sino-British Scientific Co-operation Bureau, likewise found Lingnan's infrastructure to be deficient. According to his travel notes, there was "very little going on in sci[ence], but 3 shipments of microscopes [were] recently smuggled in from HK [Hong Kong]." The library was "very small but very neat, on top of hill." My father, as the only Western faculty member, seems to have been charged with showing Needham around, for during the two days he spent at Lingnan, the two of them dined together at least three times, including once for breakfast "with Rhodes [*sic*] and his Chinese wife & v[ery] shy little boy." I was then six years old.[38]

With our relocation to Tai Tsuen, my mother had given up her job with the Maritime Customs. She continued, though, to serve as President Lee's secretary, earning $1,000 a month in Chinese National Currency. My father's monthly salary of US$100, at the exchange rate of 30 Chinese dollars (or *yuan*) to 1 US dollar, came to CN$3,000. With a total monthly income of CN$4,000, we as a family were able at first, my father reported, "to live comfortably enough as comforts go here. At least we get enough food."[39] That would soon not be the case.

Wartime inflation, caused by the Nationalist government printing money to meet its budgetary needs, was most keenly felt by Chinese salaried workers, like my mother. My father, though he was paid in US dollars, was affected as well, for two reasons. One was that his employer, the American trustees, insisted on converting his pay into Chinese currency using the official exchange rate. More than once he wrote to Wannamaker about

Journals, South-East China, April 8–July 1, 1944, entry for 18 April 1944, available at nri.cam.ac.uk, the website of the Needham Research Institute, University of Cambridge, under "Joseph Needham in Wartime China" (last accessed 16 December 2017); Sha Dongxun, *Guangdong kang-Ri zhanzheng jishi*, pp. 513, 557.

37. E. Bathurst to L. K. Little, Kukong, 1 October 1943, Kukong Semi-Official Correspondence, 1943–1946, 679(1)/32499, Maritime Customs Archives, Second Historical Archives of China; Y. L. Lee to ODW, Kukong, 11 January 1943, Box 93, TLUA–HYL.

38. George B. Cressey to Clarence E. Gauss, Chungking, 1 June 1944, enclosure re Lingnan University, Folder 842 (May to Aug), Box 55, UD 10, US Embassy in China, 1843–1945, RG 84, Records of the Foreign Service Posts of the Department of State, USNA–CP; Needham, Travel Journals, South-East China, entries of 19 and 20 April 1944; Huang Yanyu, "Mingguo sa niandu zhi sasan niandu jiaowu gaikuang" [An overview of academic affairs, 1941–1944], in *Kangzhan qijian de Lingnan* [Lingnan during the war of resistance] (n.p.: 1946?), pp. 32–33.

39. HGR to ODW, Kukong, 16 October 1943, Box 96, TLUA–HYL.

the "miserable 30 to 1 [exchange] rate when American soldiers, thousands of them, are paid in [American] currency which they change in the black market at 80 to 1." As a result, the buying power of his salary was reduced by around two-thirds: instead of $8,000 in Chinese National Currency, his US$100 bought him only CN$3,000. Furthermore, according to economist Chang Kia-ngau, "the index of the exchange rate . . . lagged far behind that of the general price level," as prices increased on average more than 300 percent a year from 1941 to 1945. In other words, prices were rising much faster than even the market exchange rate.[40] Thus, in November 1943, writing to his cousin Anna Pugh, my father commented on "the high cost of food." Three months later he wrote to Wannamaker: "Prices continue to skyrocket . . . Even with the increased exchange rate I shall be comparatively poorer than when I arrived here." Indeed, though the official exchange rate had been raised to 40 to 1 in January, it was still significantly less than the black market rate of 86–110 *yuan* to the dollar.[41] In late March 1944, in a letter to Wannamaker, President Lee confirmed our family's economic plight: "From all I have reported to you regarding the cost of living and the prices around here in the past few months, you must be quite aware of the fact that what the Trustees are paying Dr. Rhoads is far from enough."[42]

Prior to his return to China, there had been doubts about my father's capacity to cope with the difficulties of life as a refugee behind the Japanese lines, prompted perhaps by his health problems in Hong Kong and then his hypochondria in the Stanley internment camp. In February 1943, when my father was pleading to be sent back to China, Olin Wannamaker had asked history professor Henry Brownell for his opinion. Brownell, who had been with my father in Hong Kong and later at Stanley, was bluntly skeptical: "With all Rhoads['s] superior training and talent in literature his personality detracts much from his usefulness and, I hate to say it, I question whether he will adapt himself to the very different circumstances in North Kwangtung. . . . Most telling of all," according to Brownell, "Rhoads tells me that his wife . . . doubts the advisability of his trying to live as all have to do in North Kwangtung or coming to China until after the war is over."[43] However, aside from the problem of inflation, my father, contrary to earlier doubts about his ability to deal with the difficulties of wartime China, seems instead to have thrived. In a long letter to Wannamaker, dated 16 October 1943, he was remarkably—even uncharacteristically—upbeat.[44] "I am honestly amazed at the amount of work which had been done on this new campus in the way of building and making furniture and other necessary equipment for some sort of comfortable living. . . . it is hard for a newcomer to believe that a little more than a year ago there was nothing on these hillsides except a few matsheds."

He wrote of his own work and that of his department:

> I am teaching six courses myself, running the department of English, supervising a senior thesis and acting as the librarian of the University. All in all, this amounts to what I should call a double load. . . . I think it is rather interesting that my own department is now

40. HGR to ODW, Kukong, 16 October 1943, Box 96, TLUA–HYL; Chang Kia-ngau, *The Inflationary Spiral: The Experience in China, 1939–1950* ([Cambridge, MA]: Technology Press of Massachusetts Institute of Technology and New York: John Wiley & Sons, 1958), pp. 12, 53.

41. Anna E. D. Pugh to ODW, Bala Cynwyd, 20 January 1944, and HGR to ODW, Kukong, 16 February 1944, Box 97, TLUA–HYL. On the foreign exchange rate in wartime China, see Arthur N. Young, *China's Wartime Finance and Inflation, 1937–1945* (Cambridge, MA: Harvard University Press, 1965), pp. 154–155 and Table 59, Part B.

42. Y. L. Lee to ODW, Kukong, 25 March 1944, Box 97, TLUA–HYL.

43. Henry Brownell to ODW, Swarthmore, PA, 19 February 1943, Box 93, TLUA–HYL.

44. HGR to ODW, Kukong, 16 October 1943, Box 96, TLUA–HYL.

regarded as the strongest in the University. Actually we have one full-time teacher engaged by the Chinese administration[,] and the Registrar gives us four hours of his time. The rest of the work—and we are giving a complete normal program—is made possible by my own heavy load and an almost equally heavy one carried by Mrs. Kunkle and the kindness of Dr. Kunkle in allowing us some of the time of two of his teachers . . . My wife is also teaching a section of sub-Freshman English without pay. Actually, you see, three quarters of our work costs the administration nothing.

Julia Kunkle had taught at Lingnan previously; her husband was the president of the Canton Union Theological College, which, like Lingnan, had relocated to Tai Tsuen during the war.

My father also wrote about the students:

In some ways Lingnan seems to me to be a far healthier institution than at any time during the several years that I have known it. The spirit of the students, on the whole, is excellent. Most of them have learned what it means to be a bit hungry, to be a bit dirty, to wash their own clothes and to carry their own water; all in all, they are not the rotten little snobs some of them were in Canton and around Hong Kong. Similarly, I think there seems to be a more genuine intellectual atmosphere than formerly. Now that they do not have books, far more of them are eager to read and the books we do have are in constant use.

The "spirit of the students" of which he spoke was perhaps best exemplified by their response to famine. In the fall of 1943, the local rice crop failed, and the price of rice and other commodities, which had been rising in Qujiang since the beginning of the year, rose yet again, so that prices in Qujiang were higher even than in Guilin and Chongqing. According to Customs Commissioner Bathurst, writing in November, "many items are now almost 50% higher than Kweilin prices which in turn were 32% higher than Chungking prices for August 1943." The crop failure had brought on the worst famine of the Republican era in Guangdong Province and may have killed more than one million people.[45] However, with the cooperation of the Ninth War Zone in neighboring Hunan Province, the school authorities were able to purchase a large quantity of rice in Changsha and had it transported by train to Sin Yan Miu. But then the grain had to be taken the final two kilometers from the train station to the university, and this had to be done quickly and without any motorized transport. The students all rose to the challenge. Along with the faculty and staff and their dependents (including, if I recall correctly, myself as a five-year-old), they formed a human chain and, using buckets and bags, successfully moved all eight hundred *dan* 石 (or 52 tons) of rice within a few hours.[46]

The work my father did at Tai Tsuen during the 1943–1944 school year seems to have been much appreciated by those on the ground. Edward Lockwood, the American secretary of the YMCA in Qujiang, wrote that "Prof. Rhodes [*sic*] has done a great deal towards raising the morale of the Faculty"; J. Stewart Kunkle, head of the Canton Union

45. E. Bathurst to L. K. Little, Kukong, 9 November 1943, Kukong Semi-Official Correspondence, 1943–1946, 679(1)/32499, Maritime Customs Archives, Second Historical Archives of China. On the 1943 famine in Guangdong, see Peck, *Two Kinds of Time*, pp. 21, 554; Van de Ven, *China at War*, p. 188; and Liang Biqi and Ye Jinzhao, comps., *Guangdong de ziran zaihai* [Guangdong's natural disasters] (n.p.: Guangdong renmin chubanshe, 1993), pp. 33–35, 170, 183.

46. Yang Yimei, "Li Yinglin shiqi de Lingnan daxue" [Lingnan University at the time of Y. L. Lee], *Guangdong wenshi ziliao*, no. 51 (1987): 89–90; Wu Zhande, "Min yi shi wei tian" [People regard food as heaven], *Dacun suiyue*, p. 56; Li Ruiming (Lee Sui-ming) and Emily M. Hill, *Nanguo fenghuang: Zhongshan daxue Lingnan (daxue) xueyuan* [A phoenix of South China: The story of Lingnan [University] College, Sun Yat-sen University] (Hong Kong: Commercial Press, 2005), p. 50.

Figure 5.3: "Students doing group exercises on the grounds of Lingnan University," April 1944. Photo by Joseph Needham. Image courtesy of the Needham Research Institute, Cambridge.

Figure 5.4: "Two students standing at a notice board at Lingnan University," April 1944. Photo by Joseph Needham. Image courtesy of the Needham Research Institute, Cambridge.

Theological College, similarly wrote that "when I see the fine work and influence of Dr. Rhoads I wonder that you [the New York trustees] do not send out more American teachers of large experience and understanding." President Y. L. Lee, too, put in a good word to the trustees for my father, despite his earlier reservations: "He [Rhoads] has done very well. You must try to hold him at least for the next two or three years."[47] Although my father's agreement with the American trustees had clearly specified that it was for only one year, when Wannamaker wrote to him in May 1944 offering him, in very apologetic tones, "a 50% increase in the very nominal support the Trustees are at present giving to you," it sounded as if he would be kept on for at least another year.[48]

External events soon decided otherwise. Since the fall of Wuhan and Guangzhou in October 1938, the conflict in China had been more or less stalemated, with the Japanese occupying most major cities in the north and coastal cities in the south and the united front of Chinese Nationalists and Communists controlling the countryside and the interior. In the spring of 1944, however, the war suddenly sprang back to life, as the Japanese launched Operation Ichigō ("No. 1") in a desperate effort "to force the Allies to the negotiating table by scoring a clear victory." It was to be, according to scholar Hara Takeshi, "the largest military operation carried out in the history of the Japanese army."[49] The offensive was aimed, in part, at wiping out the pesky airbases in southern and south-central China from which the US Fourteenth Air Force, under General Claire Chennault, had been attacking Japanese shipping in the East China Sea. It was also intended to split the southeastern part of Free China from the western part by driving down the Guangzhou–Hankou and the Hunan–Guangxi railroads and linking up with Japanese forces in Indo-China. If it succeeded, this campaign would establish a land route for supplies from Southeast Asia to Japan, replacing the sea route, which by then was being crippled. By late May 1944 the Japanese army, advancing southward from central China, had reached Changsha, which it captured on 18 June. Hengyang and possibly Qujiang would be the next targets.[50] After seven years, the war had finally come to the interior of southwestern China, which up until then "had largely escaped the direct impact of the fighting." Though repeatedly bombed, it had not been invaded.[51]

At Lingnan, President Y. L. Lee on 30 May received official orders "to conduct final examinations for all our colleges as well as middle school within one week" and then "to evacuate as soon as possible." A couple of weeks later, when Changsha had fallen, the American and British governments told "their nationals in eastern China to evacuate westward." As President Lee later recounted, "this meant the immediate scattering of our faculty and their families and all the students."[52] It was then that my father, my pregnant mother, and I, together with Ah Hoh, abandoned Lingnan and set out for Chongqing in West China. For the third time in six years, we were on the run again. As everyone hastened

47. E. H. Lockwood to ODW, Kukong, 12 November 1943, Box 96, and J. S. Kunkle to ODW, Kukong, 5 January 1944, and Y. L. Lee to ODW, Kukong, 1 February 1943, Box 97, TLUA–HYL.
48. ODW to HGR, New York, 9 May 1944, Box 98, TLUA–HYL.
49. Van de Ven, *China at War*, p. 181; Hara Takeshi, "The Ichigō Offensive," in Peattie, Drea, and Van de Ven, eds., *Battle for China*, p. 392.
50. Hara, "Ichigō Offensive," pp. 392–393; Van de Ven, *China at War*, pp. 179–190; Edward H. Lockwood to Joe [Kidd], Kukong, 10 June 1944, Edward H. Lockwood Papers, University of Michigan Library.
51. Lary, *Chinese People at War*, p. 152.
52. Y. L. Lee to ODW, Kukong, 7 June 1944, Box 98, and "President's Report to the Members of the Board of Directors of Lingnan University for the Year 1943–1944," Kukong, 19 December 1944, Box 143, TLUA–HYL; Edwin Ride, *BAAG: Hong Kong Resistance, 1942–1945* (Hong Kong: Oxford University Press, 1981), p. 248.

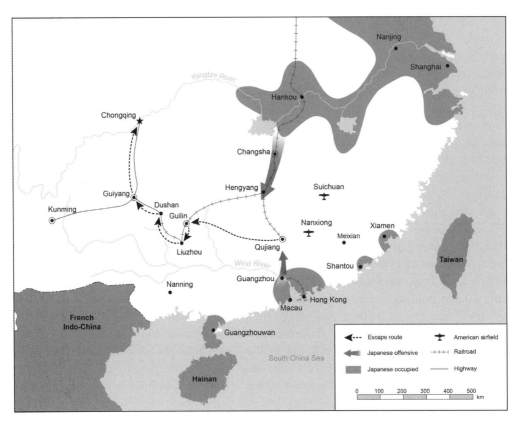

Map 5.1: Japan's Ichigō Offensive, and our escape route to Chongqing, summer 1944. Map by Ada Au-Yeung.

to leave, welcome news arrived from Europe: the Allies had landed in Normandy, thus opening up a second front against the Germans.[53]

According to Anna Pugh, based on two letters from my father, we "left Kukong the end of June by truck—the railroads had been torn up—and arrived in Chungking the first of August after a very interesting but rather hazardous journey by truck, train and truck again." The only other thing definitely known about our month-long escape from Qujiang to Chongqing was that we went by way of Guiyang, the capital of Guizhou Province, where at the end of July my father renewed his Chinese visa for another year. By then, both my father and my mother were experienced refugees.[54]

The departure from Qujiang must have been chaotic. Graham Peck, who passed through the city in early June, wrote that "the Kukong people had been warned to prepare for a compulsory evacuation within two weeks, but it was hard to leave without heavy bribes to officials. The government had commandeered most of the cars and boats which were the means of getting out to the inaccessible and safer northern parts of the province. The only other exit was up the railway to Hengyang and [then down to] Kweilin." However, by late June, Changsha had fallen to the Japanese and Hengyang was being threatened, and trains were no longer running from Qujiang, for the tracks had been

---

53. Needham, *Travel Journals, South-East China, April 1–July 1, 1944*, entry of 7 June.
54. Anna E. D. Pugh to ODW, Bala Cynwyd, PA, 7 December 1944, Box 100, TLUA–HYL; HGR's passport, p. 21.

torn up as a defensive measure.[55] So it was that we "left Kukong . . . by truck." Perhaps my father, as he had the year before on his way back from America, was able to wangle a ride with American military personnel as they abandoned their airfields to the north and east of Qujiang. Overland travel by truck in southwestern China during the war was not easy. As a British YMCA secretary recalled, "If you were lucky, you found a truck that used petrol. (All petrol had to come up the Burma Road, and after Pearl Harbour, over 'The Hump,' by air.) The second choice was a truck or bus running on alcohol made mostly from sugarcane. Failing that there were vehicles running on charcoal gas: up a steep hill it was almost as fast to walk." My father was later to wax nostalgic about "banging about on the tail end of a charcoal burning truck." Fortunately, according to the British YMCA secretary, "the motor highways were mostly recently constructed, not very wide, with a dirt surface."[56]

But where would we have gone "by truck" in late June? There were, at the time, five highways leading out of Qujiang, including one to the north and one to the west.[57] With Hengyang under assault by the Japanese, the northern route was out. Thus, the most likely escape route for us would have been to go west via Lianxian and Hexian (also known as Babu) to Guilin; according to Needham, this road was "said to be passable, but has long been derelict, and the bridges certainly unsafe." From Qujiang to Lianxian, YMCA secretary Edward Lockwood wrote, was "a two days['] ride by truck" over rough roads; then from Lianxian to Hexian was a newly constructed 150-kilometer highway, but one that reportedly "was destroyed two years ago."[58] However we did it, we probably got to Guilin by the middle of July.

At Guilin, the trains were still running, but they were even more jampacked than those earlier in Qujiang. According to US Vice Consul Richard M. Service,

> After June 15, when thousands of refugees from Hunan were joined by other thousands at Kweilin who desired to evacuate to Liuchow and Kweichow by rail, it became extremely difficult to find space on trains. Congestion was such that all trains until the first week in July were not only literally packed to capacity inside but carried hundreds of persons on the roofs of cars and clinging to every handhold. Reservations were valueless unless the space was physically occupied and forcibly held by the ticketholder from the moment the car was unlocked. In the face of this situation foreign civilians in Kweilin who desired to go overland to Kweichow encountered great difficulty, often waiting eight or ten hours at the station for chronically late trains, only to be out-pushed by huge crowds of panic-stricken Chinese who clambered through windows and fought for standing room in aisles and toilets.

Despite such difficulties, it was probably at Guilin that we changed from traveling by truck to traveling by train. If so, at this point our evacuation route essentially retraced

55. Peck, *Two Kinds of Time*, pp. 568–569; E. Bathurst to L. K. Little, Kukong, 16 June 1944, Kukong Semi-Official Correspondence, 1943–1946, 679(1)/32499, Maritime Customs Archives, Second Historical Archives of China.

56. Paton, *R. O.: Life and Times of Bishop Hall*, p. 116; HGR to ODW, [Chungking], 3 June 1945, Box 102, TLUA–HYL.

57. *Qujiangxian gaikuang* [Survey of Qujiang County] ([Qujiang]: Guangdongsheng Qujiangxian zhengfu, August 1941), pp. 32–33.

58. Needham and Needham, *Science Outpost*, p. 220; Edward H. Lockwood to Joe Kidd, Kukong, 2 August 1944, Edward H. Lockwood Papers, University of Michigan Library; Huang Chih Chien to L. K. Little, Meihsien, 26 July 1944, Kukong Semi-Official Correspondence, 1943–1946, 679(1)/32499, Maritime Customs Archives, Second Historical Archives of China; on the Linxian–Hexian highway, see Chinese Ministry of Information, *China Handbook, 1937–1945: A Comprehensive Survey of Major Developments in China in Eight Years of War*, rev. and enl. ed. (New York: Macmillan Company, 1947), p. 219.

in reverse a portion of the route my father had taken the year before: southwestward on the Hunan–Guangxi line from Guilin to Liuzhou, where according to Vice Consul Service "congestion was reportedly greater than at Kweilin," and then northwestward on the Guizhou–Guangxi line from Liuzhou to the railroad's terminus, which in the past year had been extended beyond Jinchengjiang to Dushan, over the border in Guizhou Province.[59]

Figure 5.5: "British Military Mission lorry, and refugees, during retreat from Guilin, 1944." Image courtesy of John E. Stanfield and Historical Photographs of China, University of Bristol (www.hpcbristol.net).

Figure 5.6: "Evacuation of Kweilin: Refugees at the Kweilin railroad station wait for transportation," 1944. From Charles F. Romanus and Riley Sunderland, *Stilwell's Command Problems* (Washington: Office of the Chief of Military History, Department of the Army, 1956), p. 373.

---

59. Richard M. Service to US Embassy, Kweilin, 15 July 1944, enclosed in Arthur R. Ringwalt to US Embassy, Kweilin, 16 July 1944, Folder 300 General, Box 44, UD 10, US Embassy in China, 1843–1945, RG 84, Records of the Foreign Service Posts of the Department of State, USNA–CP.

Huang Hsing Tsung 黃興宗, who had interpreted for Joseph Needham during his tour of universities in southeastern China, has described their experience getting from Liuzhou to Dushan around this same time. Because "the avalanche of refugees had already started" and "all the westbound trains were full," it took two days of "hanging around the platform" at the Liuzhou station before we "finally managed to board a train." Then, the train "made many irregular stops along the way. At times we had to wait for hours before the train started again. It seemed a miracle that we arrived at Tushan on 4 July." A trip of 246 miles on the single-track railroad had taken five days! Those who were less fortunate made the trek from Liuzhou to Dushan by other means, as depicted so vividly by journalist Theodore H. White in his historical novel *The Mountain Road*: "Up this road, as far as the eye could see, an endless procession of people, rich and poor, people dressed in rags, in silken gowns, in uniforms, riding in rickshaws, on carts, on trucks, in buses, on horseback, on foot, continued to flow toward the safety beyond the hills."[60]

Dushan was then the end of the line for the Guangxi–Guizhou railroad. For the rest of our journey we would have traveled once again by truck, first to Guiyang, where (as previously noted) my father had his visa extended at the end of July. Six years earlier, Richard Dobson, the British cigarette salesman, had driven along this recently built road. He described Guizhou as "a backward, out-of-the-way, underdeveloped province. . . . The land is consistently mountainous and barren, so uninviting that much of it has been left to the Miao [ethnic minority]. . . . High up on the hillsides one could see their wretched huts, and fields of stunted corn hacked desperately out of the rock. In the valleys corn was the main crop. . . . The roads on which I was travelling had been built only after my arrival in China [in 1936]; before, the only way to get from Kweiyang to the outer world was to walk."[61]

Near Guiyang, which Dobson found to be "a surprisingly big city," the highway forked. One road headed west to Kunming (which was the one my father would have taken the year before); the other went north to Chongqing (which would have been the one we took now). This leg of our journey may have been the easiest and fastest, as the 325-mile Chongqing–Guiyang highway had been built less than ten years earlier to facilitate Chiang Kai-shek's annihilation campaigns against the Communists. As we went north, we would have gone through Zunyi, which Dobson described as "a dull little town" and which was where, ten years earlier, during their retreat known as the Long March, Mao Zedong had come to power within the Chinese Communist movement. North of Zunyi, as the road climbed steadily, we would have experienced "the thrill of negotiating the famous Seventy-two Turns, where the highway made 72 consecutive hairpin bends to [ascend] the side of a steep mountain." Having reached the top, we would have arrived in Sichuan Province; down before us would have been "a long wooded gorge with line upon line of hills still lying across [our] path."[62]

Only two or three days after leaving Guiyang, we would have reached the highway's terminus, Haitangxi 海棠溪, on the south bank of the Yangtze. Looming on the far bank of the mile-wide river was Chongqing, "like the pointed prow of a ship, thrusting

---

60. Huang Hsing Tsung, "Pursuing Science in Hong Kong, China and the West," in *Dispersal and Renewal*, ed. Matthews and Cheung, p. 139, and "Peregrinations with Joseph Needham in China, 1943–44," in *Explorations in the History of Science and Technology in China*, ed. Li Guohao et al. (Shanghai: Shanghai Chinese Classics Publishing House, 1982), pp. 69–70; Theodore H. White, *The Mountain Road* (New York: William Sloane Associates, 1958), p. 14.

61. Dobson, *China Cycle*, p. 104.

62. Dobson, *China Cycle*, pp. 107–108, and Huang, "Peregrinations with Joseph Needham in China, 1943–44," p. 62.

downstream between the Kialing and Yangtze Rivers" (in the words of the budding author Han Suyin).[63] As there was no bridge spanning the river until 1980, the final step on our month-long trek would have involved a ferry across the Yangtze.

Where we had spent the nights along the way, during our own "long march," is unclear. A British YMCA official wrote that "much depended on whether there was a China Travel Service hotel, or a friendly mission or church, or some agency with a spare bed (as it might be, the Friends' Ambulance Unit or the Chinese Industrial Cooperatives). Failing this, it was a case of the necessarily over-pressed local inns, none of which were inviting, and some horrid." According to a Friends Ambulance Unit official, who made the trek in the opposite direction in April 1943, "We ate and slept as best we could—in filthy little village inns, in luxurious guest houses run by the government, in comfortable and prayer-ful [*sic*] missionary stations and curled up in the truck cab on the highway or among the bales and boxes under the tarpaulin." In September 1943 the British writer Robert Payne, likewise going from Chongqing to Guiyang, spent his first night sleeping by the side of the road, another night at a China Inland Mission hostel at Zunyi, and his third night at a little hotel in Guiyang.[64]

As it turned out, the Japanese, after capturing Hengyang with difficulty on 8 August, did not continue advancing down the Guangzhou–Hankou railroad. Instead, they headed down the Hunan–Guangxi railroad, seizing both Guilin and Liuzhou in November and linking up with friendly forces from Indo-China soon afterward. Thus, Qujiang was not overrun after all, and Lingnan was able, in the fall of 1944, to resume operations at its several campuses in northern Guangdong. But my father was no longer around for the new school year. James Henry, Lingnan's former provost, who had been repatriated and was now back in China with the US Office of Strategic Services, wrote Wannamaker in mid-August: "I am afraid we shall lose the Rhoads. I heard they were on the way to the Capitol [*sic*; i.e., Chongqing] and if they reach there, especially if another baby is expected, you can't expect them to go back."[65]

The university's reprieve, however, was for a semester only, because in January 1945 a new Japanese offensive finally succeeded in capturing Qujiang. Students and faculty and administrators were forced to scatter again, this time for good. President Y. L. Lee and others retreated to Meixian (now Meizhou), three hundred miles to the east and away from the Japanese attack, with hopes of reopening the university yet one more time.[66] The various offices of the Guangdong provincial government as well as the Maritime Customs Service scattered to the east and west as well.

---

63. Han Suyin, *Destination Chungking* (Boston: Little, Brown and Company, 1942), p. 206.
64. Paton, *R. O.: Life and Times of Bishop Hall*, p. 117; John Rich to Clarence [Pickett] et al., Chengtu, 20 April 1943, Letter No. 5, Folder Letters from John Rich, Foreign Service 1943—Country China (Letters from J. Perry to FAU Reports to National Office), AFSC Archives; Robert Payne, *Forever China* (New York: Dodd, Mead and Company, 1945), pp. 437–446.
65. James M. Henry to ODW, [Kweilin], 17 August 1944, Box 99, TLUA–HYL.
66. Corbett, *Lingnan University*, p. 147.

6

With the US Government in Chongqing (1944–1945)

Chongqing (Chungking) is a mountainous city at the confluence of the Yangtze and Jialing rivers. The wartime capital of China, it had been the seat of Chiang Kai-shek's national government since the end of 1937. Protected by mountains forming the Sichuan Basin, the city had been safe from a land assault by the Japanese but not from aerial bombardment. Thus, in the first years of the war, Chongqing, like Qujiang in Guangdong but on a much larger scale, had been "bombed almost daily by swarms of a hundred planes, sometimes releasing a thousand bombs in a few seconds," according to historian Dick Wilson. "Only the fact that heavy fog every winter kept the Japanese bombers away for half the year prevented it from being smashed out of existence."[1] But the bombing had tapered off after the outbreak of the Pacific War in December 1941.

In the winter of 1944–1945, however, Chongqing's immunity from a land assault was challenged from the south by Japan's Operation Ichigō. That offensive, which had driven us out of Qujiang at the end of June, had resumed. After taking Guilin and Liuzhou in November, the Japanese had advanced up the mountain road and railroad from Liuzhou into southern Guizhou Province, capturing the railhead at Dushan on 5 December. Guiyang, the provincial capital, thus came under threat, and if Guiyang were lost, then, as one of the characters in Ba Jin's wartime novel *Cold Nights* observed, the Japanese would be "only two days away from Chungking by car"—a fact that was confirmed by our recent refugee experience. According to historian Parks Coble, "Free China . . . appeared on the verge of collapsing." General Albert C. Wedemeyer, Chiang Kai-shek's new American chief of staff, "was so alarmed by the Japanese advance on 10 December that he reported . . . that the fall of both [Kunming and Chongqing] was imminent." Indeed, in Ba Jin's novel, the publishing house and the bank where the two main characters were employed began taking steps to transfer their operations to Lanzhou, in northwestern China. Fortunately, the Japanese forces were overextended and did not advance much beyond Dushan, which the Nationalists soon recaptured. The panic in the capital city generated by the initial loss of Dushan soon subsided.[2] Nevertheless, Operation Ichigō had long-term consequences for Chiang Kai-shek and his regime. According to historian Hara Takeshi, it had "inflicted

---

1. Dick Wilson, *When Tigers Fight: The Story of the Sino-Japanese War, 1937–1945* (New York: Viking Press, 1982), p. 153.
2. Pa Chin, *Cold Nights*, trans. Nathan K. Mao and Liu Ts'un-yan (Hong Kong: Chinese University Press; Seattle and London: University of Washington Press, 1978), pp. 33, 66, 79; Coble, *China's War Reporters*, pp. 119–121; Asano Toyomi, "Japanese Operations in Yunnan and North Burma," in Peattie, Drea, and Van de Ven, eds., *Battle for China*, p. 384.

an estimated 750,000 casualties on the Nationalist army and thus fatally weakened it for the postwar confrontation with its Communist rivals."[3]

Prewar Chongqing, like Qujiang, had been a sleepy backwater, but after it was chosen as China's wartime capital, hundreds of thousands of "downriver people" had come pouring in. From two hundred thousand before the war, the population ballooned to a million.[4] As Joseph Needham observed, wartime Chongqing was "an extremely sprawling place, running along at different levels for miles."[5] This urban sprawl was composed of three parts: the Lower and the Upper cities within the old city, some of whose walls were still intact in the early 1940s, and what might be called the New City to the west.

The Lower City (Xiabancheng 下半城), south of the ridge that bisected the old walled city from east to west, took in the steep slopes rising up some two hundred feet from the narrow strip of land along the banks of the Yangtze. "A thousand Chungking alleyways darted off down the slopes of the hills from the two main roads," wrote journalists Theodore White and Annalee Jacoby. "They twisted and tumbled over steps that had been polished smooth by the tramp of centuries of padding straw-sandaled feet. The native Szechwanese [Sichuanese] lived in these alleys as they had for centuries; they held aloof from the worldly downriver Chinese and were suspicious of them." According to Eric N. Danielson, writing in 2005, "These steep hillsides are still today characterized by ramshackle houses hanging from cliffs and endless flights of stone steps, with whole neighborhoods inaccessible by any means of transportation other than on foot." Despite such obstacles, the Lower City had long been the commercial and administrative center of Chongqing; six of the walled city's nine gates, for example, were located there, as were the offices of the prefectural and county magistrates during the Qing dynasty.[6] By the late 1920s, however, the Lower City had been eclipsed in importance by the Upper City (Shangbancheng 上半城), "located on the heights of the peninsula's ridge." This was where many of the downriver people, along with well-to-do native Sichuanese, lived and worked and shopped.[7] Finally, west of the old city, beyond the Tongyuan Gate 通遠門, on land that had once been taken up by graveyards, lay the vast new suburban administrative center, which had been built up by the Nationalists and their wartime refugee regime and was now "filled with the villas of high party and government officials."[8]

Tying the whole city together was a four-mile-long roadway whose different segments went by different names as it ran from east to west through the Upper City and the New City: Zhonghua Road 中華路 (now Xinhua Road 新華路), Minsheng Road 民生路, and the four sections of Zhongshan Road 中山路. Everett D. Hawkins (1906–1970), then new to the city, described this roadway, which was served by express and local buses, in terms that would be familiar to his relatives in Manhattan: beginning at the tip of the peninsula where the two rivers met (which he equated with the Battery), then westward to Xiaoshizi 小什字 ("the Wall St. of the city"), then Duyoujie 都郵街 ("Times Square with

---

3.   Hara, "Ichigō Offensive," p. 402.

4.   White and Jacoby, *Thunder Out of China*, p. 6.

5.   Needham and Needham, *Science Outpost*, p. 35.

6.   White and Jacoby, *Thunder Out of China*, p. 6; Eric N. Danielson, "Revisiting Chongqing: China's Second World War Temporary National Capital," *Journal of the Royal Asiatic Society Hong Kong Branch* 45 (2005): 175; Wei Yingtao, comp., *Jindai Chongqing chengshi shi* [Modern urban history of Chongqing] (Chengdu: Sichuan daxue chubanshe, 1991), p. 460.

7.   Danielson, "Revisiting Chongqing," p. 175; Wei Yingtao, *Jindai Chongqing chengshi shi*, pp. 460, 473–474.

8.   Danielson, "Revisiting Chongqing," p. 180; Wei Yingtao, *Jindai Chongqing chengshi shi*, pp. 464–465; Chang Jui-te, "Bombs Don't Discriminate? Class, Gender, and Ethnicity in the Air-Raid-Shelter Experiences of the Wartime Chongqing Population," in Flath and Smith, eds., *Beyond Suffering*, p. 60.

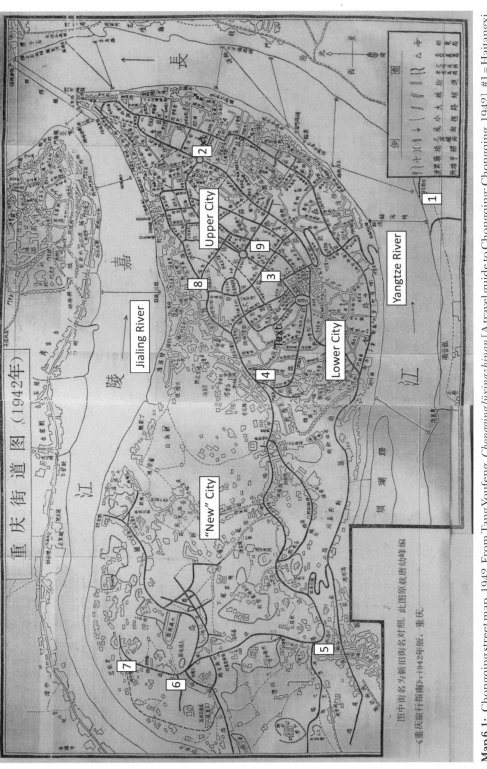

Map 6.1: Chongqing street map, 1942. From Tang Youfeng, *Chongqing lüxing zhinan* [A travel guide to Chongqing; Chongqing, 1942]. #1 = Haitangxi, terminus of Sichuan–Guizhou highway; #2 = Xiaoshizi; #3 = Duyoujie; #4 = Tongyuan Gate; #5 = Lianglukou/OWI office; #6 = Shangqingsi; #7 = Chiu Chin Middle School (old site of OWI); #8 = Methodist Union Hospital; #9 = 214 Bao'an Road (our residence in the Upper City).

Figure 6.1: "Chung Chen[g] [中正] Road, a busy street in the Chongqing banking district," January 1944. From the Library of Congress, Prints and Photographs Division, NYWT&S Collection [LC-USZ62-131091].

some big, really fine shops and some theatres in the neighborhood"}, then Liangluko 兩路口 ("125th St."), and finally Shangqingsi 上清寺 ("way up town").[9]

With its mountainous topography, Chongqing was a city of steps. In the absence of bridges, nearly everyone reached the city by cross-river ferries and was immediately confronted by the sheer mountainous cliffs of the Lower City. As an Indian journalist wrote of his arrival in early 1942, "Three hundred steps were facing me, for Chungking is nothing if not steps. I did a few and then thought it wiser to take a [sedan] chair." More stairs awaited once the Upper City had been reached. According to John Melby, an American diplomat, "From the Embassy to the street [in the New City] is exactly 106 steps—I counted them—and the only way up or down is to walk. The whole city is like that."[10]

Dorothy Needham, Joseph Needham's wife and colleague, has left a vivid description of Chongqing's street scene in 1944:

> Terrific crowds of people, all in blue, grey, a few black or brown. Babies in bright scarlet.
> Countless activities right on the pavement. Graceful carrying-poles. People, even young

9.   Wei Yingtao, *Jindai Chongqing chengshi shi*, pp. 471–472; Everett D. Hawkins to "Mother and Kidlets in New York," [Chungking], 23 September 1944, Folder Letters Sent 1944, Box 1, Everett D. Hawkins Papers, 1900–1972, RG 30/130, Oberlin College Archives, Oberlin, OH.

10. D. F. Karaka, *Chungking Diary* (Bombay: Thacker & Co., 1942), p. 15; John F. Melby, *The Mandate of Heaven: Record of a Civil War, China, 1945–49* (Toronto: University of Toronto Press, 1965), p. 35.

girls, often heavily burdened. . . . Water very scarce, often turned off at the main because of inadequacy of electric power for pumping. Long queues of coolies waiting with buckets at hydrants. People live extremely crowded, in houses, huts, parts of bombed houses, perched everywhere on the cliffs, often accessible only by narrow, steep, roughly paved lanes, or by steps. Everywhere unprotected edges, with perpendicular drops. Rickshaws, often with finely muscular pullers, sedan-chairs, horsedrawn carriages with bells, cars, buses, army trucks. People mostly neat, even if gowns fantastically patched, but many very ragged about. Mostly look cheerful, and on the whole healthy, though a good deal of skin disease to be seen. Shops clean and well-arranged. All sorts of things usually of poor quality but very high prices.[11]

Adding to the wartime city's multitude of downriver folk were thousands of Americans. For after 1941 the United States had joined the anti-Japanese war and become China's principal diplomatic and military ally. It consequently had a big and growing presence in Chongqing, as represented by numerous American agencies, both civilian and military. My father readily found work here. On 12 August 1944, within a couple of weeks of our arrival in the city, he had signed on with one of these American agencies, the Office of War Information.[12]

The OWI was principally, though not exclusively, a propaganda agency of the US government. My father had been in contact with the OWI previously. A year and a half earlier, after he had been repatriated to America and was desperately seeking a way to get back to China, he had approached the agency as one option, "asking whether in the event of my going back, I could be of any service to the Office of War Information as a kind of listening post. I am quite confident that through the access I would have, with my wife's help, to the bamboo wireless, I could gather reliable information about the occupied areas of South China directly from loyal Chinese now in those places. I believe also I could manage to get more of our own information into Canton and Hongkong for distribution there."[13] It is unclear whether, when my father did get to Qujiang, he did any work for the OWI, but it is apparent that when he was cut loose from Lingnan by the Ichigō offensive and wound up in Chongqing, he turned to the OWI again.

"The various roles of the OWI," according to Wilma Fairbank (1909–2002), "included psychological warfare against the enemy and the 'projection of America' to allied and neutral nations. During the war years it had become a large and far-flung bureaucracy which, in its purely informational role, distributed news and features, motion pictures and filmstrips, produced radio programs, circulated exhibits, established libraries and reading rooms, and made translations of American books." Her own cultural relations program at the US embassy was "operating on a shoestring." In contrast, the OWI in China—known in Chinese as Meiguo xinwenchu 美國新聞處 (American Information Service)—was "rich in American hardware, talent, and funds," she wrote enviously. "It was equipped with a radio network, photo labs, movie projectors, duplicating and other office machines, and all the technicians necessary to operate and service them."[14] In late

---

11. Needham and Needham, *Science Outpost*, p. 236.
12. China Division, Monthly Personnel Report, 1–31 August 1944, Folder Chungking Letters 13–30 September [1944], Box 660, NC 148 387: Reports of the Office of Communications . . . , Letters and Reports from Outposts, RG 208, Records of the Office of War Information, USNA–CP.
13. HGR, Bala Cynwyd, to ODW, 10 October 1942, and to James Linen, 21 October 1942, Box 91, TLUA–HYL. Linen was an official with the OWI.
14. Wilma Fairbank, *America's Cultural Experiment in China, 1942–1949* (Washington: US Department of State, Bureau of Educational and Cultural Affairs, 1976), pp. 145–146. On the OWI in China, see Matthew D. Johnson,

1944, soon after my father joined the organization, the China Division of the OWI had on its payroll 34 Americans and 276 Chinese.[15]

The China Division was headquartered in Chongqing. In 1944–1945, it had three regional branches: one in Chengdu, one in Kunming, and one in Yongan, Fujian. Administratively, it was headed by the veteran journalist F. McCracken (Mac) Fisher (1907–2000) from the time of its formation in 1942 until he was succeeded, in March 1945, by William L. Holland (1907–2008), formerly the executive secretary of the Institute of Pacific Relations (an early "think tank"). As Wilma Fairbank noted, the agency basically had two sections; one involved psychological warfare (PW), directed mainly at Japanese enemy soldiers in the field, and the other was "purely informational." My father, in Chongqing, worked on the information side as "chief of English publications" and— perhaps drawing on his experience on the staff of *The Pennsylvanian* a quarter-century earlier—as editor of the *American Digest*.[16]

The American Digest was a weekly mimeographed newsmagazine, fourteen or fifteen pages in length. Published in English, it was composed of "articles from magazines and newspapers which come from the States on microfilm." For example, the issue for 6 October 1944 (Vol. 5, No. 14), the first one for which my father was responsible, reprinted six articles: one each from recent issues of *Time* ("Tycoon Mayer and Tycoon Nobel"), *Newsweek* ("Numbers Please"), and the *American Mercury* ("The Miracles of Penicillin"), and three other items.[17] The *Digest* also published special issues on such newsworthy subjects as the Dumbarton Oaks Conference in the fall of 1944 (where the United Nations was founded), the Yalta Conference in February 1945 (where the Allies carved up postwar Europe), and the death of President Franklin D. Roosevelt on 12 April 1945.[18] Each regular issue also included a "two-page round up of the news," prepared by Elmer Newton (ca. 1896–1953), the OWI's news editor, which was lauded as "the most trustworthy and informative weekly summary now being published." The *Digest* itself was "probably the only publication published in Free China today that is not censored by the Chinese Kuomingtang [*sic*]."[19] It was distributed free of charge "among the foreigners in China and to a limited number of English speaking Chinese" as "a means of keeping the

"Propaganda and Sovereignty in Wartime China: Morale Operations and Psychological Warfare under the Office of War Information," *Modern Asian Studies* 45 (2011): 303–344, and Mark Francis Wilkinson, "To Win the Minds of Men: The American Information Service in China, 1941–1945" (MA thesis, University of Maryland, 1977).

15. China Division, Monthly Narrative Report for September 1944, Folder Chungking Letters 13–30 September [1944], Box 660, NC 148 387: Records of the Office of Communications . . . , Letters and Reports from Outposts, RG 208, Records of the OWI, USNA–CP. A list of American personnel attached to OWI, China Division, 4 December 1944, in Folder China Personnel June thru December 1944, Box 663, has eighty-two names; nineteen of these people were "awaiting transportation [to China]."

16. Elizabeth Jorzick, "China, July 15–August 31, 1944," Folder Outposts Chungking, Box 1, NC 148 6J: Records of the Historian, Outpost Records, 1942–1946, RG 208, Records of the OWI, USNA–CP; HGR, Curriculum Vitae and Testimonials, 28 December 1951, in my personal collection.

17. "China, August 22, 1944," Folder China Reports of OWI Activities, 1943–1945, NC 148 6I [Eye]: Records of the Historian: China, Burma and India Theater, 1942–1945, and China Division, Monthly Narrative Report for October 1944, Folder Chungking Letters 11–30 November 1944, Box 662, NC 148 387: Records of the Office of Communications . . . Letters and Reports from Outposts, RG 208, Records of the OWI, USNA–CP.

18. Everett D. Hawkins, "Monthly Summary for February 1945," Folder Outposts Chungking, Box 1, NC 148 6J: Records of the Historian, Outpost Records, 1942–1946, and George E. Taylor to William T. Turner, Washington, D.C., 14 June 1945, Folder George Taylor 1943–1945, Box 3018, NC 148 521: Records of the San Francisco Office . . . General Records of the Chief, Philip Lilienthal, 1942–1946, RG 208, Records of the OWI, USNA–CP.

19. Everett D. Hawkins, "Monthly Summary for February, 1945," Folder Outpost Chungking, Box 1, NC 148 6J: Records of the Historian, Outpost Records, 1942–1946, and James L. Stewart, A Report on the China Division of OWI, 1 October 1944, Folder Chungking Letters, 1–10 October 1944, Box 661, NC 148 387: Records of the Office of Communications . . . Letters and Reports from Outposts, RG 208, Records of the OWI, USNA–CP.

foreign especially the American community well informed on happenings in this country [i.e., the US] and on the battle fronts." Its circulation in 1944–1945 of 4,500 to 5,000 copies was limited only by the availability of paper, which was in critically short supply during the war. Many subscription requests had to be turned down. Nevertheless, each copy had multiple readers. As a result, "the number of readers of each issue of the *Digest* may be placed at 30,000. By any American standard this is no circulation at all; by Chinese standards it is good."[20] (I have been unable to locate any copies of the *Digest*.)

Besides editing the *American Digest*, my father, as chief of English publications, had three other responsibilities with the OWI. One was to distribute to local American and Chinese organizations and institutions, such as the Friends Ambulance Unit and the Chinese Industrial Cooperatives (Indusco), spare copies of books and magazines received from America. Another was to oversee the Public Reference Files, which maintained "classified files of typewritten copies of press and magazine articles," which could be read on site or borrowed for a week. According to my father, "Three to four representatives of responsible organizations consult these files each day." Finally, as he had been at Lingnan at Tai Tsuen, he was head of the Library Department and in charge of the Public Reading Room, which was stocked with books and current magazines. In December 1944, he reported, "Library visitors continue to number about 60 a day." By March 1945, after the library moved "just around the corner" into more spacious quarters, the number of visitors had increased to two hundred a day. "There seems . . . to be no way of keeping pace with the demand," he reported. "Within two days of opening[,] the new room was over-crowded, with as many as sixty persons present at one time during the late afternoon and early evening, this in spite of utterly inadequate lighting."[21]

The OWI was located in Chongqing's New City. It had started out in the Shangqingsi neighborhood near the end of the fourth section of Zhongshan Road ("way up town," according to Everett Hawkins), where it shared with the Office of Strategic Services (OSS) a four-story twenty-five room building on the spacious grounds of an American Methodist school, the Chiu Chin (Qiujing) Middle School 求精中學 (also known as the Chungking High School). (The school had evacuated to a distant suburb of the city in 1939 to get away from the Japanese air raids.) By the time we arrived in Chongqing, the OWI had relocated to the Lianglukou neighborhood at 149 Zhongsan Road 中三路 (as the third section of Zhongshan Road is known colloquially), which Hawkins called "Chungking's uptown Broadway" and "125th Street." Nearby were the US Embassy, at 99 Liangfuzhi Road 兩浮支路, and the residence of the American ambassador (Clarence Gauss), at 2 Jialing New Village 嘉陵新村.[22]

---

20. Gerald Winfield, "OWI Program in China: A Report and Tentative Suggestions," [1943?], Folder Gerald Winfield, Box 3019, NC 148 522: Records of the San Francisco Office . . . Correspondence with Outposts in China, July 1944–1945, Elizabeth Jorzick, "China, April 15 May 15, 1944," Folder Outposts Chungking, Box 1, NC 148 6J: Records of the Historian, Outpost Records, 1942–1946, and James L. Stewart, A Report on the China Division of OWI, 1 October 1944, Folder Chungking Letters 1–10 October 1944, Box 661, NC 148 387: Records of the Office of Communications . . . Letters and Reports from Outposts, RG 208, Records of the OWI, USNA–CP.

21. China Division, Monthly Narrative Report for November 1944, Folder Chungking Letters 1–10 December 1944, Box 662, NC 148 387: Records of the Office of Communications . . . Letters and Reports from Outposts, and Everett D. Hawkins, Highlights of Information Activity for January 1945, Folder Outposts Chungking, Box 1, NC 148 6J: Records of the Historian, Outpost Records, 1942–1946, RG 208, Records of OWI, USNA–CP.

22. John King Fairbank, *Chinabound: A Fifty-Year Memoir* (New York: Harper & Row, 1982), pp. 202–203; George Atcheson Jr., to Secretary of State, Chungking, 21 November 1944, Details Concerning Living Quarters at Embassy, Folder 124.1 Quarters—Office and Residential, Box 42, UD 10: US Embassy (Legation) in China, 1843–1945, RG 84, Records of the Foreign Service Posts of the Department of State, and Everett D. Hawkins, Highlights of

The OWI compound at Lianglukou had at least three buildings. The four-story main building, which the OWI rented in January 1945, was intended "to provide working space for about fifteen Americans plus approximately twenty-five [Chinese] typists, stenographers, translators, etc." A spacious Public Reading Room occupied the first floor. According to Hawkins, the director of information, "Howard Rhoads is the master of the second floor with his own office, the morgue or quiet research library, the *American Digest* room and the microfilm room, where typewriters clatter for two shifts each day. Liu Tsun-chi [劉尊棋] and the Translation Department are in command of the third floor. . . . The fourth floor is given over to files for old papers and living quarters for some of the servants." On the street outside the main building were a large bulletin board as well as a loudspeaker for Chinese-language radio programs that were retransmitted from San Francisco in the mornings and evenings. Two other buildings in the compound were a new two-story dormitory, which according to the original design was "to house the fifteen Americans, since hotel or other accommodations are not available in war-crowded Chungking," and a smaller building that would "provide living quarters for the [Chinese] messengers, janitors and watchmen."[23]

In a letter to his wife, William Holland, who had succeeded Mac Fisher as head of the OWI's China Division in the spring of 1945, described the compound as follows:

> The place (both office and dormitories) has grown immensely since 1943 [when he last visited Chongqing] and is now really quite handsome and comfortable. I'm housed in a quite pleasant fair sized room in a new building with a good view, good service, plenty of hot water (not in the room) and a garden which should be lovely very soon . . . We have an excellent mess, considered the best in Chungking, and apparently a very capable lot of servants. . . . It's much better than I was prepared for.

His own room was on the second floor of the dormitory building, while the communal bathroom was on the ground floor. Nearby was the "old hostel," where the dining room and lounge were located.[24]

Housing in wartime Chongqing (as in Qujiang) was, as noted, very tight. When we first arrived in the city and before my father was hired by the OWI, we most likely found temporary lodging on the south bank of the Yangtze, opposite the city proper. That was where most foreigners then lived and where most foreign businesses were located; it was there, too, that the US embassy had been housed—in the compound of the Standard Oil Company—before relocating to Chongqing's New City.[25] It is probable that when my father joined the OWI, we moved across the river, but there was as yet no housing for him at the compound; the new dormitory was not yet finished. Thus, when my sister Janet was born on New Year's Day 1945, our address on her report of birth was given as 214 Pao An Road 保安路 (now Bayi, or August First, Road 八一路). This building, which no longer

---

Information Activity for January 1945, Folder Outposts Chungking, Box 1, NC 148 6J: Records of the Historian, Outpost Records, 1942–1946, RG 208, Records of the OWI, both in USNA–CP.

23. Elmer Davis to Sen. Homer T. Bone, Washington, 8 March 1943, Everett D. Hawkins, Highlights of Information Activity for January 1945, and H. P. Peters to Barrett, Report on Trip, London, China & India, 24 January 1945, all in Folder Outposts Chungking, Box 1, NC 148 6J: Records of the Historian, Outpost Records, 1942–1946, RG 208, Records of the OWI, USNA–CP.

24. W. L. Holland to Doreen P. Holland, [Chungking], 10 March [1945], Folder 61, Box 1, W. L. Holland Papers, University of Massachusetts Library.

25. Evans Fordyce Carlson, *Twin Stars of China: A Behind-the-Scenes Story of China's Valiant Struggle for Existence by a U.S. Marine Who Lived and Moved with the People* (1940; reprint, Westport, CT: Hyperion Press, 1975), p. 298; Dobson, *China Cycle*, p. 110.

Figure 6.2: The OWI's four-story main building in Chongqing, 1945. From Folder Outpost, General, 1945, Box 3019, NC 148 522, RG 208, Records of the Office of War Information, USNA–CP.

Figure 6.3: "Front Gate of Office of War Information, Chungking," 1945. From Folder Outpost, General, 1945, Box 3019, NC 148 522, RG 208, Records of the Office of War Information, USNA–CP.

exists, was near Duyoujie (Hawkins's "Times Square"), in the heart of Chongqing's Upper City. The hospital where my sister was born, the Methodist Union Hospital, was nearby, on Linjiang Road 臨江路 in the Daijiaxiang 戴家巷 neighborhood. In 1939, to escape the Japanese aerial bombardments, the hospital had moved to the Gele mountains 歌樂山 in the distant western district of Shapingba 沙坪壩, but by mid-1944 its maternity wards were back at their old site.[26] On account of her birthplace, my sister was given the Chinese name Lo Yu Bik 路渝璧, meaning Jade from Chongqing.

26. Janet Rhoads's Report of Birth, Chungking, 24 January 1945, in my personal collection; "Methodist Union Hospital Report for 1939," in West China Conference of the Methodist Church, *Year Book & Official Journal, 1939* (1940), pp.

Likewise, when in the fall of 1944 I was six and a half years old and ready for first grade, the school I was sent to was not far from our home in Chongqing's Upper City. This was the Chee Min (Qiming) Boys' School 啟明小學, which too was founded by and affiliated with the West China Mission of the Methodist Episcopal Church. It was in the Jiaochangba 較場壩 neighborhood, in "almost the exact geographical center of the [old] city." Like the hospital, the Chee Min School had moved out of the city in the early years of the war, but it must have returned to its old location by 1944. Housed in a three-story building constructed in the mid-1920s, it enrolled both boarders and day students. I would have been a day student. The school, renamed under the Communists as the August First Road Primary School 八一路小學, was torn down around 2000 to make way for a residential high-rise.[27]

The medium of instruction at the Chee Min Boys' School was Chinese. It was most likely the Sichuanese dialect of Mandarin Chinese, whereas I had grown up in Hong Kong and Qujiang speaking Cantonese with my mother and Ah Hoh. Nevertheless, despite my initial unfamiliarity with Mandarin, I did quite well at school. According to my report card, printed on the thin, coarse paper of wartime China, I had classes in reading and writing, arithmetic, art, and music. My grade-point average for the first semester was 89.96, and I was ranked third in a class of 55.[28] Strangely, I have no personal recollection whatsoever of attending this school.

Sometime after my sister was born, we left Chongqing's Upper City and moved to the New City. In a long letter to Olin Wannamaker in early June 1945, my father mentioned that we were then living "in the official compound."[29] We made the move probably around the time that the new OWI library at Lianglukou was opened to the public in late January. And we most likely moved into the new two-story dormitory in the compound that had been designed to house Americans working for the agency and where William Holland was to live. It is unclear whether, after our move, I continued to attend the Chee Min School. (I have no report card for the second semester.) Perhaps not, because it would have meant a long commute to the school from the OWI compound. Perhaps, instead, I was home-schooled by my parents (most likely by my mother).

Unlike in Hong Kong and in Qujiang, my mother had no formal employment in Chongqing. She undoubtedly had her hands full getting ready for her daughter's birth and then caring for her two children. Assisting my mother and living with us was Ah Hoh, the amah or nanny, who, according to my father, "has been a pearl without price ever since my wife took her over in Hongkong," even though, he added without explanation, she "doesn't like me at all."[30]

The OWI was a civilian agency, but it was an agency at war. Nearly all of its American employees were men, two of whom, as Holland mentioned in a letter to his wife, were married to "Chinese girls" and "one [clearly referring to my mother] has a 7 year old very

---

194–195; R. E. Diffendorfer, Memo re Chungking Union Hospital, 1 December 1944, in Roll #1, Missionary Files, Methodist Church, 1912–1949, China (microfilm ed., Scholarly Resources), United Methodist Archives Center, Drew University, Madison, NJ. The hospital is now the Second Affiliated Hospital of Chongqing Medical University.

27. W. A. McCurdy, Chungking, to J. R. Edwards, 27 March 1925, to F. D. Gamewell, 21 October 1925, and to Corresponding Secretaries, Board of Foreign Missions of the M. E. Church, 1 August 1930, all in Roll #11, Missionary Files, Methodist Church, 1912–1949, China (microfilm), United Methodist Archives Center, Drew University; Li Danke, personal communications, 31 October 2014 and 5 June 2015.

28. ER's report card, Chee Min School, Chongqing, 27 January 1945, in my personal collection.

29. HGR to ODW, [Chungking], 3 June 1945, Box 102, TLUA–HYL.

30. HGR to ODW, [Chungking], 3 June 1945, Box 102, TLUA–HYL.

Figure 6.4: "OWI New Hostel for Staff, Chun[g]king, 1945." From Folder 39, W. L. Holland Papers. Image courtesy of Pat Holland and the Department of Special Collections and University Archives, W. E. B. Du Bois Library, University of Massachusetts Amherst.

attractive boy." The men often wore military uniforms, though (Everett Hawkins wrote) "with U.S. O.W.I. on the shoulders and collar in place of the military rank." And they kept to a military schedule. According to Holland, "They work a full 8 hour day here, from 8 to 5 with a rising bell at 6:45! It's not as bad as it sounds, however. There are so many army bugles blowing at 6 that I wake up anyway and then the boy comes in with a big pot of glowing charcoal, like a hibachi in Japan, to warm up the room."[31] In the case of our family, Ah Hoh would have taken the place of Holland's "boy."

In his June 1945 letter to Wannamaker my father commented (with tongue somewhat in cheek) on our new environment and its effect on me, including what he called "the linguistic difficulties" that I was having:

> The boy seems to flourish in a heathen illiterate way, speaking Cantonese like a native, Szechwanese like an old master, and atrocious English, flavored with all the routine words and phrases of a military establishment, which he picks up in the washroom. A few more months of this and he will be completely unfit to associate with respectable people. . . . Edward, because we wear GI clothes most of the time, has some sort of notion that I am in

---

31. W. L. Holland to Doreen P. Holland, [Chungking], 10 March [1945], Folder 61, Box 1, W. L. Holland Papers, University of Massachusetts Library; Everett D. Hawkins to "Mother," [Chungking], 17 December 1944, Folder Letters Sent, 1944, Box 1, Everett Day Hawkins Papers, RG 30/130, Oberlin College Archives.

the army and is humiliated that I have no stripes on my sleeve. Sergeants are his gods, with corporals running second. Generals he ignores or surveys with contempt.[32]

The OWI compound, as previously noted, was close to the US embassy, and "down the street from the Embassy," according to diplomat John Melby, "there is a park with a high concrete tower for parachute jumping."[33] This is one of the few things I do seem to recall of life in Chongqing. I must have been enthralled with watching (presumably Chinese) soldiers practice their parachute jumps from the tower.

In that same letter to Wannamaker, my father reflected on his first ten months with the OWI. "[Mac Fisher] I had liked well enough and also respected as a good newspaper man. But the coming of Bill Holland . . . has meant that one side of my work, a rather vague sort of cultural relations job, is being built up far beyond what it was when I took it over." This led him to work closely with Wilma Fairbank, who had just arrived at the US embassy as the cultural relations officer, as there was considerable overlap between their two operations. My father added that as a consequence of his work with the OWI, "while I still have longer hours at a desk than I like, I also have wider and more varied academic contacts than ever before," including some at Yenching University at its wartime campus in Chengdu. Moreover, "I occasionally go to dinner at the Academia Sinica [Nationalist

Figure 6.5: My father with my baby sister and me, the OWI compound, Chongqing, 1945.

32. HGR to ODW, [Chungking], 3 June 1945, Box 102, TLUA–HYL.
33. Melby, *Mandate of Heaven*, p. 35.

China's premier research institution], where I have two or three friends." Due perhaps to this widening network of contacts among Chinese intellectuals, he became more aware of the political situation around him. "The entanglements of Chinese politics are completely fascinating and I spend a great deal of time just getting straightened out by my scouts."[34]

Finally, my father told Wannamaker in June 1945, "We are all quite well, not enjoying Chungking, but living very comfortably." One reason for not enjoying Chongqing was the weather, which he elsewhere wrote was "very bad." It was an opinion shared by many others. According to journalists White and Jacoby, "There were only two seasons in Chungking, both bad. From early fall to late spring the fogs and rains made a dripping canopy over the city; damp and cold reigned in every home. The slime in the street was inches thick . . . Everyone shivered until summer came; then the heat settled down, and the sun glared. Dust coated the city almost as thickly as mud during the wintertime. Moisture remained in the air, perspiration dripped, and prickly heat ravaged the skin. . . . Swarms of bugs emerged."[35] A sunny day was such a rarity in winter that, as the local saying went, "dogs bark at the sun." It was, of course, precisely this damp and foggy weather that had curtailed the Japanese aerial bombardments for much of the year.

As an additional discomfort, there were the air-raid alarms. It is true that long before we arrived in Chongqing in August 1944 the Japanese air raids had all but stopped, and many medical and educational institutions that had been evacuated to the distant suburbs in the early years of the war, such as the Methodist Union Hospital and the Chee Min Boys' School, had returned to the city. As one character in Ba Jin's novel *Cold Nights*, set in Chongqing in 1944–1945, remarked, "The Japanese haven't bombed here for two years." Nevertheless, there were still occasional air-raid alarms. One of these occurred in mid-December 1944 and required rapid evacuation into tunnels dug into the city's hillsides.[36] This, too, I seem to remember. As I recall, we shared a shelter with a group of shackled prisoners. No bombs, however, were dropped.

Yet another source of discomfort was the inflation, which had worsened steadily. The price index (with 1937 = 100) had been 22,800 in December 1943; by August 1945, according to historian Parks Coble, it had risen more than tenfold to "a staggering 264,700."[37] But unlike at Qujiang, my father was well-compensated for his work: "A grateful government pays us well," he told Wannamaker. His annual salary with the OWI was US$3,800, with an additional $2,000 in living allowance, for a total of $5,800. This was considerably more than his Lingnan salary of $1,200. Nevertheless, he described the cost of living in Chongqing as "horribly expensive—last month's bill [presumably for all household expenses] was CN227,800 dollars. Even at a black market rate of 900 [to 1] this is steep, and you may well be happy," he told Wannamaker, "that I am off the Lingnan payroll at the moment."[38] As another indicator of the magnitude of the inflation, recall that a year and a half earlier the *yuan*-to-dollar exchange rate had been 86–110 to 1. Even at an

---

34. HGR to ODW, [Chungking], 3 June 1945, Box 102, and 18 July 1945, Box 103, TLUA–HYL.
35. HGR to ODW, [Chungking], 3 June 1945, Box 102, and Anna E. D. Pugh to ODW, Bala Cynwyd, 7 December 1944, Box 100, TLUA–HYL; White and Jacoby, *Thunder Out of China*, pp. 9–10.
36. Pa Chin, *Cold Nights*, pp. 1–5, 39, 46–49; Pan Xun and Zhou Yong, comps., *Kangzhan shiqi Chongqing dahongzha rishi* [A chronological record of aerial bombardment of Chongqing during the War of Resistance] (Chongqing: Chongqing chubanshe, 2011), pp. 395–404.
37. Coble, *China's War Reporters*, p. 105.
38. HGR to ODW, [Chungking], 3 June 1945, Box 102, TLUA–HYL; China Division, Annual Personnel Report as of 31 December 1944, Folder Chungking Letters 1–10 December 1944, Box 662, NC 148 387: Records of the Office of Communications—Letters and Reports from Outposts, RG 208, Records of the OWI, USNA–CP.

Figure 6.6: "Midnight in the dugout"—OWI officials passing time inside air-raid shelter, Chongqing, December 1944. From Box 5, RG 30/130, Oberlin College Archives. "Mac" Fisher is at rear, reading by candlelight; Everett Hawkins is at right front.

exchange rate of 900 to 1, our monthly bill of CN$227,800 was equivalent to US$253, or 52 percent of our monthly income of $483.

William Holland, like everyone else, commented often on the inflation. August 1943: "Prices are crazy. . . . It is said an Arrow shirt costs more than a plane trip from Chungking to Kunming." March 1945: "Prices were high in 1943 but now they're fantastic." April 1945: "Prices have been going up so fast lately that our living allowance here has been increased from $87 to $102 (US) a month, which is a relief though hardly adequate." As historian Matthew Combs points out, with the cessation of the Japanese aerial bombardment, inflation had become "the only effect of the war that reached into the daily lives of Chongqing's people."[39]

We were in Chongqing for only the last part of the war. Years earlier, the city had "throbbed with the strength of a nation at war" (in the words of journalists White and Jacoby), but by the time we arrived, it had become "a city of unbridled cynicism, corrupt to the core."[40] Adding to the disillusionment among both Chinese and Americans were growing strains in US-China relations. When the United States entered the war as an ally of China, Chiang Kai-shek had agreed to the appointment of an American general, Joseph W. Stilwell, to serve as his chief of staff. Stilwell was never shy about expressing his frustration with Chiang's unwillingness to commit his troops against the Japanese. From Chiang's perspective, however, the Japanese were bound to be defeated; what he needed now was to preserve his military strength for the coming struggle with the Communists. Their quarrel came to a head in mid-October 1944, a couple of months after our arrival in Chongqing, when Chiang persuaded President Roosevelt to recall Stilwell and replace him with the less abrasive Albert Wedemeyer. At almost the same time, Clarence E. Gauss,

39. W. L. Holland to Doreen P. Holland, Chungking, 27 August [1943], 10 March [1945], and 1 April 1945, Folders 60 and 61, Box 1, W. L. Holland Papers, University of Massachusetts Library; Matthew T. Combs, "Chongqing 1943: People's Livelihood, Price Control, and State Legitimacy," in Esherick and Combs, eds., *1943: China at the Crossroads*, p. 304.
40. White and Jacoby, *Thunder Out of China*, pp. 18, 19.

an experienced diplomat, was replaced as US ambassador by Patrick J. Hurley, a political appointee with strongly pro-Chiang views. Meanwhile, the US army had managed to send an "observer group" to Yan'an, the capital of the Communist-held area in northwestern China. Their glowing reports of life in Yan'an contrasted sharply with the gloom-and-doom accounts emanating from Chongqing.

By then, the end of the war was in sight. Japan's military successes with the Ichigô offensive had been offset by the loss in July 1944 of Saipan Island in the Pacific, which brought the Japanese home islands within range of American bombers. After Germany surrendered in early May 1945, the Americans were able to concentrate their firepower on Japan, and at the Yalta Conference the Soviets agreed (secretly) to join the fight against Japan in three months' time. In a letter to Wannamaker in early June 1945, my father was already contemplating life in the postwar world.[41]

Nevertheless, the war ended much more swiftly than anyone anticipated. It had been thought that the Allies would have to invade Japan and that the Japanese military would mount a stiff resistance. But the dropping of the two atomic bombs on Hiroshima and Nagasaki on 6 and 9 August, coupled with the Soviet Union's entry into the war as promised, convinced the Japanese government on the 10th to indicate its willingness to capitulate. "News of the victory over Japan . . . reached Chungking in the evening [of the 10th]," Wilma Fairbank recalled, and sparked a spontaneous "happy hysteria." Without waiting for an official announcement, "the population poured out into the streets, and the uproar of a million human voices vied with the honking of truck horns and the shrilling of sirens." The *New York Times* added, "Jeeps and trucks carrying American GI's received thunderous acclamations."[42] The official announcement came five days later, on 15 August, when Emperor Hirohito took to the radio to call on the Japanese people to "endure the unendurable." This was followed by the formal surrender, which took place on 2 September aboard an American battleship in Tokyo Bay. In China, the following day, 3 September, was declared a national holiday to commemorate the victory over Japan. As Ba Jin described the scene in Chongqing, "In the streets smiling crowds welcomed the victory parades; airplanes performed many stunts and scattered celebration leaflets."[43] I, too, must have joined in the joyous celebrations, but once again I have no recollection.

China's War of Resistance against Japan (1937–1945) had lasted eight long years—the entirety of my life up until then.

---

41. HGR to ODW, [Chungking], 3 June 1945, Box 102, TLUA–HYL.
42. Fairbank, *America's Cultural Experiment in China*, p. 145; "Chinese Jubilant; Soviet Aid Hailed," *New York Times*, 11 August 1945, p. 3; White and Jacoby, *Thunder Out of China*, pp. 277–278; and Pa Chin, *Cold Nights*, p. 161.
43. Pa Chin, *Cold Nights*, p. 166.

7

Back Home in Guangzhou (1945–1948)

The end of the anti-Japanese war did not, regrettably, mean an end to conflict in China. Instead, it brought back to the surface the long-simmering rivalry between Chiang Kai-shek's Nationalists and Mao Zedong's Communists. As the war ended, each side raced to take over territory that the Japanese had occupied. The Communists generally gained the upper hand in the countryside of northeastern and northern China; the Nationalists, in the cities and in central and southern China. Postwar US policy tried to mediate between the two Chinese parties, and for about a year armed conflict was averted. But by July 1946 open warfare between the Nationalists and the Communists had broken out again.

Fortunately for us, the fighting largely took place in North China and the Northeast, where the Communists were concentrated; South China was largely under Nationalist control and relatively peaceful. A small group of Communist guerrillas had operated in the East River region of Guangdong during the war, but as part of the overall ceasefire agreement concluded between the Nationalists and the Communists in January 1946 these guerrillas had been "repatriated" to Yantai, Shandong, in northern China. They left Guangdong in June 1946 aboard three US Navy landing craft.[1] These three postwar years of our lives in China, compared with what had gone on before and what was to come afterward, were rather uneventful.

With the end of the anti-Japanese war, there was a mass exodus from Chongqing, as most downriver people, including the Americans, made their way home as quickly as they could. Thus, Chiang Kai-shek and his Nationalist government returned to their prewar capital of Nanjing, though not until May 1946, when the water level of the Yangtze had risen enough to permit shipping.[2] We, too, went "home" to Guangzhou, where we had not lived in seven years.

My cousin Luo Ren once told me that my father was one of the first Americans to reach Guangzhou after the war. I initially found that hard to believe, but it turns out to have been true. According to chemistry professor Hoh Shai Kwong, who had remained behind in the Japanese-occupied city and been charged by Provost James Henry with keeping an eye on the Lingnan campus, my father arrived, by plane, on 5 September, six days after American troops liberated the Japanese civilian internment camp in the city. He had been sent from Chongqing to set up a branch of the Office of War Information. This move had been in the works for at least a month and a half. Japan's eventual defeat

1. Chan Sui-jeung, *East River Column: Hong Kong Guerrillas in the Second World War and After* (Hong Kong: Hong Kong University Press, 2009), esp. ch. 6.
2. K. P. S. Menon, *Twilight in China* (Bombay: Bharatyia Vidya Bhavan, 1972), pp. 120, 164.

Figure 7.1: Japanese surrender ceremony, Sun Yat-sen Memorial Hall, Guangzhou, 16 September 1945. Image courtesy of the Alabama Department of Archives and History. Seated at center of table is Chinese General Zhang Fakui; to Zhang's left is Chinese General Gan Lichu 甘麗初, and to his right is US General Harwood C. Bowman; standing, facing them, is Japanese General Tanaka Hisakazu.

was by that time all but certain; indeed, in mid-July he had informed Olin Wannamaker, somewhat cryptically, that "present plans call for me to set up an operation in the area with which I am most familiar as soon as it becomes possible." When he arrived in Guangzhou, Chinese Nationalist troops had not yet appeared; "the Japanese army [was] still in actual control of the city."[3] It was not until 16 September, in a ceremony held at the Sun Yat-sen Memorial Hall in Guangzhou, that the commander of the Japanese forces in Guangdong, Tanaka Hisakazu, formally surrendered to Zhang Fakui 張發奎 (1896–1980), the commander of the Second Army Group.[4]

Even then, as an internee recalled as he awaited repatriation to his native New Zealand, "A strange feature of Canton during those waiting days was the presence of armed Japanese still about the streets. . . . It was a strange spectacle, a month after V-J Day, to see Japanese soldiers and Chinese National troops, both fully armed, doing police duty in full view of one another in the same city block." Though subsequently disarmed, there were still many Japanese troops around Guangzhou for months afterward. In March 1946 botany professor Yung Chi-tung 容啟東 (1908–1987) at Lingnan commented that a detachment of Japanese prisoners of war had been hired "to repair some of our athletic fields at the cost of one package of local cigarettes per man per day, plus a very small

3.   HGR to ODW, [Chungking], 18 July 1945, Box 103, and Canton, 22 December 1945, Box 104, TLUA–HYL; He Shiguang and Jia Huilin (William W. Cadbury), "Guangzhou liushou zhi jingguo" [An account of stewardship in Guangzhou], in *Kangzhan qijian de Lingnan*, p. 54.

4.   Zuo Shuangwen, *Hua'nan kangzhan shigao*, pp. 175–177. Tanaka was executed in 1947 as a war criminal.

amount of money. They are very efficient laborers, much cheaper than hiring Chinese laborers. Besides, it makes us feel good to see that they have to repair some of the destructions they have done to us."[5]

Passing on information from my father, my mother in Chongqing was able to cable the American trustees in New York that President Y. L. Lee had returned to the campus (from Meixian) and that the Canton Hospital and the Lingnan campus were both in "good condition." She also forwarded President Lee's urgent request for funds "for bringing staff back."[6] The rest of our family rejoined my father in late October 1945, when my mother, my baby sister, and I—and most likely Ah Hoh, too—flew on an Air Transport Command (ATC) plane from Chongqing to Guangzhou via Kunming. It was our first airplane ride.[7]

In Guangzhou, my father continued to work, but only on a half-time basis, for the Office of War Information, which in the postwar era was renamed the United States Information Service (USIS) and placed under the State Department. Led by John King Fairbank (1907–1991), the Harvard historian and Wilma's husband, who had joined her in October 1945, the China division of the USIS had relocated its headquarters from Chongqing to Shanghai; it now had ten regional branches, of which the Southeast China Branch in Guangzhou was one.[8] The branch was headed initially by Christopher Rand (ca. 1912–1962), a journalist who previously had run the intelligence-gathering operation for the OWI in Yongan, Fujian. Shortly afterward, at the beginning of November, when Rand had been transferred to Shanghai, he was succeeded by Elmer Newton, with whom my father had worked in Chongqing. By then, according to an administrative report, "this branch of the USIS [was] finally in full swing . . . We have an audience for everything we have to say, limitless spectators for everything we have to show, and a market for all our wares."[9]

My father served, mostly under Elmer Newton, as Deputy Director and Cultural Relations Officer of the Southeast China Branch of the USIS. According to another administrative report, his duties were characterized as entirely "information and cultural": specifically, 20 percent in press and publications, 30 percent in libraries and institutes, 20 percent in exchange of persons, and 30 percent in cultural reporting. This was similar to what he had done in Chongqing. His half-time salary was US$2,300 a year (slightly more than he had been paid in Chongqing, perhaps because of the increase in administrative responsibilities). In a letter of recommendation John Fairbank later wrote, "Dr. Rhoads handled some of our library program and contact with Chinese intellectuals and impressed me as the best type of American academic specialist—sensitive to human values, efficient as a worker, and with a keen intellectual interest in his work." Though his job with the USIS was supposed to be concluded at the end of 1945, my father was

---

5. E. G. Jansen, *Jade Engraved: New Zealand Missionaries and Their Chinese Colleagues in Japan's "China Incident"* (Christchurch: Presbyterian Bookroom, 1947), p. 215; Chi-tung Yung to ODW, Canton, 6 March 1946, Box 108, TLUA–HYL.

6. CKR to ODW, radiogram, Chungking, 24 September 1945, Box 103, TLUA–HYL.

7. Chi-tung Yung to ODW, Canton, 6 March 1946, Box 108, TLUA–HYL. Yung flew on the same flights as us.

8. Fairbank, *Chinabound*, p. 300.

9. Christopher Rand to "Dearest M," [Shanghai], 4 November 1945, Folder 1, Box 44, and Rand to W. L. Holland and Brooks Darlington, Shanghai, 7 November 1945, Folder 3, Box 45, Christopher Rand Papers, Howard Gotlieb Archival Research Center, Boston University, Boston, MA; and Monthly Report for October 1945, Folder Outposts China—Canton Branch Office, Monthly Reports, 1945, Box 6, NC 148 6J: Records of the Historian, Outpost Records, 1942–1946, RG 208, Records of the OWI, USNA–CP.

persuaded to continue, still on a half-time basis, for another six months in an "advisory or consultative" role.[10]

Meanwhile, even before leaving Chongqing, he had been rehired by the American trustees to teach at Lingnan University. In 1943, when he returned to China, my father had been given only a one-year contract because of doubts about his temperament, collegiality, and administrative skills. His year with Lingnan in Qujiang followed by the year with the OWI in Chongqing, however, had greatly changed him, as he himself recognized. At Qujiang, as he later wrote to Olin Wannamaker, "I got to know a number of my Chinese colleagues better than I had known them before," and "the very nature of the life we were leading created a sort of identification with the university such as I had not felt in Hongkong, for obvious reasons, nor in Canton, for reasons likewise rather obvious—my personal affairs for one thing, and for another the fact that after all my Canton connection was rather short." (He had been in Guangzhou hardly more than two years before his evacuation to Hong Kong.) Possibly aware of former criticisms of his inadequacies as an administrator, he cited his work with the OWI in Chongqing: "I have learned a number of tricks at this job that I never tumbled to at Lingnan and have neither the dislike nor fear of an administrative job that I formerly had." As Wannamaker commented, in a letter to the president of the Board of Trustees, "He [Rhoads] holds a rather important position in the OWI in Chungking, giving him responsibilities of an administrative character such as he previously needed and also the necessity of dealing with many people of all sorts. I think he has greatly improved as a personality."[11]

Consequently, on the recommendation of both President Y. L. Lee and the *de facto* provost James Henry, Olin Wannamaker in February 1945 offered my father an appointment to the Lingnan faculty "on a permanent basis," that is, "on the same terms with the appointments of all other permanent members of the faculty, including insurance and salary reserve and travel allowance for yourself and your family." This was sort of equivalent to academic tenure; he would no longer be on probation. In early June, while still in Chongqing, my father formally accepted the offer: "I have decided definitely to return [to Lingnan] . . . The terms mentioned in your letter to me are acceptable in every way."[12] As a married teacher with two children, he would receive, if he were a full-time employee, a salary of US$170 per month (or $2,040 a year). This was about half of what the USIS was paying him, but in addition to his base salary he would receive "a furnished home, free of rent, and the medical, dental, and oculist care for the family," as well as "a reserve of $200 per year; and payment of premium on a $5,000 twenty-payment life insurance policy."[13] He and the family would also receive, in 1947, a year-long paid furlough in the United States, something that, due to circumstances, he had never enjoyed since being hired in 1936. He thus rejoined the Lingnan faculty in October 1945, though only on a half-time basis until the following June because of his continuing work with the USIS.

---

10. Charles S. Millet, Organization and Administrative Report as of April 1, 1946, Folder Canton, 1946, 000-125.3, UD 2286: US Consulate, Canton, Classified General Records, 1937–1948, RG 84, Records of the Foreign Service Posts of the Department of State, USNA–CP; HGR to ODW, Canton, 22 December 1945, Box 104, 11 April 1946, Box 106, and 25 June 1946, Box 109, TLUA–HYL; HGR, Curriculum Vitae and testimonials, 28 December 1951, in my personal collection.

11. HGR to ODW, [Chungking], 3 June 1945, and ODW to Harold B. Hoskins, New York, 22 June 1945, Box 102, TLUA–HYL.

12. ODW, New York, to HGR, 8 February 1945, and to Henry C. Brownell, 23 February 1945, Box 101, and HGR to ODW, [Chungking], 3 June 1945, Box 102, TLUA–HYL.

13. ODW to Williams and Cooper, New York, 14 February 1946, Box 105, TLUA–HYL.

Even before the Japanese surrender, President Y. L. Lee, from his Meixian refuge in eastern Guangdong, had hurriedly dispatched an agent (Lai Shau Pan 黎壽彬 [1905–??]) to the campus to lay "claim to all the property by means of seals on the doors and windows of the buildings." By so doing he had prevented wholesale looting. Lee himself, as my mother reported, arrived in Guangzhou soon afterward. The campus, which had been occupied since 1942 by the now disbanded pro-Japanese Guangdong University, had survived the war in relatively good shape, unlike other parts of Guangzhou city, "where large areas [were] entirely destroyed or heavily damaged." According to university historian Corbett, "None of the buildings had been destroyed, but some had suffered from the weather and others from termites . . . Many pieces of equipment were missing from the laboratories. In the library . . . one-fifth of the books had disappeared."[14]

We were thus able as a family to move into the "furnished home" provided for in my father's contract as a member of the permanent faculty. We were assigned to Residence No. 47, one of the red brick buildings with green tiled roofs for which the campus is noted. It was known informally among the foreigners as the "MacDonald House." Its previous occupant, Wilfred MacDonald, a professor of mathematics since 1911, had died in 1943 while interned in Guangzhou. This large two-story house with spacious grounds and lush vegetation sat atop the crest of the small hill (Ma Kong Ding) in the northeastern part of the campus where many other Western faculty members with families were housed and that some facetiously called the "foreign concession." (See Figure 3.2.) Built in the early 1920s, it, like the other single residences nearby, had a living room, dining room, study, kitchen, pantry, and two porches on the first floor, and three bedrooms, two sleeping porches, a bathroom, and a shower on the second. It had also a basement and an attic.[15] The house was far more spacious and luxurious than anything our family could have afforded had my father been living and working as a college professor in the United States. It was a far cry from the rowhouse in West Philadelphia where he had grown up. It has now been declared a Guangdong Cultural Relic.

My father was on hand when the university, after seven years in exile, resumed operations on the old Hong Lok site on 1 November 1945 with 630 students. Lingnan was one of the first refugee universities in the country to return to its original campus. According to historian Jessie Gregory Lutz, "most" of the Christian colleges in China had "decided to delay transfer to the home campus until the spring or fall of 1946." Hong Kong University, too, did not reopen until the fall of 1946; "even then," writes its official historian, "its teaching activities were to be on a very limited scale until 1949."[16] With the Japanese no longer a threat, President Y. L. Lee requested of the American trustees that ownership of the university property revert to the Chinese directors, as had been the case before 1938.[17]

---

14. Sz-to Wai, "The Lingnan Exile," Canton, 29 December 1945, Box 143, and Henry S. Frank, Comments on the Current Situation of Lingnan University, 13 May 1946, Box 109, TLUA–HYL; He Shiguang and Jia Huilin, "Guangzhou liushou zhi jingguo," p. 54; Corbett, *Lingnan University*, p. 148.

15. William W. Cadbury to Catharine Jones Cadbury, Canton, 27 February 1946, Folder 1946, Box 10, Collection 1192, Cadbury & Cadbury Papers, Haverford College Library; Yu Zhi, ed., *Kangle honglou* [Red Buildings on Hong Lok Campus] (Hong Kong: Shangwu yinshuguan, 2004), pp. 238–241; Henry Refo, "Midwest China Oral History Interviews," *China Oral Histories*, Book 95 (1980), p. 10, http://digitalcommons.luthersem.edu/china_histories/95 (accessed 13 June 2017).

16. Y. L. Lee to ODW, Canton, 11 November 1945, Box 104, TLUA–HYL; Jessie Gregory Lutz, *China and the Christian Colleges, 1850–1950* (Ithaca: Cornell University Press, 1971), p. 403; Cunich, *A History of the University of Hong Kong*, vol. 1: 435.

17. Y. L. Lee to ODW, Canton, 11 November 1945, Box 104, TLUA–HYL.

Figure 7.2: Our house, Residence No. 47, in the northeast section of the Lingnan campus, late 1940s.

During the 1945–1946 school year, the first after the war, my father divided his time between the Lingnan campus, where he lived and taught, and the USIS office, which was in Guangzhou city, first at 62 Tai Ping Kai 太平街 (now Renmin South Road 人民南路) and later at 18 Kung Yuen Road 公園路. As he wrote in April 1946, "I have been going over to the city five afternoons a week, using a jeep which is assigned to me, but keeping very irregular hours." He would sometimes give our neighbor, Dr. William Cadbury, a lift to the Canton Hospital. The Pearl River Bridge, linking the city and Ho Nam Island, had survived the war largely intact, though its drawbridge feature had been disabled. (My father would have had to give up the use of the jeep once he left the USIS.) Though nominally on a half-time basis at Lingnan, he wrote, "I have been teaching full time, in fact an overload, attending to all administrative duties [as department chair] and serving on two committees which hold long weekly meetings." He noted, however, that his connections to the USIS, which had a book program that he oversaw, were extremely beneficial to Lingnan: "I have been able to supply the entire freshman English class with reading material in English classes at a time when such things cannot be obtained thru ordinary channels. I have seen also that the Lingnan library got the first crack at any stuff we [at USIS] had for distribution."[18] The university library had been decimated during the Japanese occupation.

During most of this first postwar school year, my father was one of only three Westerners on the Lingnan faculty and the only one who was a member of the permanent Western staff. Provost James Henry, though also living on campus, was then employed as the deputy director of the local office of UNRRA, the United Nations Relief and Rehabilitation Administration; he could serve Lingnan only "in a side-line advisory capacity."[19] When Henry Frank returned from the US in late April 1946, he took over Henry's administrative duties at Lingnan as vice provost.

The immediate postwar period was a time of hardship and shortages for nearly everyone in China. In the spring of 1946, to help the eight hundred members of the staff, "both those who went to the interior and those who remained at Lingnan," Dr. William Cadbury, who had just come back to Lingnan in February, organized a clothing drive. He solicited used clothing from his many Quaker supporters in the Philadelphia area, which he had shipped to him. The drive was so successful that the donations, totaling "over twenty-three tons [!!!]," filled his house "to the roof . . . leaving me only one small corner in the dining room, and my bedroom." He thereupon asked a number of "Lingnan ladies," including my mother, to serve on a committee to help sort and distribute the used clothing and to ensure that "there shall be no graft and no pilfering in this distribution."[20] Electricity, too, was in short supply. The university's own generator had been taken away by the Japanese in 1942; as a result, as Professor C. T. Yung explained, "We are now depending on electric power from the city . . . At best we can have only 6 hours of power per day, and nights without lights are almost the rule rather [than] the exception."[21]

Our family shared in all this distress. As my father wrote plaintively to Wannamaker in June 1946, "we are now in a somewhat desperate position as to necessary household equipment, bedding, and so forth. My Chinese colleagues here, I am afraid, cannot understand that I cannot get material by the van load from America merely by pressing a button. If Mrs. Pugh could get together one fairly large box or suitcase of things suggested in my letter to her and these could be brought to Canton by a returning Lingnan family, I would naturally be glad to pay all transportation and customs charges." Anna Pugh, his cousin, was able to oblige, and a shipment was scheduled to depart for China in late August.[22]

Additionally, according to Vice Provost Henry Frank, "Rhoads finds that milk for his children is a very large item [of expenditure]."[23] This was due, in part, to the continu-

---

18. HGR to ODW, Canton, 11 April 1946, Box 106, TLUA–HYL; on the locations of the USIS office, Wang Yidun, "Zhanhou Meiguo xinwenchu yu Guangzhou Jidujiao qingnianhui de guanxi he huodong" [The relationship between the USIS and the Canton YMCA and their joint activities in the postwar years], *Guangzhou wenshi ziliao*, no. 28 (1983): 202.

19. Y. L. Lee to ODW, Canton, 11 November 1945, Box 104, and Henry S. Frank, Comments on the Current Situation of Lingnan University, Canton, 13 May 1946, Box 109, TLUA–HYL. The other two Western faculty members were Mrs. J. Stewart Kunkle (English) and J. Elliott Fisher (Sociology).

20. William W. Cadbury to Catharine Jones Cadbury, Canton, 21 February and 27 February 1946, and Cadbury to Friends, Canton, 7 April 1946, Folder 1946, Box 10, Collection 1192, Cadbury & Cadbury Papers, Haverford College Library.

21. Chi-tung Yung to ODW, Canton, 6 March 1946, Box 108, TLUA–HYL.

22. HGR to ODW, Canton, 25 June 1946, and ODW to Anna Pugh, 22 July 1946, Box 109, TLUA–HYL.

23. Henry S. Frank to ODW, Canton, 12 October 1946, Box 110, TLUA–HYL.

ing problem of inflation. Bad as it had been during the war, inflation steadily worsened afterward. As economist Chang Kia-ngau explains, "after the end of the war the government not only again failed to balance the budget but even expanded its expenditures further, thus increasing the deficit." In the few short months between August 1945 and February 1946, the official exchange rate between the Chinese *yuan* and the US dollar weakened from 668:1 to 2,020:1.[24] As the exchange rate deteriorated, prices correspondingly soared. In early March 1946, Professor C. T. Yung complained that "one of the chief and most serious difficulty [*sic*] in keeping the university going is the mounting high cost of living. Prices of rice had gone up 400% since my return to Canton [four and a half months earlier]. . . . We are indeed financially much worse off than we were in Kukong and Pingshek." Writing a month later, my father concurred: "I am afraid we have terrible times ahead. Cholera is spreading here like wildfire and famine threatens. And always the inflation. . . . Morale in general is low."[25] Nevertheless, in June 1946, after having served close to two years (one in Chongqing and one in Guangzhou), my father left the USIS and rejoined the Lingnan faculty on a full-time basis.[26] In recognition of the hard times in China, the New York trustees, on the recommendation of Vice Provost Frank, approved in November 1946 an increase in the salary of the Westerners on the Lingnan staff by one-third. My father's annual salary was raised from $2,040 to $2,724.[27]

By 1947–1948, the third school year since the end of the war, Lingnan was largely back on its feet, and in some respects it was doing better than ever. The university was now composed of five colleges: Arts, Science and Engineering, Agriculture, Medicine, and Theology (due to Lingnan's affiliation with Kunkle's Union Theological College).

Figure 7.3: My father and I and our two dogs in yard of Residence No. 47, ca. 1947.

24. Chang, *Inflationary Spiral*, p. 107; "Exchange Rates during August, 1945 to July, 1946 Obtained from United Clearing Board," enclosed in Homer C. Loh to Henry S. Frank, Shanghai, 1 February 1947, Box 113, TLUA–HYL.
25. Chi-tung Yung to ODW, Canton, 6 March 1946, Box 108, and HGR to ODW, Canton, 11 April 1946, Box 106, TLUA–HYL.
26. HGR to ODW, Canton, 25 June 1946, Box 109, TLUA–HYL.
27. HGR to ODW, Canton, 25 June 1946, Box 109, Henry S. Frank to ODW, Canton, 12 October 1946, Box 110, and ODW to Frank, New York, 13 November 1946, Box 111, and Personnel Budget, Fiscal Year July 1, 1947–June 30, 1948 (Forecast as of Jan. 29, 1947), Box 150, TLUA–HYL.

Student enrollment (which in 1936 had been 560) had climbed above one thousand, of whom more than 30 percent were women. The teaching staff numbered 154 (twice what it had been before the war).[28] Many of the prewar Western faculty members had returned to the campus, with the New York trustees underwriting fourteen positions and various Christian mission boards supporting at least seven other Western faculty members. (The missions providing faculty members were United Brethren [2], American Maryknoll [2], French Catholic [1], English Methodist [1], and American Presbyterian [1]).[29] By 1947–1948, too, the Student Exchange Program, suspended in 1938, had been revived, with nine participants.[30] Because James Henry was still tied up by off-campus duties—he was now an adviser to the governor of Guangdong Province (and Chiang Kai-shek's brother-in-law), T. V. Soong 宋子文—Henry Frank became the full-fledged provost in March 1948.[31]

In 1947–1948, too, my father was a full professor and chair of the Western Languages and Literature Department. Complaints were no longer voiced about his bureaucratic skills; perhaps he had, indeed, improved as an administrator. Under him were five regular instructors, only two of whom were native speakers of English (Associate Professor Ruth [McCullough] Mack and Instructor Augusta Walker), neither of whom were part of the "permanent" faculty. Ruth Mack, with an MA from Radcliffe in 1931, had taught previously at Lingnan, in 1931–1936, and had returned for two more years, 1946–1948; Augusta ("Polly") Walker (ca. 1914–2000) was a 1945 MA from the University of Michigan. It was one of my father's enduring frustrations—and that of Olin Wannamaker in New York as well—that they had great difficulty finding qualified Americans willing to come out to China to teach English. As he told Wannamaker back in 1945, "It is, in my opinion, a matter of the greatest urgency that the English department be built up as a largely foreign staffed department as quickly as possible, though my idea for the future is that we should henceforth have one or two Chinese members." Indeed, the rest of the department was made up of Chinese. The other three members of the regular teaching staff of the Western Languages Department were Assistant Professors H. K. Chung 鍾香舉 and K. Y. Chou 周光耀 (Lingnan BA, 1941) and Instructor Y. M. Cheung 張亦文 (Lingnan BA, 1929). In addition to English, the department offered two years of French, taught by "a Roman Catholic Sister supported by the Order of Notre Dame."[32]

Only about thirty-five students majored in English, in contrast to 216 in Economics and Business Administration and 149 in Civil Engineering, which were the two most popular departments at the university. Nevertheless, "in the present curriculum requirements four hundred odd students are taught in the [English] department each semester."[33] English, in short, was a service department, but with most classes at Lingnan taught in English it performed a very valuable service. It was not, unlike some departments in the sciences, a

28. Report of the Special Planning Committee on Lingnan Policy, ca. 1 January 1948, Part III, Present Status of Lingnan, Box 144, TLUA–HYL.

29. Total Western Salaried Personnel, 1937–1938 [*sic*; 1947–1948], Box 152, TLUA–HYL.

30. Corbett, *Lingnan University*, p. 152.

31. Corbett, *Lingnan University*, p. 151.

32. HGR to ODW, Canton, 22 December 1945, Box 104, and Portrait of Lingnan, College of Arts, English Department, enclosure in Lee E. Winters to ODW, Canton, 10 June 1948, Box 120, TLUA–HYL; List of Faculty and Administrative Staff, Fall 1948, Folder 3257, Box 182, China College Files—Lingnan University, RG 11, United Board Archives, YDSL. Professor H. K. Chung's educational background is not known.

33. Portrait of Lingnan, College of Arts, English Department, enclosure in Lee E. Winters to ODW, Canton, 10 June 1948, Box 120, and Report of the Special Planning Committee on Lingnan Policy, ca. 1 January 1948, Box 144, TLUA–HYL.

research department. There is no record that my father himself carried out any scholarly research during his stint at Lingnan.

He did, however, at one point try to interest the university administration in setting up a daily press monitoring service, based on what the OWI in Chongqing had done. As explained by Provost Frank, the idea was to have "translations made every day of such items in the vernacular press as would help us to keep in touch with the local situation in so far as this is reflected in newspaper items." My father went so far as to prepare, as a model, a three-page "Memorandum on the Student Strike of May 2 and 3, 1947."[34]

The precipitant for this two-day student strike at Lingnan was an assault on the university bus shuttling between the Hong Lok campus and the Canton Hospital in Guangzhou city by soldiers stationed at a conscription center near the university's South Gate. Though no students had been injured in the fracas, the student body as a whole demanded a formal apology from the commanding officer of the conscription center. When that was not forthcoming, the students called for a strike—one that encompassed "all departments and grades from the first year of the primary school on"—and they made a personal appeal to General Zhang Fakui, the leading military figure in postwar Guangzhou. In the end, General Zhang, who was generally well regarded, persuaded the students to call off their strike; in return, he agreed to come to Lingnan and address the student body. One of the points he made in his talk to the students was that "whereas a strike in the National Sun Yat-sen University [國立中山大學] bothered him not at all, he was concerned about so unusual an occurrence as a strike at Lingnan."[35]

Indeed, the postwar era from 1945 to 1949 was one of almost incessant student activism throughout China. According to political scientist Suzanne Pepper,

> students were involved in scores of individual protests, strikes, and incidents. Some of these developed over political issues, others over academic and school-related matters. In addition to these more or less isolated protests, four major demonstrations, or student tides (*hsueh-ch'ao* [學潮]), as they were called, aroused nationwide attention and response. . . . The students' primary demands were an immediate end to the Civil War, an end to US backing for the [Nationalist] Government in that war, and a shift in public expenditure from military to civilian needs.[36]

The student strike at Lingnan in May 1947 coincided with the beginning of the third of Pepper's four "student tides," called the Anti-Hunger Anti-Civil War Movement (*fan ji'e fan neizhan yundong* 反飢餓反內戰運動), but it may have been related to it only tangentially. According to Henry Frank, writing at the end of May, there had been attempts from off campus "during the past weeks" to get the Lingnan students "to join anti-civil-war demonstrations." The outside agitation may have come from Sun Yat-sen University, across the river in Guangzhou city, where in late May the students were to call a three-day strike in support of the Anti-Hunger Anti-Civil War Movement.[37] By then, however, the Lingnan student strike had come to an end. It thus seems to have been an isolated protest and not part of the national student tide. As General Zhang Fakui said in his speech to the

---

34. Henry S. Frank to ODW, Canton, 28 May 1947, Box 114, TLUA–HYL.

35. Henry S. Frank to ODW, Canton, 28 May 1947, and enclosure, "Memorandum on the Student Strike of May 2 and 3, 1947," Box 114, TLUA–HYL; see also Yang Yimei, "Li Yinglin shiqi de Lingnan daxue," pp. 91–92. On General Zhang Fakui, see Boorman and Howard, *Biographical Dictionary of Republican China* 1: 56–61.

36. Suzanne Pepper, *Civil War in China: The Political Struggle 1945–1949* (Lanham, MD: Rowman & Littlefield Publishers, 1999), p. 42.

37. Henry S. Frank to ODW, Canton, 28 May 1947, Box 114, TLUA–HYL; Pepper, *Civil War in China*, p. 64.

Lingnan students, their school, unlike Sun Yat-sen University, was not known as a hotbed of student activism.

Lingnan was involved in one other postwar protest movement. It, too, was a localized event, unconnected to any of the above-mentioned student tides; it was, nevertheless, perhaps the most serious uprising in the city during the entire postwar period. It was prompted by the attempt in January 1948 by the British in Hong Kong to tear down the Kowloon Walled City (Jiulong saicheng 九龍塞城). Located within the New Territories north of Kowloon Peninsula, the settlement had long been the site of a Chinese military garrison. When the New Territories were turned over as a leasehold to Britain in 1898, the walled city, rather unusually, had remained under Chinese jurisdiction and control. Subsequent efforts over the years by the British to extend their authority over the enclave had been stoutly resisted by its residents. The Kowloon Walled City came to be seen as, in the words of historian John Carroll, "a powerful symbol of Chinese sovereignty in British Hong Kong."[38]

When the British, having regained control of Hong Kong from the Japanese, tried yet again in January 1948 to tear down the walled city and turn it into a park, it sparked an anti-British response in Guangzhou. A protest parade was organized for 16 January and included students from Lingnan. As in 1925 the demonstrators headed for Shameen. Formerly an Anglo-French leasehold, Shameen had reverted to Chinese rule during the Second World War. As a result, rather than simply threatening to attack Shameen (as they had in 1925), the demonstrators could now march onto the man-made island with impunity. They headed for the British consulate at the west end of the island. According to Dr. Cadbury, "First students in two lots passed by throwing stones & shouting, but then came a detachment of '3 peoples principles' youth in uniforms." (The Three People's Principles Youth Corps [Sanmin zhuyi qingniantuan 三民主義青年團], founded in 1938 by Chiang Kai-shek, was an adjunct to the Nationalist Party.) "They brought kerosene & set fire to the British consulate & other British properties, manhandled the British Consul & other personnel & prevented police & fire companies from coming to the rescue for 2 hours. The beautiful consulate buildings were burned to the ground." In addition, according to Cadbury, "Posters were pasted up even on our campus denouncing British imperialism." This attack on Shameen succeeded yet again in preventing the British in Hong Kong from demolishing the Kowloon Walled City, which was to survive as a no-man's-land for almost another fifty years. It was not torn down until 1994, on the eve of Hong Kong's retrocession to Chinese rule.[39]

A press monitoring service like the one my father had suggested might have helped the foreign community at Lingnan (and beyond) comprehend such unsettling events as the 1947 Lingnan student strike and the 1948 attack on Shameen. Few, if any, of the Westerners on the faculty were able to read Chinese with any facility, though some of them might have been conversant in Cantonese. The press monitoring service, however, would have been of little use to the Chinese administrators and professors, who were playing an expanding role in the life of the university. Vice Provost Henry Frank had expressed mild interest in my father's proposal, but there is no evidence that the service was ever established.

---

38. Carroll, *Concise History of Hong Kong*, p. 71.
39. William W. Cadbury to Ben [Cadbury], Canton, 25 January 1948, Folder 1948, Box 10, Collection No. 1192, Cadbury & Cadbury Papers, Haverford College Library; Yang Yimei, "Li Yinglin shiqi de Lingnan daxue," pp. 97–98; Carroll, *Concise History of Hong Kong*, pp. 187–188.

Meanwhile, by 1947–1948 the ongoing inflation had metastasized into "hyperinflation" (defined as an inflation rate of more than 50 percent a month). It was a major contributing factor in the student unrest. In Guangzhou, the price index (with 1937 = 100), which already stood at 561,091 in December 1946, had shot up to 9,419,215 by December 1947. The price index for Guangzhou for a later period is not available, but in Shanghai by July 1948 it had climbed yet further, to 287,700,000! Fortunately, our family was to some extent insulated from the corrosive effects of this hyperinflation because my father, unlike his Chinese colleagues, was paid in US dollars, which he was now able to convert into Chinese *yuan* at the market rate, whereas previously in Qujiang he had been constrained by the artificially low official exchange rate. Still, with the price index outpacing the exchange rate and his annual salary unchanged at US$2,724, it was a challenge even for a foreign family to keep up with the rising cost of living. As Henry Refo, a teacher at the True Light Middle School, recalled, "My salary amounted to about a million [Chinese] dollars a month. I would go to the bank with a wicker basket [to receive his pay] and put the money, which was in packages of thousands of dollars, in my wicker basket and take it home. Then I would dispose of it as fast as I could"—lest it lose any more value.[40]

As for my mother, on our return from Chongqing, she was able to reunite with her sister Chi Kin and with their father, whom she had not seen since her departure for Qujiang after the fall of Hong Kong; she had left both of them in Japanese-occupied Guangzhou. In 1943 Chi Kin and her family, having been prevented from joining her son Luo Wen in Free China, had gone to Macau instead. They returned to Guangzhou after the war and remained there until and beyond the Communist takeover in 1949. Ngan Heung Cho and his two families spent the rest of the war years in Guangzhou under the Japanese occupation. In 1946 he and his wife, Sam Gwu, and their four children returned to Hong Kong, where they lived in the Wan Chai neighborhood of Hong Kong Island.[41] His concubine, Wong Sam Mui, continued to live at the ancestral village, Ngan Bin Tsuen.

By then, due to a series of economic reverses, beginning with the worldwide Depression, followed by the war with Japan and China's postwar fiscal collapse, Ngan Heung Cho had fallen on hard times and was working at an import-export firm in Hong Kong.[42] At that point, according to my uncle Ki Ping, he finally got a bit of luck. A business associate had sold him "a shipment of sand" that gold dealers had used to make molds for casting gold ingots. It was thought that the sand might contain enough residual gold to be worth extracting, but it turned out that the sand had something even more valuable than gold: wolfram, the main source of tungsten, which, as my uncle points out, was "very much in demand worldwide by manufacturers of electric bulbs and weaponry."[43]

Though living in Hong Kong, my grandfather had made sure to hold on to the twenty-seven pieces of property in his native village of Ngan Bin Tsuen that he had managed to buy (or buy back) during the years when he had prospered. In doing so he had fulfilled a promise he had made to his mother long ago to recover what had been unjustly taken from her. These properties, consisting of land and houses, were held in the name of the "benevolent society" (*shantang* 善堂) he had established, the Kyun Sin Tong 拳善堂. The society was so named, according to my uncle, because Ngan Heung Cho had "with his

40. Chang, *Inflationary Spiral*, pp. 372–373; Henry Refo, "Midwest China Oral History Interviews," p. 34.
41. Ngan Ki Ping, "Gei Changshun de beiwanglu (Part II)," 22 April 2016.
42. Ngan Ki Ping, "Zi yuan," p. 3; Luo Ren, "Huohong de nianyue" [Years and months that were fiery red], *Binshe* (Class of 1954), 2 (June 1998), p. 5. The latter is the alumni newsletter of the Class of 1954, Lingnan University.
43. Ngan Ki Ping, "Further to My Most Recent Reply re Memo #4 Today," 19 June 2015, and "Memo #6," 21 June 2015.

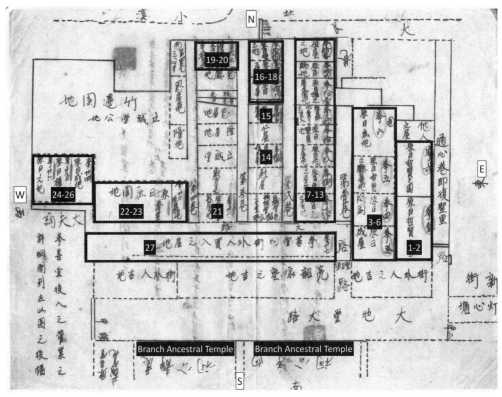

Figure 7.4: Sketch map of my grandfather's holdings in Ngan Bin Village, 1947. Courtesy of Ngan Ki Ping. The main ancestral hall, if I recall correctly from my 2016 visit, lies slightly to the north and west of the branch halls, just off the left edge of the map.

bare hands 赤手空拳 [*chishou kongquan*] made his fortune and reputation in the business community."[44]

In 1947, my grandfather drew up a fascinating document spelling out the distribution of these properties in Ngan Bin Village. On the back of the document is a hand-drawn map showing the precise locations of these twenty-seven lots. He provided for all eleven of his surviving children, including (though on a reduced scale) his daughters. Six lots (#1–6) were to be divided between the two oldest sons, No. 7 and No. 9 in birth order; seven lots (#7–13) were to go to the three younger sons, Nos. 14, 15, and 17; and three lots (#16–18) were set aside for the six daughters, Nos. 2, 4 (my mother), 8, 11, 12, and 18, as a place for their "old maids residence" (*gupo wu* 姑婆屋), if in their old age they should be widowed or unmarried. Some of the remaining lots were designated for his grandchildren (probably only those with the Ngan surname, hence excluding me).[45] This document was rendered in triplicate, with one copy each given to the three sons of Sam Gwu (Nos. 14, 15, and 17), with whom he was living in Hong Kong. It might be noted that, while this reflected gender discrimination, there was no discrimination against the offspring of the concubine, Wong Sam Mui; her children (Nos. 8, 9, 11, and 12) were

---

44. Ngan Ki Ping, personal communication, 2 September 2014.

45. "Qizhi ji gedi guanye zhi xiangxi kailie" 其之及各弟管業之詳細開列 [A detailed listing of properties overseen by Kei Chee and his younger brothers], 1947, courtesy of Ngan Ki Ping.

treated the same as the children of the principal wives. Indeed, it was there in one of the houses in Ngan Bin Village that her son (No. 9) had been allotted that Wong Sam Mui lived during the war and "for decades" afterward.[46]

Meanwhile, my mother returned to work as a stenographer and typist, now for Henry Frank at the American Foundation office. This was the same work she had done for Provost James Henry before the war, for President Y. L. Lee during the war (first in Hong Kong and later in Qujiang and Tai Tsuen), and for Customs Commissioner Edgar Bathurst in Qujiang. Much of Frank's typed correspondence with the New York trustees in 1946 carried the identifying tag "HSF:ckr."[47] However, the vice provost was understandably uncomfortable with this arrangement. As he explained, in a handwritten postscript to a typed letter to Wannamaker, "Mrs. Rhoads has been very good about taking dictation and typing letters for me, but there is a great deal of stuff (including parts of this postscript) which I do not feel justified in turning over to any local person."[48] In response, Wannamaker was able to resurrect a prewar, pre-Depression practice and send out "a confidential American secretary" in the person of Ethel Montgomery (1893–1984), formerly the office manager in New York, who arrived on campus in November 1946. Succeeding her in 1947–1948 was Jean Miller Worcester (1908–2000), a former naval officer.[49] With their arrival, there was no further need for my mother's stenographic services in the American Foundation office. She may, however, have worked in a similar capacity for President Y. L. Lee, at least for a while during these postwar years. She also helped Dr. Cadbury, our neighbor, with some of his correspondence.[50]

At home my mother oversaw a small staff of domestic servants to care for my baby sister, to market and cook, to clean house, to do the laundry, and to tend to the yard. Chief among them was Ah Hoh. As previously noted, Ah Hoh had originally worked for Henry Frank and his family but had spent most of the war years with us in Hong Kong, Qujiang, Tai Tsuen, and Chongqing. After the war, when the Frank family were finally able to return to Lingnan, Ah Hoh was placed in an awkward position: should she stay with us or should she go back to the Franks? For whatever reason, she stayed with us. She was the housekeeper; according to Austin Frank, she did not cook.[51] She—and perhaps some of the other servants too—most likely lived in the basement of our house. I have no recollection as to the number of servants we employed. I imagine that, in addition to the general housekeeper (Ah Hoh), they would have included, at least, a babysitter, a gardener, and a cook. As to what the cook prepared for our meals, here too I have no recollection. Western households typically ate Western food, but we were not exactly a Western household. What I do remember is eating lots of Chinese food, which I love, particularly Cantonese favorites, like *lop cheong* 臘腸 (sausage) and *ham yu* 鹹魚 (salted fish), along with white rice.

---

46. Ngan Ki Ping, personal communication, 20 December 2014.
47. See, for example, Henry S. Frank to ODW, Canton, 29 June 1946, Box 107, TLUA–HYL.
48. Henry S. Frank to ODW, Canton, 25 May 1946, Box 109, TLUA–HYL.
49. ODW to Clinton N. Laird, New York, 30 September 1946, Box 108, ODW's Memorandum to Harold B. Hoskins, "Matters for discussion at luncheon conference today," 20 June 1946, Box 109, Ethel Montgomery to Friends in Room 904, Canton, 10 November 1946, Box 110, and Total Western Salaried Personnel, 1937–1938 [*sic*; 1947–1948], Box 152, TLUA–HYL.
50. William W. Cadbury to Paul, George and John, Canton, 3 March 1947, Folder 1947, Box 10, Collection No. 1192, Cadbury & Cadbury Papers, Haverford College Library.
51. Austin Frank, personal communications, 7 and 18 July 2013; Marian (Frank) Zeitlin, personal communication, 17 July 2013.

Figure 7.5: My sister and one of our servants in yard of Residence No. 47, ca. 1947. Note chicken in yard.

In the postwar years my mother was able to pursue her interest in the piano. It was almost certainly around this time that she studied with Harry Ore, the Latvian composer and pianist living in Hong Kong, to whom she may have been introduced when she was a student at True Light Middle School. Ore would come to Guangzhou once or twice a month to give lessons to students at Lingnan and elsewhere. In June 1948, as we were about to depart for a year's leave in the United States, he presented her with—and inscribed—three of his compositions for the piano, including "Variations on a Japanese Song" and "A Message from Latvia." My mother also hosted "music meetings" of the Lingnan Women's Auxiliary at our home. And she performed in public on at least two occasions, once at a Sunday morning service in August 1946, where she played the "Largo" from Antonin Dvorak's New World Symphony, and the other time at a concert at Swasey Hall in November 1947.[52]

My mother also involved herself in other aspects of the social life of the university. As previously mentioned, she, along with several other "Lingnan ladies," was asked to serve on a small committee that Dr. Cadbury had organized in the spring of 1946 to help

52. William W. Cadbury to Daughters, Hong Kong, 1 April 1946, Folder 1946, Box 10, William W. Cadbury diaries, entries of 11 August 1946 and 29 November 1947, Box 52, and [Lingnan] Women's Auxiliary, List of meetings, 1947, Folder International Women's Club of Canton, Box 67, Collection No. 1192, Cadbury & Cadbury Papers, Haverford College Library.

distribute the used clothing that his supporters in the US had collected and shipped to him. For the Women's Auxiliary, in addition to the music meetings, my mother hosted "staff meetings," "sewing meetings," and the women's Red Cross.[53]

My father, too, joined in the social life of the university, which revolved around the Wednesday evening prayer meeting, the Friday afternoon staff tea, and the Sunday morning church service. The Wednesday "prayer meetings" seem to have been rather loosely construed; in some instances they were akin to faculty meetings (though mostly for the Western faculty). According to Dr. Cadbury's diaries, my father led at least two prayer meetings, one (in March 1947) on "sacred poems beginning in the 16th century up to 20th," and the other (in June 1948) on China and America. At one other meeting, where Tokyo-born entomologist J. Linsley Gressitt (1914–1982) read one or more letters from some (possibly missionary) friends in Japan, my father, having just come from a cocktail party in Shameen and having had a little too much to drink, "began to fire a series of questions as to 'What missionaries are trying to do in Japan,'" much to the consternation of Dr. Cadbury, a devout Quaker.[54] My father and mother also hosted, every semester, one of the Friday afternoon staff teas.[55] There is no evidence, however, that they attended the Sunday church service, aside from my mother's piano recital mentioned earlier.

Despite the missionary origins of Lingnan University, my parents' lack of interest in religion was not unusual among the Westerners then on campus. This was already apparent in the mid-1930s, when zoologist Franklin Wallace was on the faculty. When asked about this situation by Robert J. McMullen, Executive Secretary of the United Board for Christian Colleges in China, President Y. L. Lee reportedly replied that "the greatest difficulty in strengthening the religious life on the campus was the utter indifference of members of the American faculty." McMullen even found fault with James Henry, the school's nominal provost, who reportedly "never attends church and virtually never occupies the pulpit." And when he brought this matter up with anthropologist Charlotte Gower (1902–1982) and with my father, he was much distressed to find both of them "completely indifferent." Olin Wannamaker in New York, writing to Henry Frank, offered a defense of James Henry's religious belief—"It emphasized inner life and conduct toward other persons rather than a church relationship"—and took note that there were, in fact, many members of the American staff "who have and manifest a strong religious influence—you and Mrs. Frank, the Brownells, the Cadburys, the Hoffmanns."[56]

The issue of the role of Christianity at Lingnan came up again in the spring of 1948, when Y. L. Lee resigned after eleven years as president of the university and Chen Su-ching 陳序經 (1903–1967) was chosen as his successor. A native of Hainan Island and an alumnus of the Lingnan Middle School, S. C. Chen had graduated from Fudan University in Shanghai in 1925 and earned his PhD degree in political science from the University of Illinois in 1928, with a dissertation on "Recent Theories of Sovereignty." He had taught

53. See Folder Miscellaneous—Lingnan University 1/3, Box 66, and Folder International Women's Club of Canton, Box 67, Collection No. 1192, Cadbury & Cadbury Papers, Haverford College Library.

54. Wallace, "Midwest China History Oral Interviews," pp. 27–29; William W. Cadbury diaries, entries of 12 March 1947, 26 May and 2 June 1948, Box 52, Collection No. 1192, Cadbury & Cadbury Papers, Haverford College Library.

55. William W. Cadbury diaries, entries of 10 October 1947 and 30 April 1948, Box 52, Collection No. 1192, Cadbury & Cadbury Papers, Haverford College Library.

56. Wallace, "Midwest China Oral History Interviews," p. 30; ODW to Henry S. Frank, New York, 5 September 1946, Box 110, TLUA–HYL. Gower taught at Lingnan from 1938 to 1941; after repatriation in 1942, she joined the US Marine Corps and worked for the Office of Strategic Services and later the Central Intelligence Agency.

at Lingnan in the early 1930s before joining the faculty of Nankai, the highly regarded private university in Tianjin, where he rose to become the right-hand man of its founding president, Zhang Boling. Among contemporary Chinese intellectuals, Chen stood out as a proponent of "wholesale Westernization" (*quanpan xihua* 全盤西化). Despite his impressive administrative and academic credentials, his selection as Lingnan president by the predominantly Chinese Board of Directors did not sit well, at least initially, with the American trustees. Olin Wannamaker, in New York, even deemed Chen's nomination "a bit dangerous." The reason for their concern was that he was not, unlike all three of his predecessors (James Henry, Chung Wing Kwong, and Y. L. Lee), a baptized Christian, nor was he "a member of any church." (Indeed, in 1964 he would state that he was never a Christian.) Nonetheless, his supporters insisted that he was "a Christian at heart."[57] Backed by the Chinese directors, Chen Su-ching took office as Lingnan's president on 1 August 1948.

Finally, as for myself, when we came home to Guangzhou, I resumed my schooling. Having started out at the Chee Min Boys' School in Chongqing, I most likely continued my education in a Chinese school. Lingnan University's primary school, established for the children of the Chinese faculty and staff, was down the hill from our house; from 1945 to 1947 I probably attended its second and third grades (I have no report cards from, and no personal recollection of, this period.) Unlike the school in Chongqing, the Lingnan primary school would have taught in Cantonese, with Mandarin possibly as an auxiliary course. Simultaneously, I must have been home-schooled in English by my mother, for among my personal possessions are workbooks for first-grade readers, "Fun with Dick and Jane" and "Our New Friends."

During the year we were in Chongqing, I had had to learn Mandarin, or at least the Sichuan dialect of Mandarin. Once back in Guangzhou I reverted to speaking Cantonese, not only at school but also at home with my mother and with Ah Hoh and other servants. All my friends, too, were Chinese—there were no boys my age among the children of the Western staff—and with them I spoke Cantonese. Perhaps the two boys who were my closest friends then were the son of the university president Y. L. Lee and the son of chemistry professor Hoh Shai Kwong. With my father, however, I had to speak English. My father eventually learned enough spoken Cantonese to understand it and to be able to get around town on his own, but it was a rudimentary knowledge of the language. (He did not read Chinese.) Thus, when my father spoke to me, or to my mother, it was in English.

In the fall of 1947, the university reopened its Western School. There had been such a school on campus prior to the war, but it had fallen by the wayside during the ensuing upheaval. It was resurrected in 1947 on the initiative of two faculty wives, Martha (Griggs) Frank (1903–1995) and May (Leung) Chang (1909–1998), and the newly returned English professor, Ruth (McCullough) Mack. These three mothers had started "a small 'pick-up' Western School" in February 1947 for their own children as well as for USIS Chief Elmer Newton's twelve-year-old son. Later in the year Vice Provost Henry Frank, Martha's husband, convinced the American trustees to build on these efforts by hiring two schoolteachers in America and restarting "a full-fledged Western School." Faculty children could attend for free, but by charging tuition for children from off-campus

57. ODW to James M. Henry, New York, 21 April 1948, and Henry S. Frank to ODW, Canton, 11 May 1948, Box 119, TLUA–HYL; Wang, *Managing God's Higher Learning*, pp. 8–9, 66–67; Chen Xujing, "Youguan Lingda yu Zhong Rongguang de jidian huiyi" [Some recollections regarding Lingnan University and Chung Wing Kwong], *Guangzhou wenshi ziliao*, no. 13 (1964): 38, 50.

(e.g., among missionaries, foreign business people, and government officials), the school would almost pay for itself.[58] Roma (Mitchell) Melanphy (1896–2000), a widow with long teaching experience in the Berkeley, California, school system, was hired for one year to teach in the school's lower grades and to serve as its principal. The school, which had eight grades divided between two rooms, was in the Jackson Lodge, four houses down the eucalyptus-lined lane from our house.[59] Western children who were older than eighth grade were often sent off to the American School in Shanghai.

In anticipation of my father's furlough (or sabbatical) in the US the following school year, I was transferred from the university's Chinese primary school to the Western School when it opened in late September 1947. (Interestingly, my parents had not enrolled me in the "pick-up" Western School the previous spring.) The school had thirty-two pupils, five of whom were faculty children: Laura Chang, Marion Frank, the two daughters of Ruth Mack, and myself. I was put in the fourth grade, with Mrs. Melanphy as my teacher. Looking ahead to our year abroad, Vice Provost Frank in October wrote, "Young Edward's problem of adjustment will be very much simpler as a result of our having a Western School here this year. This is his first opportunity to spend very much time in the company of English-speaking children and his use of English and his responsiveness to those who speak it are increasing daily."[60]

Like me, the two Mack sisters were products of an interracial marriage. It may be recalled that their mother had taught at Lingnan in the early 1930s and had married their father, Mack Kwok Chun, in 1935. They and their mother had spent the war years in the US, while their father had taught at Lingnan's College of Agriculture at Ping Shek. In 1946 Ruth Mack had returned to Lingnan to teach in the English Department, bringing the two girls with her.

Attitudes in China toward mixed-race children such as us were themselves mixed. On the one hand, some Chinese looked favorably upon race mixing (particularly if the races to be mixed were yellow and white). For the visionary Confucian thinker Kang Youwei at the turn of the twentieth century, "hybridization essentially serves as a mechanism for eugenic improvement and [racial] revitalization," as historian Emma Jinhua Teng put it. And as previously noted, the former president of Lingnan, Chung Wing Kwong, had espoused similar ideas. On the other hand, according to Teng, "The racialized character of modern Chinese nationalism had a distinctly negative impact on Eurasians, calling into question their Chineseness and making issue of their descent from foreigners who had subjected China to humiliation."[61]

The more general view, among both Westerners and Chinese, was the negative one. As summarized by Norwood Allman based on his experiences as an American lawyer in Shanghai, "The children of such unions are the real sufferers. They are the victims of a cruel and perhaps senseless social ostracism. Rarely are they accepted as equals by either the Chinese or by nationals of the white parent. They are half-castes or Eurasians,

58. Henry S. Frank to ODW, Canton, 8 May 1947, Box 114, TLUA–HYL. May Chang was the wife of chemistry professor Frederic C. Chang.
59. Roma J. Melanphy to ODW, Napa, CA, 21 July 1947, Box 115, and ODW to Melanphy, telegram, New York, 7 August 1947, Box 114, "Committee on Public Safety" re "Western School," 26 July 1948, and Henry S. Frank to Jettye F. Grant, Canton, 9 August 1948, Box 120, TLUA–HYL.
60. Henry S. Frank to ODW, Canton, 27 October and 4 December 1947, Box 116, and "Committee on Public Safety" re "Western School," 26 July 1948, Box 120, TLUA–HYL.
61. Emma Jinhua Teng, *Eurasian: Mixed Identities in the United States, China, and Hong Kong, 1842–1943* (Berkeley: University of California Press, 2013), pp. 120, 199.

names which carry a certain stigma to some insensate residents in the Orient."[62] Chinese terms for "Eurasians" carry a similar stigma, as spelled out by literary scholar Vicky Lee. "Eurasians were (and occasionally still are) often referred to in derogatory Chinese terms like *tsap chung* [雜種] (half-caste), *da luen chung* [打亂種], *tsap ba lang* [雜巴冷] (mixed/ messed up breed). Other Chinese terms like *boon tong fan* [半唐番] and *wun hyut yih* [混血 兒] are less derogatory but still suggest a kind of genealogical abnormality."[63] However, I, for one, do not recall being ostracized or stigmatized for being Eurasian. Perhaps this was because I was living in the cocoon-like environment of a university campus.

Though originally due for his furlough in 1947–1948, my father had postponed it for a year, in part because "the department is not in good enough shape for him to be away next year." But he did not want to delay it any further, because of me; he was anxious, as Henry Frank wrote Wannamaker, "to place his son Edward (aged 9) in school where he will need really to learn English and become fluent in it."[64] Fortunately, Olin Wannamaker had persuaded Paul A. Grieder (1899–1992), Professor of English at Montana State University, to come back to Lingnan for a year on a Fulbright Fellowship.[65] (Like Ruth Mack, Grieder had taught at Lingnan previously.) That cleared the way for my father to take his sabbatical in the fall of 1948.

---

62. Allman, *Shanghai Lawyer*, p. 192.
63. Vicky Lee, *Being Eurasian: Memories Across Racial Divides* (Hong Kong: Hong Kong University Press, 2004), p. 18. My thanks to Bruce A. Chan, for confirming, in a personal communication, 24 March 2017, that "Vicky [Lee]'s Cantonese terms pretty well cover the whole range of colloquial terms for mixed-race persons" and for providing the Chinese characters for those terms.
64. Henry S. Frank to ODW, Canton, 4 March 1947, Box 113, TLUA–HYL.
65. Corbett, *Lingnan University*, p. 150.

8

An American Interlude (1948–1949)

The year we were away from Lingnan, 1948–1949, was a particularly momentous one in China. Popular support for Chiang Kai-shek's Nationalist government, particularly among the urban population, evaporated, as the regime continued to fail to solve the problem of hyperinflation. In August 1948 it finally got rid of the Chinese National Currency, replacing it with the "Gold Yuan" (*jinyuan* 金圓), at a conversion rate of three million (!!!) *yuan* of old currency to one new Gold Yuan note, and it set the new foreign exchange rate at four Gold Yuan to one US dollar. But according to historian Odd Arne Westad, "By the end of October it was clear to everyone that the August reforms had collapsed, and with them the last vestiges of ordinary economic activities in and around the cities. . . . the Gold Yuan started to depreciate even more rapidly than its predecessor."[1]

Soon thereafter, the military tide turned decisively against Chiang and the Nationalists and in favor of Mao Zedong and the Communists. Having already established their control over the countryside in northeastern and northern China, the Communists began driving the Nationalists out of their urban strongholds. Shenyang, the major city in Manchuria, fell to them in November 1948, followed quickly by Tianjin and Beijing in January 1949. The Communists then swept southward across the North China Plain, crossing the Yangtze River on 20 April and capturing Nanjing, Shanghai, and Hankou soon afterwards. Amid such tribulations, Chiang Kai-shek, in January, stepped down as President of the Republic of China and was replaced by Vice President Li Zongren. In late April, after Nanjing had fallen, Li Zongren relocated the national capital to Guangzhou. Meanwhile, Chiang, having fled to Taiwan, kept his more important post as head of the Nationalist Party.[2]

At Lingnan, too, the year was one of change. It was the first year of the presidency of Chen Su-ching. At the time of his appointment there had been concerns in some quarters about Chen's Christian convictions and his suitability as Y. L. Lee's successor. A year later, however, Provost Henry Frank happily reported to the American trustees that the new president, "although not a professing Christian, [had] gained the confidence of the various mission bodies in Canton, both for himself and for the Christian purpose and character of Lingnan, to an extent not equalled for decades."[3] While we

---

1. Odd Arne Westad, *Decisive Encounters: The Chinese Civil War, 1946–1950* (Stanford: Stanford University Press, 2003), pp. 182–185; Shun-hsin Chou, *The Chinese Inflation, 1937–1949* (New York: Columbia University Press, 1963), p. 146.
2. Westad, *Decisive Encounters*, pp. 185–255.
3. Corbett, *Lingnan University*, p. 152.

were away, S. C. Chen lived in our otherwise empty house. It is unclear whether Ah Hoh worked for President Chen in our absence, or what she did. Meanwhile, in New York, Olin Wannamaker, the longtime director of the American trustees, retired in February 1949; he was succeeded by James Henry, the former provost of the university, who had resigned as adviser to Governor T. V. Soong and returned to America.

In Hong Kong, as we awaited our departure for America, we ran into Gilbert Baker. Baker, who had previously taught at Lingnan and had baptized me there, was now the chaplain at St. John's University in Shanghai. He and his wife stood as my sister Janet's godparents as she was baptized at St. John's Cathedral.[4]

My father took his year-long furlough in Philadelphia. We traveled to the US aboard the SS *Cape San Martin*, a freighter (a cargo ship that carried a few passengers as well). (For the Lingnan trustees, who paid for our transportation, freighters were preferable to the more costly passenger liners.) The ship departed Hong Kong on about 30 July, a few days after my sister's baptism. For me personally it was a wrenching experience to leave Ah Hoh, the amah who had brought me up and who had been with me for close to ten years, from Hong Kong to Qujiang and Chongqing and back to Guangzhou. Perhaps even more than my mother she was the person to whom I had felt the closest attachment. I cried and cried as we left the harbor. The ensuing voyage took thirty-three days. We stopped at Honolulu, went through the Panama Canal, and arrived at New Orleans on 2 September 1948.[5] "On the trip over," my mother recounted, "Howard had a restful time; Edward had the grandest time—he even ran the boat for half an hour, painted the boat and did all sorts of things—and has expressed the desire of being a sailor when he grows up; Jenny had two French playmates part of the way, was not seasick, but found it too long a trip sometimes; but poor me! I was seasick whenever we ran into trade winds and suffered altogether about two weeks and had the worst spell after Honolulu."[6]

As a native-born American citizen, my father, of course, had no difficulty entering the United States. My sister and I, though born abroad and with an alien for a mother, both claimed to be citizens by descent from him. But our claims to citizenship were possibly contingent. Under the US Nationality Act of 1934, there was an important residency requirement for us: we had to live in the United States for at least five years continuously previous to our eighteenth birthday; otherwise, we would lose our citizenship.[7] This proviso did not jeopardize our citizenship claim in 1948 since neither my sister nor I was then within five years of our eighteenth birthday, but it might in the future. So in 1947, our father had written to the American consulate in Guangzhou arguing that a new nationality law, enacted in 1940, had set this residency requirement aside under the following circumstance: "if the American parent is at the time of the child's birth in the employ of the United States Government or of a recognized educational, missionary, or philanthropic organization whose principal place of business is in the United States." This exemption clearly applied to my sister, because when she was born in 1945 our father was working for the US Office of War Information. But did it apply to me? My father contended that it

---

4.   Gilbert Baker to his parents, Hong Kong, 30 July 1948, Folder 24, Box 5, RG 8, China Records Project, Miscellaneous Personal Papers Collection, YDSL.

5.   HGR to ODW, Canton, 8 July 1948, Box 120, and Philadelphia, 13 September 1948, Box 121, TLUA–HYL; "Port and Shipping," *New Orleans Times-Picayune*, 3 September 1948, p. 46; CKR's Republic of China passport, in my personal collection.

6.   CKR to Dr. and Mrs. William W. Cadbury, Philadelphia, n.d. [but letter postmarked 22 December 1948], Folder Last names O-S, Box 42, Collection No. 1192, Cadbury & Cadbury Papers, Haverford College Library.

7.   ER's "Report of Birth" for ER, 13 June 1938, in my personal collection.

Figure 8.1: Aboard the *Cape San Martin*, with deckhands and some fellow passengers, summer 1948.

Figure 8.2: My mother, my sister, and I at the Panama Canal, summer 1948.

did, because at the time of my birth in 1938 he was employed by the Trustees of Lingnan University. Though "the principal place of business" of Lingnan University could hardly be said to be in the United States, he argued that it was the trustees that had hired him and paid his salary, and the trustees were based in New York City. He succeeded in making his case. The consulate agreed that my sister and I were both American citizens and were not subject to the residency requirement. To reinforce this point, someone appended to the official letter a handwritten notation: "Mr. Rhoads—If necessary we shall keep them forever clothed in American flags to preserve their citizenship!"[8] My sister and I thus were able to travel to the US on my father's passport as American citizens.

---

8.   HGR to the American Consulate-General, Canton, 8 July 1947, Oscar V. Armstrong to HGR, Canton, 15 July and 14 October 1947, all in my personal collection.

Our mother, on the other hand, was traveling on a Chinese passport that had been issued by the Chinese Ministry of Foreign Affairs in Chongqing on 30 December 1944. Extended in January 1948 for one year, it was valid for travel specifically to the "U.S.A. via India & all necessary countries & ports enroute." A month later the American consulate in Guangzhou issued her a visa allowing her to enter the United States as a Temporary Visitor. Her stamped passport indicates that she was granted "shore leave" when we stopped in Honolulu and that she was admitted into the United States at New Orleans on 3 September 1948, the day after the ship docked.[9]

After New Orleans, the *Cape San Martin* was supposed to sail on to Philadelphia, but for some reason it went no farther. We had to disembark and travel the rest of the way by train. Because my father was in the employ of the Lingnan trustees, nominally a Christian organization, we were "entitled to the half fare railway rate granted to clergymen."[10] Philadelphia was, of course, my father's hometown. It was where he was born and had gone to school and gotten his doctorate. It was where his parents and grandparents were buried, and where his closest relative, his cousin Anna Pugh, lived with her husband and family.

Immediately upon our arrival in early September, my father had two main tasks. One, made urgent by the fact that the academic year was about to begin, was to find me a school. In this regard my father was able to have his colleague and neighbor at Lingnan, Dr. William Cadbury, pull some strings on my behalf. A medical missionary, Cadbury had been with Lingnan since 1909, when it was still the Canton Christian College. By 13 September my father was able to report, "I have got Edward into the Friends' Select School . . . This was possible only through the good offices of Cadbury, who went to work on his various friends and relatives in Quaker circles and got them to make room for Edward over others on a long waiting list."[11] Friends' Select was (and still is) a historic private Quaker coeducational college-preparatory school located two blocks northwest of City Hall. My application for admission, filled out by my father, noted that I had "lived all [my] life in China" and that I was particularly weak in English, both spoken and written. Nevertheless, I was placed into the fifth grade, though perhaps as a special or visiting student rather than as a regular student (there are no report cards in my school records). My sister, then three and a half years old, was enrolled in the kindergarten.[12] Tuition fees at Friends' Select for the two of us were $325 and $200.[13] In late December my mother wrote to reassure Dr. and Mrs. Cadbury at Lingnan that I was "doing more than satisfactory work."[14]

My father's other main task, even more urgent, was to find convenient and affordable lodging. Because such a place would have to be within walking distance of the Friends' Select School, he looked primarily in Philadelphia's Center City. As he wrote Wannamaker in mid-September, "In the week I have been here I have done little besides walking my legs

9.   CKR's passport, in my personal collection.

10. ODW to Augusta Walker, New York City, 23 August 1947, Box 114, and HGR to ODW, Philadelphia, 13 September 1948, Box 121, TLUA–HYL.

11. HGR to ODW, Philadelphia, 13 September 1948, Box 121, TLUA–HYL.

12. ER's Application for Admission, Friends' Select School, 7 September 1948, courtesy of Dick Hoffman. The school has now dropped the apostrophe from its name.

13. ODW, Memo for conference with Mr. Hayes re "Furlough budget of Dr. Rhoads," 4 October 1948, Box 121, TLUA–HYL.

14. CKR to Dr. and Mrs. William W. Cadbury, Philadelphia, n.d. [but letter postmarked 22 December 1948], Folder Last names O-S, Box 42, Collection No. 1192, Cadbury & Cadbury Papers, Haverford College Library.

Figure 8.3: Friends' Select School, Fifth Grade, 1948–1949. From the school's yearbook, *The Record* (1949). I am sitting by the window in the right rear corner.

off and my shoes through in search of a place to live." At first we stayed at an unnamed "Methodist sponsored" hotel at $12 a day for rooms. (This may have been the Robert Morris Hotel, at 17th and Arch Streets.) Shortly afterwards he got us two rooms at the Morris Apartments, on 13th Street between Spruce and Pine Streets, about seven blocks south of Friends' Select. This he described, somewhat ambiguously, as "once quite a nice Quaker place but for some years rather on the edge of complete respectability." Though the rent at the Morris Apartments, at $40 a week, was half that of the Methodist-sponsored hotel, he told Wannamaker that it was still "far too much." Nevertheless, we were at the Morris Apartments for the next three months, and I well remember walking through the ground-floor tunnels of City Hall on the way to and from school.[15]

Finally, in mid-December, my father caught "something of a break on the housing." He was able to sublet the apartment of an unnamed "acquaintance, a portrait painter who is following the society trade down to Florida." Located on the south side of Rittenhouse Square, the apartment "is no bigger than the one we now have, but a bit more cheerful and much less expensive." Whereas the rent at the Morris had come to about $160 a month, this new place was "$100 a month completely furnished and with utilities included except for telephone, which I shall have to carry. The rub is that our agreement is until April 1 only; so, if she comes back then, we shall have to move on."[16] When the portrait painter did return in mid-April, we were back at the Morris, where we lived for the last four months of our stay in Philadelphia.[17]

---

15. HGR to ODW, Philadelphia, 13 September 1948, Box 121, TLUA–HYL.
16. HGR to ODW, Philadelphia, 29 November 1948 and 12 December 1948, Box 121, TLUA–HYL.
17. HGR to James M. Henry, Philadelphia, 9 April 1949, Box 123, TLUA–HYL; CKR, US Departing Alien Tax Return for 1 January to 19 August 1949, in my personal collection.

The expense of sending two kids to a private school and residing in Center City meant that we were living on a tight budget. Our travel from Lingnan to Philadelphia and back was paid for by Lingnan's American trustees, who also gave us a monthly allowance for living expenses. As Wannamaker explained to the chair of the trustees, "For a number of years the fixed allowance for a family during the furlough year has been at the rate of $225 per month plus $50 as assistance in covering the rental item. We have budgeted Dr. Rhoads with his family, including two children, at that rate plus $30 per month as the allowance for the two children." These sums, however, totaling $305, were at least $95 less than our monthly expenses, which my father calculated came to $400 to $425. At a trustees meeting in mid-October, Wannamaker managed to get the total monthly salary and allowances raised to $350, which was an increase of 15 percent but still $50 to $75 shy of what we were spending. Meanwhile, my father, as Wannamaker assured the chair of the trustees, had "expressed the complete willingness to undertake part-time work of some kind, probably teaching."[18] Indeed, during the spring semester of 1949 he was employed as a part-time teacher of English at Temple University.[19]

For my mother, living in America could not have been easy. Not that she, unlike me, had any problem with the English language, as one can tell from her letters (see, for example, her account quoted above of our voyage across the Pacific). But for the first time in her life, she had to fend for herself. It is true that as a New Woman of China she had always worked outside the home; she was never what the Chinese call a *huaping* (花瓶, flower vase), that is, someone who is pretty but useless. Nevertheless, she had also had a lot of domestic help. With Ah Hoh and other servants, she had never had to look after children, to clean house, to shop for groceries, to cook. Life as an American housewife would have been a new and not necessarily enjoyable experience for her.

During our year in Philadelphia, we visited often with my father's cousin, Anna Pugh, and her husband Al in suburban Bala Cynwyd. If my memory is correct, we attended at least one University of Pennsylvania football game at Franklin Field in the fall of 1948, and saw my cousin Jack Pugh, a trombonist, perform in the Penn marching band. I also became a big fan of the Philadelphia Phillies professional baseball club, as the Phillies in 1948 and 1949 began to put together a winning team that came to be called the Whiz Kids, centering on pitcher Robin Roberts and outfielder Richie Ashburn. The Whiz Kids went on, in 1950, to win the National League championship for Philadelphia, though by then I was no longer around to cheer them on. (Philadelphia had another major-league baseball team, the Athletics; I was not a fan of the A's.) Before we left, my mother had the pleasure of attending the last concert of the 1948–1949 season by the Philadelphia Orchestra under the direction of the legendary Eugene Ormandy. And as she wrote in late May 1949, "The children are looking forward to the circus this Saturday."[20]

As my father's furlough year began to wind down, the political situation in China was becoming yet more unfavorable to the Nationalists. The Communists, after crossing the Yangtze and capturing Shanghai, Nanjing, and Hankou in April and May 1949, were "advancing in the West and in the South, although at a slower pace than in the spring." In early July they took Zhejiang Province, most of Fujian, and Hunan and were poised

---

18. HGR to ODW, Philadelphia, 3 October 1948, ODW, Memo for conference with Mr. Hayes, 4 October 1948, and ODW to HGR, New York, 22 October 1948, Box 121, TLUA–HYL.
19. HGR, Curriculum Vitae and testimonials, 28 December 1951, in my personal collection.
20. CKR to Ethel Montgomery, Philadelphia, 24 May 1949, Box 123, TLUA–HYL. Having served as Provost Frank's secretary at Lingnan, Montgomery had returned to the New York office.

to invade Guangdong. But even as they overran all of these Nationalist-held areas, the Communists seemed receptive to the continued presence of the Christian colleges in China.[21]

Thus, while many Westerners were fleeing China, my father was emphatic about his desire to go back. As James Henry, Wannamaker's successor as American Director, informed Provost Henry Frank in early February, "I wrote Dr. Rhoads and had a reply yesterday. They are definitely planning to return and this in spite of a second strong urging from Elmer Newton to join the latter's staff in the Voice of America's China Program." (Elmer Newton, it may be recalled, had been my father's superior at the Guangzhou office of the US Information Service right after the war.) In a letter to James Henry in late April, my father reiterated "that when I told you a couple of months ago that we wished to go back to Canton, the decision was final."[22]

In any case, he may not have had much of a choice. Aside from the offer from Elmer Newton, details of which are not available, my father, given his age (49), would have had a difficult time landing a suitable teaching position in the US. Furthermore, even if he had been successful in a job search, my mother's year-long visa as a Temporary Visitor would not have allowed her to remain in the US, though she had had her passport extended to December 1950 by the Nationalist Chinese consul general in New York City. Accordingly, my parents booked tentative passage on a ship leaving San Francisco for Hong Kong at the beginning of August. This allowed us "some time to look round a bit [i.e., do some sightseeing] in the first half of the summer" before we had to leave.[23]

This is not to say that my parents were not worried about what might await us in China. In late May, following the Communist takeover of Shanghai, my mother noted, "the US Consulate [in Guangzhou] is advising all unnecessary Americans and the dependents of necessary ones to leave Canton." And in mid-July, prompted by unspecified news reports that some foreigners in Shanghai had been prevented by the Communists from leaving the country, my father voiced multiple concerns about the future to James Henry in New York: "My personal opinion is . . . that we are all going to be eliminated or be made—in effect—prisoners in China with no chance of getting out when we ourselves decide that we have had enough. Just how my family will emerge from this whole mess—if my fears are correct—is more than I can see. My guess is that Chinese wives of Americans will not be permitted to leave the country if and when the Americans are [allowed to leave], or are kicked out. And it is not impossible that should the Chinese permit them to go[,] the American government might not accept them." (It is unclear what news reports my father may have been referring to; the *New York Times* in early July 1949 reported no prohibition on foreigners leaving Shanghai.) With regard to my father's last concern, Henry's reply tried to be reassuring: "I got the definite impression the last time I was down in Washington that there was no cause for anxiety in a case like yours of the U.S. Government discriminating in the case of Mrs. Rhoads."[24]

My father's gloomy assessment of his personal situation did not sit well with James Henry, who confided to Henry Frank that his letter "is somewhat typical of him" and

21. Westad, *Decisive Encounters*, pp. 282–285; Lutz, *China and the Christian Colleges*, pp. 445, 450.
22. James M. Henry to Henry S. Frank, New York, 9 February 1949, Box 122, HGR to Henry, Philadelphia, 27 April 1949, Box 123, TLUA–HYL.
23. HGR to James M. Henry, Philadelphia, 27 April and 4 May 1949, Box 123, TLUA–HYL; CKR's passport, in my personal collection.
24. CKR to Ethel Montgomery, Philadelphia, 24 May 1949, Box 123, HGR to James M. Henry, Philadelphia, 18 July 1949 and Henry to HGR, New York, 19 July 1949, Box 124, TLUA–HYL.

"has left a rather bad taste in my mouth." Adding to Henry's irritation in dealing with my father was the matter of my schooling. In late May, my father had written to inquire if the Western School on the Lingnan campus would be in operation on our return. The school, resurrected in 1947, had continued, during our absence, in 1948–1949, but its future was unclear. "If it is not to be I think I ought to investigate the possibility of leaving Edward here. He has had so little regular schooling that I wouldn't want him to run wild for another year at his present age." Henry replied bluntly, "I am not at all sure that I could get any special educational grant for you from the Trustees." That ended the possibility of my being left behind.[25]

We departed Philadelphia on 9 August and, traveling by train across the country (again at the clergy's reduced rate), arrived at San Francisco a couple of days later. While awaiting the ship that would take us to Hong Kong, my father received yet more disturbing news: "Last night's radio report that the U.S. consulate is winding up in Canton only adds to the confusion in which I am, and have for a long time been, moving. We shall of course go to Hong Kong anyhow." Thus, on 20 August we set sail aboard the Pacific Transport Lines freighter *China Transport*.[26]

Compared with the *Cape San Martin*, which had caused my mother much seasickness, the *China Transport* proved to be a much more comfortable ship. The ship went by way of Japan, which had yet to recover from the devastation of the recent war and was still under American occupation. During a layover in Yokohama, my father wrote, "We had a few hours in Tokyo, which I now regret. I would much rather remember it as it was in 1936

Figure 8.4: Aboard the *China Transport*, with an unidentified fellow passenger, on our way back to China, summer 1949.

25. HGR to James M. Henry, Philadelphia, 30 May and Henry to HGR, New York, 1 June 1949, Box 123, Henry to Henry S. Frank, New York, 20 July 1949, Box 124, TLUA–HYL.

26. HGR to James M. Henry, Philadelphia, 31 July 1949, Box 124, and CKR to Henry, Philadelphia, 4 August 1949, and HGR to Henry, San Francisco, 18 August 1949, Box 125, TLUA–HYL; "To Sail From Here," *San Francisco Chronicle*, 20 August 1949, p. 9.

. . . Yokohama is pretty ghastly." We finally reached Hong Kong on 11 September, three weeks after leaving San Francisco.[27] We arrived "home" in Guangzhou two days later, "having come in," as my father happily wrote James Henry, "quite uneventfully."[28] Among the many things that he had groused about to Henry was the possibility that we might be barred from entering China; as it turned out, when we arrived at Guangzhou the city was still in the hands of the Nationalists, though barely.

27. HGR to James M. Henry, San Francisco, 18 August 1949, and Yokohama, 6 September 1949, Box 125, TLUA–HYL; CKR's passport, in my personal collection.

28. Henry S. Frank to James M. Henry, Canton, 28 August 1949, Frank to Amerfound, cablegram, Canton, 16 September 1949, and HGR to Henry, Canton, 28 September 1949, Box 125, TLUA–HYL.

The Communists Take Over (1949–1951)

Upon our arrival in Guangzhou in mid-September 1949, we returned to our old home at Residence No. 47, while President S. C. Chen, who had been living there in our absence, moved to the nearby Residence No. 54, also known as the Cadbury House or the William Penn Lodge.[1] William Cadbury, the Quaker medical doctor who had pulled strings to get me into Friends' Select School, had retired after forty years at Lingnan and gone home to Moorestown, New Jersey. Ah Hoh came back to work for and live with us.

In the month preceding our return, much had happened. The Communists were fast approaching Guangzhou. When in mid-August the US consulate in Guangzhou announced that it was closing down, "most American business people left, including the U.S.I.S. and the American Consul with his staff," according to Joseph Hahn, the Maryknoll missionary and Lingnan teacher. At the university, Henry Frank, as the resident director of the American Foundation, had called "a meeting of all the U.S. citizens on the campus, faculty as well as students," to discuss the situation. Afterwards, a few of the Westerners among the Lingnan faculty and staff opted to join the exodus; they included Ruth Mack of the Western Languages Department and Jean Worcester, the private secretary whom the New York trustees had provided Henry Frank. Also, the student exchange program, which had been revived two years earlier, was again suspended. "Most" of the Western faculty, nevertheless, "decided to stick it out." Additionally, Gilbert Baker, who had taught at Lingnan in 1936–1938, had left St. John's University in Shanghai and returned to teach at the Union Theological College, which was now a constituent part of the university. On 1 September Lingnan began a new school year with a near record enrollment of more than 1,200 students.[2]

The new academic year was Chen Su-ching's second as university president. His administrative team included physicist P. C. (Percy) Feng 馮秉銓 (1910–1980) as academic dean, linguist Wong Li 王力 (1900–1986) as dean of the College of Arts, and Henry Frank as dean of the College of Science. Frank was moreover the university's provost and, as noted, the resident director of the American Foundation. As such, he served as the intermediary between President Chen and the American trustees in New York. According to university historian Corbett, President Chen, in his hiring policy, favored Westerners "in English and the natural sciences, including anthropology, but not in economics,

---

1. Henry S. Frank to James M. Henry, Canton, 28 August 1949, Box 125, TLUA–HYL.
2. Hahn, Diary Report for August 1949, Maryknoll Mission Archives; Minutes of the Executive and Policy Advisory Committees, 20 September 1949, Folder 3243, Box 180, China College Files—Lingnan University, RG 11, United Board Archives, YDSL; Baker, *Flowing Ways*, p. 160.

Figure 9.1: Lingnan's commencement ceremony, 13 June 1949. From Folder 5806A, Box 405, RG 11, Special Collections, YDSL. Dean P. C. Feng is handing out diplomas, while President Chen Su-ching watches.

sociology, or history, where Chinese teachers were preferable because they could make specific applications to Chinese conditions with which they were more familiar than foreigners could be." Taking advantage of the political and military turmoil in North China, he was able to lure a number of prominent scholars to join him in the South. His prize recruits included the historian Chen Yinque (or Yinke) 陳寅恪 (1890–1969) and the mathematician Jiang Lifu 姜立夫 (1890–1978). As a result, Lingnan became known as one of the top universities in China. This was, in many respects, Lingnan's golden age.[3]

We arrived back on campus two weeks into the semester. My father resumed teaching and serving as head of the Western Languages Department. With Ruth Mack's departure, he became the only native speaker of English in the department. According to his new contract, his annual salary was to be (as it had been since 1947–1948) US$2,724, plus (as before) rent-free housing on campus, complete medical and dental care for him and his family, and "full transportation to the United States at the end of his present five-year term, or earlier if called home by the Trustees." In addition, "In case he should be called

---

3.   Corbett, *Lingnan University*, pp. 152–156; Li Ruiming (Lee Sui-ming), comp., *Lingnan daxue* [Lingnan University] (n.p.: Lingnan [daxue] choumu fazhan weiyuanhui, 1997), p. 117; Li and Hill, *Nanguo fenghuang*, p. 93; Steven Tung Au, *Lingnan Spirit Forever: A Mission in Transition, 1951–1990; From Trustees of Lingnan University to Lingnan Foundation* (New Haven: Lingnan Foundation, 2002), p. 3.

home by the Trustees, on account of the present situation in China," he and his family would be given a "regular furlough allowance, of approximately $4,200.00 a year."[4]

My mother, too, resumed working at Lingnan. In the immediate postwar period she had been a typist and stenographer for Henry Frank at the American Foundation office, but in 1946 she had been replaced by the confidential secretary sent from New York. After Jean Worcester's departure, however, Frank had been forced to type his own letters, because no one else was willing to come to China as Worcester's replacement due to the unsettled political and military situation. Consequently, within a week of our return to the campus, Frank approached my mother about "doing some correspondence for me." Thereafter, for the next twelve months, many of his typed letters to the New York office once again carried the typist tag "HSF:ckr." The 1949–1950 budget of the American trustees for the field staff provided for a full-time secretary in the American Foundation office, with an annual salary of US$1,200, or slightly less than half my father's salary.[5]

Meanwhile, there was, again, the issue of my schooling. The Western School at Lingnan, which had been revived for a couple of years (1947–1949), had ceased operations once more. So when we returned to Guangzhou, I was placed back in a Chinese school after having undergone two years of Western schooling. I was re-enrolled in the university's primary school, where I repeated fifth grade. Joining me in the Chinese school, in the same class, were two other former pupils from the Western School, Laura Chang and Marian Frank. Among our Chinese classmates were president Chen Su-ching's fourth son and chemistry professor Hoh Shai Kwong's second son; the latter was a close friend of mine. (Another close friend from before seems to have left, following his father's resignation as university president; the Lee family may have moved to Hong Kong.) Also in attendance at Lingnan's Chinese Primary School, though in lower grades, were Gilbert and Martha Baker's two children, David and Anne, and the daughters of entomology professor J. Linsley Gressitt. The Bakers were living in House No. 49, the next building from us and the very same house that Baker had lived in when he first taught at Lingnan in 1936. My sister, who was enrolled in the kindergarten, has "a vague memory of walking to school" with Anne Baker.[6]

On Friday, 14 October 1949, a month and a day after we arrived back on campus and two weeks after the formal proclamation in Beijing of the founding of the People's Republic of China, the Communist army, sweeping southward from Hunan and meeting little resistance, finally "liberated" Guangzhou. That afternoon, as the university's first social tea of the academic year at President Chen's house was winding down, attendees heard a loud explosion from across the river. The Nationalists, as they retreated, had blown up the Pearl River Bridge, the icon of republican Guangzhou, which had survived the Japanese war more or less intact. They offered no other opposition. As physicist Arthur Knipp wrote the next evening, "There has been a general feeling of relief all day that the changeover has taken place so quickly, apparently with little disorder in the city."

---

4.   James M. Henry, *Affirmation*, New York, n.d., in my personal collection.
5.   Henry S. Frank to James M. Henry, Canton, 19 September 1949, Box 125, and Details of Proposed [Field] Budget for 1 July 1949–30 June 1950, Box 150, TLUA–HYL.
6.   Henry S. Frank to James M. Henry, Canton, 28 November and 2 December 1949, Box 126, TLUA–HYL; Baker, *Flowing Ways*, p. 161; Janet Pinkowitz to ER, email communication, 27 April 2018. Another of our schoolmates, in the sixth grade, was Zhong Nanshan 鍾南山, who later became one of China's most prominent scientists; it was he who in 2003 "discovered" the SARS coronavirus and in 2020 raised the alarm on the virus that causes COVID-19. I have no personal recollection of him.

Figure 9.2: A contingent from Lingnan in the parade welcoming the Liberation of Guangzhou, 11 November 1949. From Folder 44, Box 3, Brownell Papers, University of Vermont Library.

Guangzhou's tenure as the national capital had lasted five and a half months. To celebrate their triumph, the Communists in the city held a day-long parade on 11 November.[7]

For a while, the Nationalists, who had retreated to Taiwan and still possessed an air force, were able to carry out punitive air raids against Guangzhou. As social scientist Ezra Vogel explains, "Because anti-aircraft facilities were almost non-existent during the first few months after Liberation, Kuomintang planes could come and go with virtual impunity." Father Hahn's Maryknoll Mission diary recorded four such bombardments in the winter and spring of 1949–1950. In late December 1949, he noted, "we watched a dive bomber swoop down from about six thousand feet and destroy a locomotive. . . . Sometimes the planes machine-gun and kill a few people, and one gets the impression that it is wanton." In mid-January 1950, "we watched a plane dive through the clouds and shoot a bus across the river. . . . Fourteen passengers were killed, and seventeen injured." In February, Father Hahn reported "almost daily sorties by Nationalist planes, with resultant air raid warnings and stifling of transportation and traffic." Finally, on 3 March came the biggest bombardment "so far": "it seems about 300 were killed and about 400 seriously injured. The target was a R.R. station, but most of the bombs missed their mark." In the same month, however, "the Communists were able to shoot down a Kuomintang plane and after that," according to Vogel, "the problem subsided." Indeed, Father Hahn,

---

7.   Excerpts from letter from Arthur R. Knipp to Mrs. Knipp, Canton, n.d. [October 1949], Folder 25, Box 2, and Henry C. Brownell, Personal diary, Folder 9, Box 3, Brownell Papers, University of Vermont Library.

in May 1950, confirmed that "there have been no bombings of Canton since the end of March." None of these bombardments hit the Lingnan campus.[8]

During the early years of the Communist regime, the country was divided into six administrative regions: Northeast China, North China, East China, South Central China, Southwest China, and Northwest China. As the map was drawn, Guangdong was placed in the South Central region, with its headquarters in Wuhan rather than Guangzhou. As education historian Ruth Hayhoe comments, "The dynamic southern coastal part of China, which had historically been both economically open and politically radical, seems to have been purposely marginalized in this administrative division of territory." Guangzhou city itself was until 1954 centrally administered from Beijing.[9]

The initial reaction at Lingnan to Communist rule was overwhelmingly positive. There was general satisfaction with the behavior of the victorious People's Liberation Army, which, according to a certain L. C. Lee, was "well trained, well disciplined, well organized and well officered. The soldiers though ill dressed and ill equipped are friendly, courteous and chivalrous. . . . They had done what the Kuomintang should have done." There was also general satisfaction that under the Communists the hyper-inflation that had ravaged the economy during the last years of Nationalist rule was quickly brought under control. Father Hahn, in his diary report of June 1950, wrote that "the currency is very stable, and is even improving slightly. Prices are low compared with last year, and also very steady." Moreover, the Pearl River Bridge was quickly repaired and reopened to traffic in November 1950.[10] It was to remain the only highway bridge over the river until 1967.

While the Communists' long-term aims were to revolutionize the society and the economy, their immediate task was to consolidate control and re-establish public order. During the first year or so they refrained from making major changes; according to Vogel, "the oft-repeated motto" of the time was "'Temporarily maintain the existing situation; introduce reforms gradually as necessary and feasible.'" Where Lingnan was concerned, as Ruth Hayhoe notes, "Private institutions and missionary institutions maintained their identities and received some state support over the first two to three years of the new regime, with the expectation that they would gradually adapt themselves to the new guidelines." At the same time, according to Jesse Gregory Lutz, they were "still permitted to receive fiscal aid from the West."[11]

Life for the Western personnel at Lingnan went on largely as before, with only a few changes. They were, for example, required in October 1949 to give up all the firearms in their possession. Thus, Henry Brownell recorded that he turned over "1 big revolver in wooden case, 2 med[ium] revolvers, [and] 1 tiny lady's revolver." It is likely that at this time my father surrendered the rifle and ammunition he had acquired during his stint with the OWI. The Westerners were also required in February 1950 to register with the

---

8.   Ezra F. Vogel, *Canton under Communism: Programs and Politics in a Provincial Capital, 1949–1968* (Cambridge, MA: Harvard University Press, 1969), pp. 61–62; Hahn, Diary Reports for December 1949, January 1950, February 1950, March 1950, and May 1950, Maryknoll Mission Archives.

9.   Ruth Hayhoe, *China's Universities, 1895–1995: A Century of Cultural Conflict* (New York and London: Garland Publishing, 1996), p. 143; Johnson and Peterson, *Historical Dictionary of Guangzhou and Guangdong*, p. 19.

10.   L. C. Lee to Mrs. . . . [*sic*], Canton, 30 November 1949, in Folder Correspondence (primarily to WWC), Box 2, Collection 1160, Cadbury Papers, Haverford College Library, and in Folder 37, Box 1, Brownell Papers, University of Vermont Library; Hahn, Diary Report for June 1950, Maryknoll Mission Archives; Vogel, *Canton under Communism*, pp. 80–82.

11.   Vogel, *Canton under Communism*, p. 71; Hayhoe, *China's Universities*, p. 74; Lutz, *China and the Christian Colleges*, p. 461.

new government, which for some involved long interrogations. Once possessed of their resident permits, they were "allowed to move freely within the city limits," though not to travel to other cities or to Hong Kong.[12]

Life on the Lingnan campus, too, went on largely as before. Reporting in December 1949, Father Hahn wrote, "Classes continued at the university with very little interruption." According to Gilbert Baker, "There was still . . . a degree of freedom in university life. . . . Church services continued as they had always done in Swasey Hall . . . The work of the theological college [where Baker taught] continued undisturbed . . . We had an uninterrupted academic year during which I was teaching [in Cantonese] New Testament and Church history."[13] As Provost Henry Frank wrote in early November 1949,

> There has been what I should call a normal amount of demonstration, and students and staff are naturally learning as much as they can about the principles of the new regime. This has been almost entirely extracurricular and the few classes which have been called off have been for meetings called in the city to dispel propaganda rumors spread by the old gang [the Guomindang] and announce broad outlines of policy. There have been plenty of slogans posted on the campus, and while one or two have denounced American imperialism it seems generally accepted that the American teachers here are not imperialists, and no effort I could make has been able to discover any change in attitude toward us.

Among the student activists at Lingnan was my cousin, Luo Ren, the second son of my mother's older sister, Chi Kin, who was then a senior in the Lingnan Middle School. By his own account, he had earlier joined a Communist underground cell that operated out of the basement of Swasey Hall as a charitable after-school program.[14]

Lingnan's primary school too seems to have been largely left alone during the 1949–1950 school year, with only a couple of changes introduced. One of them was the *yangge* 秧歌 (Rice-sprout Song), which was taught to the pupils—and to the university community at large—right after Liberation. A song-and-dance traditionally performed by North China peasants during the lunar New Year, it had been adopted by the Communists and popularized nationwide. The *yangge* purportedly had its origins in the movements and the singing of the peasants as they transplanted rice seedlings. Though ethnographer David Holm regards this origin story as "highly questionable," the song and dance that we at Lingnan were taught clearly depicted the ten stages of grain cultivation, from preparing the field to taking the harvest to the granary. The *yangge* was presented to us as a form of group calisthenics that was appropriate to "the beginning of a new age." In mid-November, Jane (Menut) Brownell (1886–1977), wife of the history professor, commented on the students' "practicing folk dances & folk songs ad infinitum & vociferously!"[15] The other change introduced by the Communists at our primary school came in the second

---

12. Corbett, *Lingnan University*, p. 160; Henry S. Frank to "All Members of the Western Staff," Canton, 20 October 1949 (with marginal notations by Brownell), Folder 37, Box 1, Henry C. Brownell to Mr. and Mrs. R. E. Montgomery, [Canton], 8 February 1950 and to "Lautenschlager," Canton, 2 May 1950, Folder 38, Box 1, Brownell Papers, University of Vermont Library.
13. Hahn, Diary Report for December 1949, Maryknoll Mission Archives; Baker, *Flowing Ways*, pp. 162–163.
14. Henry S. Frank to James M. Henry, Canton, 4 November 1949, Box 126, TLUA–HYL; Luo Ren, "Huohong de nianyue," pp. 5–9.
15. Lingnan daxue tiyu weiyuanhui [Athletics committee of Lingnan University], "Niu yang wuqu" 扭秧舞曲 [Performing the rice-sprout song and dance], 1 November 1949, a one-page instructional sheet, in my personal collection; Jane Brownell to Margaret [Hoffmann], Canton, 18 November 1949, Folder A-C (except Cadbury), Box 43, Collection No. 1192, Cadbury & Cadbury Papers, Haverford College Library; see also David Holm, "Folk Art as Propaganda: The Yangge Movement in Yan'an," in *Popular Chinese Literature and Performing Arts in the People's Republic of China*, ed. Bonnie S. McDougall (Berkeley: University of California Press, 1984), pp. 13–14, 24.

Figure 9.3: The *yangge* (Rice-sprout Song) performed in the Liberation parade, Guangzhou, 11 November 1949. From Folder 44, Box 3, Brownell Papers, University of Vermont Library.

semester of the school year. A new course, titled "General Political Knowledge" (*zhengzhi changshi* 政治常識), was added to the curriculum; at the same time, English was dropped as a secondary subject.

According to my report cards for the year, my academic record was far from stellar. In the fall semester, I did very well in English, scoring 90 out of 100 points, but regrettably English was not considered a core subject and so was not included in the computation of a student's grade point average (GPA). In my core subjects, I did well in arithmetic (79), but not so well in Mandarin Chinese (60), history (68), geography (62), science (60), art (68), music (72), and athletics (65), with 60 as a passing grade. My GPA for the semester was 66.6, and I ranked 19th out of 31 students in the second section (*yiban* 乙班) of the class. In the spring semester, I did about the same; though my GPA, 69.12, was slightly higher, and I was again ranked 19th, it was now out of a smaller section of 26. Overall, I had met the minimum GPA of 60 for promotion to sixth grade, except that I had failed the newly introduced subject of General Political Knowledge with a grade of 53! I would need to be re-examined in the subject before I could proceed. The teacher's comments about my behavior and character: "Lively and playful. Intelligent by nature. It's a pity he can't study positively."[16]

Meanwhile, even though there had been no sign that their people on the Lingnan campus were in any danger, the trustees in New York were worried. They had been concerned even before the Communists' arrival, when the US Consul had urged all Americans

---

16. ER's report cards, Lingnan primary school, fifth grade, 1949–1950, in my personal collection. My thanks to Wang Mansheng for help in reading my teacher's handwritten comments.

Figure 9.4: Instruction sheet for performing the *yangge* dance, issued by the Athletics Committee of Lingnan University, 1 November 1949.

Figure 9.5: Fifth-grade group exercise, Lingnan Primary School, 1949–1950, with me (because of my height) at the head of the boys' line. Watching from the stand are, possibly, my sister (with the braids) and, next to her, Sylvia and Becky Gressitt.

to leave before leaving himself. In late September 1949, the executive committee of the trustees had held a "very serious discussion as to whether or not the American staff should be ordered home." As James Henry, the American Director in New York, reported to Provost Henry Frank in Guangzhou, "in spite of some possible dissent, the consensus seemed definitely in favor of ordering the women and children as far as Hong Kong. There was perhaps an evenly divided opinion as to whether we should stop at women and children."[17]

Six months later, after the Communist takeover, James Henry was no longer quite so ambiguous or ambivalent. On 30 March 1950, in a personal letter to Henry Frank, he wrote, "If you want my sincere present opinion, it is that the American staff should be evacuated as soon as at all feasible. When I say this I am thinking particularly of Fred [Frederic Chewming Chang 曾朝明 (1905–1995)] and his family, the Gressitts, and the Hoffmanns, to say nothing of the Rhoadses and the Brownells. In other words, every family where a lady is involved." One of Henry's arguments for leaving was that with President Chen's hiring spree, Western professors were no longer needed for Lingnan to function. "Lingnan has reached such a stage of development that it would put the institution in no jeopardy whatever to be deprived of American physical participation for a shorter or a longer period. This is something of which we can be well proud."[18]

Replying immediately and at length, Henry Frank told the president of the Board of Trustees that it was still the opinion of all "the persons on the Trustees' payroll" that now was not the time for them to leave.

---

17. James M. Henry to Henry S. Frank, New York, 28 September 1949, Box 125, TLUA–HYL.
18. James M. Henry to Henry S. Frank, New York, 30 March 1950, Box 128, TLUA–HYL.

> We are not saying that the time will not come when we will want to leave . . . But . . . we think that departure now or planning now for departure in the summer, would be disastrously bad timing. . . . The attitude of the Government toward Lingnan seems to be entirely benevolent. . . . We have recently had our new residence certificates issued to us after a long delay which seems to have been largely a matter of insufficient or inefficient clerical assistance in the foreign affairs office of the police department. . . . there is no longer any question that the University could continue to exist and to operate if we all left. Of course it could. But . . . it would denude the English department and the Chemistry Department of professors.

In a later letter, Provost Frank spelled out the effects on the English and chemistry departments: "Howard [Rhoads] is the only western English teacher left as it is, and if Fred [Chang] and Frances [Spieth (1923–2009)] and I, or any of us, had to leave, a well balanced and efficient [chemistry] department would be messed up." He asked that "whatever result the Trustees wish to see, they leave to SC [President Chen Su-ching] and me the devising of ways of producing it." Indeed, a visiting Methodist missionary, writing to James Henry in July 1950, claimed that "the President and all the senior Chinese members of the staff [at Lingnan] are very keen on the Americans staying. They have stood by the Americans with a fine loyalty."[19]

However, soon after the end of Lingnan's first academic year under the Communists, the political situation changed dramatically as a result of the outbreak of the Korean War (1950–1953). After 1945 the Korean Peninsula had been liberated from the Japanese occupation but divided between a Communist North and a non-Communist South. On 25 June 1950, North Korea invaded South Korea, prompting the United States, supported by the United Nations, to come immediately to the aid of the South. In addition, the US interposed its Seventh Fleet in the Taiwan Strait, thus demonstrating their support of Chiang Kai-shek and the Nationalists against the Communists. America was now at war with China's Communist ally and neighbor, and, by intervening so directly in the ongoing Chinese civil war, possibly posed a threat to China itself.

The Chinese Communist Party responded to these concerns by launching, nationally, the Campaign to Suppress Counterrevolutionaries, which Vogel describes as "by far the most violent campaign in the first two decades of Communist rule," in the course of which millions were killed.[20] Concurrently, political attacks on the United States increased exponentially. In Guangzhou in July, Father Hahn wrote, "Last week was 'peace' week, celebrated by parades of people and soldiers . . . Next week is anti-aggression week. Parades and signs all over the city, directed in large part against the U.S. . . . [T]he people . . . are told, over and over again, about the cruel invasion of American hordes against the peace-loving, law-abiding, gentle people of North Korea." On 19 July, "at 8 P.M., Lingnan had its own 'anti-aggression' meeting, for Chinese only. A speaker was imported and talked un-opposed for several hours."[21]

Against this backdrop of rising anti-Americanism on the Lingnan campus, a "bombshell announcement" (in Father Hahn's words) was made on 21 July: "All the foreign

---

19. Henry S. Frank to Alfred Hayes, Canton, 17 April 1950, Folder Canton Hospital/Lingnan University, Box 3, Collection No. 1160, Cadbury Papers, Haverford College Library; Frank to James M. Henry, Canton, 4 July 1950, and Rev. W. H. Alton to Henry, Hong Kong, 20 July 1950, Box 130, TLUA–HYL. Spieth later married another chemist, Robert Connick.
20. Vogel, *Canton under Communism*, p. 63.
21. Hahn, Diary Report for July 1950, Maryknoll Mission Archives.

women and children and a number of the men are leaving for home," much as James Henry had recommended four months earlier. Thus, Fred Chang's family left for Hong Kong and the US in mid-August, as did Henry Frank's wife and daughter and Lin Gressitt's wife and three young daughters, though Chang, Frank, and Gressitt themselves all remained behind. Historian Henry Brownell, too, left, taking his wife with him and ending a forty-two-year career at Lingnan. According to Father Hahn, this exodus had cut the foreign population on campus in half, leaving only eleven foreigners on the staff.[22] These eleven (some with family members) were Gilbert Baker (Union Theological College, with wife and three children), Fred Chang (Chemistry), Henry Frank (Chemistry), Lin Gressitt (Entomology), Joseph Hahn (Engineering), William Hoffmann (Entomology, with wife), Arthur Knipp (Physics), Dr. Frank Oldt (Public Health), George N. Putnam (1909–1991, Sociology), Frances Spieth (Chemistry), and, of course, my father (with wife and two children). Of the eleven, seven were on the payroll of the American Trustees, and four (Baker, Oldt, Hahn, and Putnam) were not.

In view of the changed situation brought on by the American intervention in the Korean War and the rise of anti-Americanism, Henry Frank decided in late July, after "several long talks" with President Chen, to go to New York to confer in person with James Henry and the American trustees. In mid-August he applied to the Public Security Bureau for an exit permit and designated physics professor Arthur Knipp, who had been with Lingnan since 1910, to act in his absence as provost and the trustees' representative. Frank expected to receive his exit permit in a few days; instead, his application was repeatedly held in abeyance, because he, unlike his wife and daughter, was not yet prepared to leave China permanently. At the end of November, he still had not heard, and had "been living out of a suitcase for three and a half months."[23] At the same time, the trustees had also decided to send James Henry to Hong Kong, where he would wait for Henry Frank to come down from Guangzhou and where he could confer with various of Lingnan's Chinese directors.[24] Henry reached Hong Kong by air at the end of August.

Though my parents had opted to stay on, they nevertheless began making contingency plans. Unlike their American colleagues, they faced not one but two sets of problems. One, of course, was getting out of China, which at this time was not too difficult. Chinese citizens, like my mother, could depart and re-enter China freely, while foreigners, like my father (and my sister and me, since we were traveling on his US passport), had to apply for an exit permit, which at that time was freely granted in most cases so long as it did not involve re-entry. The other problem, which was unique to our family, was getting into the US. This was no difficulty for my father, nor for my sister and me, since it had been established that the two of us were American citizens. My mother, however, was a non-citizen and could not enter and stay in the US without an immigrant visa. (When my mother went to the US in 1948, she had done so as a Temporary Visitor and not as an immigrant.) By this time the Chinese Exclusion Act had been repealed, and Chinese immigration was governed by the national origins quota system. Under this system the

---

22. Hahn, Diary Reports for July and for August 1950, Maryknoll Mission Archives; Arthur R. Knipp to Ethel Montgomery, Canton, 16 August 1950, Box 130, TLUA–HYL; Jane C. Brownell to Mr. and Mrs. Lincoln Brownell, Canton, 9 August 1950, Folder 38, Box 1, Brownell Papers, University of Vermont Library.
23. Henry S. Frank, Canton, to James M. Henry, 22 July 1950, Box 130, and Joseph A. Hahn to the Most Rev. Raymond Lane, "Excerpts of a letter, November 1950," Box 131, TLUA–HYL.
24. James M. Henry to Tso Iu, New York, 3 August 1950, Box 130, TLUA–HYL.

annual quota for Chinese immigrants was a mere 105. Thus, if my mother were to go the United States, she would have to apply for a visa as a non-quota immigrant.

The visa had to be applied for in person at an American consulate. Since the consulate in Guangzhou had shut down, she would have to go to the consulate general in Hong Kong. Consequently, in the late summer and fall of 1950 my mother made at least three trips down to Hong Kong to confer with American consular officials about applying for an immigration visa. And she made these trips all by herself because, as James Henry later explained, "owing to the present political situation, Dr. Rhoads could not come from Canton to Hong Kong unless he was prepared to leave Canton permanently. As the University is still in great need of his services he is reluctant to leave just now."[25]

Some or all of my mother's solo trips coincided with James Henry's stay in Hong Kong from 30 August to 10 December. He had been her boss at Lingnan in prewar days, when he was the resident director of the American Foundation. She sought out his help. Thus on 9 September, Henry wrote a letter to the US Immigration and Naturalization Service in Washington in support of her petition for an immigration visa. He also asked Olin Wannamaker, who had returned to the New York office as the acting American director while Henry was abroad, to write similarly, which he did on 18 September. When two months later my mother still had not received a reply from the US immigration authorities, she appealed to Henry once more for assistance, and he accordingly requested that the New York office make further inquiries in Washington on her behalf. Only then, in mid-November, did she find out that her petition had, in fact, been approved by the Immigration Service on 19 October and authorized by the State Department on 23 October. The problem was that the paperwork had been "mailed in the State Department Pouch to the American Consulate General, Hong Kong," but because the Hong Kong consulate was then "a mad house in these matters," it had been temporarily misplaced. My mother had been granted, as she had hoped, non-quota status as the wife of an American citizen. The only thing left to do, after she learned that her application had been approved, was to appear at the consulate to obtain the actual visa.[26]

During her several visits to Hong Kong, my mother, in addition to consulting with Henry about her personal visa problem, served as his informant and as an intermediary between him and Henry Frank, who was still stuck in Guangzhou. It was a job for which she was well-suited, for besides having worked for James Henry before the war, she had, more recently, worked for Henry Frank as well. In early September she told Henry "that in one of the leading HK Chinese papers was a terrific denunciation of Americans & the American Foundation of Lingnan by Dr. Lin—plant pathologist on the campus." ("Dr. Lin" was, almost certainly, Lin Kongxiang 林孔湘 [1910–1985], a 1941 Cornell PhD). And in mid-November, "after listening to & querying Mrs. Rhoads," Henry asked her to convey instructions to Frank on what to do next.[27] My mother's repeated trips to Hong Kong and her contacts with Henry did not go unnoticed by the Communist authorities in Guangzhou. According to Henry, she was "apparently under police surveillance," and according to Father Hahn, she had been "followed on the [Hong Kong or Macau]

25. James M. Henry to US Commissioner of Immigration and Naturalization, Hong Kong, 9 September 1950, Box 130, TLUA–HYL.

26. James M. Henry to ODW, Hong Kong, 9 September 1950, Box 130, Henry to Ethel Montgomery, Hong Kong, 19 November 1950, ODW, New York, to Henry, 24 November 1950 and to Kan Koam Ching 簡鑑清, 11 December 1950, Box 131, TLUA–HYL.

27. James M. Henry to ODW, Hong Kong, 9 September 1950, Box 130, and 15 November 1950, Box 131, TLUA–HYL.

boat, and questioned."[28] Of course, my mother was not the only person James Henry consulted during the more than three months he was in Hong Kong. Others with whom he conferred included Lingnan staff members Fred Chang, Tong Fuk Cheung, and Hoh Shai Kwong, members of the Chinese Board of Directors and, on at least one occasion, President S. C. Chen, who at Henry Frank's request had gone to Hong Kong in his stead to discuss whether the American teachers should stay or leave.[29]

Meanwhile, despite the tensions in US–China relations, Lingnan's new school year (1950–1951), the second under the Communists, had begun on an optimistic note. As President Chen wrote in October 1950, in a personal letter to former history professor Brownell, "The University started off very encouragingly with an enrolment of over 1400 . . . The attitudes of the government towards Christian schools, especially universities[,] are very much better." (Better than what, he didn't say.) Father Hahn, the Maryknoll missionary, likewise observed that "things here are still excellent for foreigners. Outside of the police restrictions on any kind of travel, things are very normal. . . . There is a restriction on in middle schools, in that they may not hold any religious services in such schools. But universities are not yet so affected."[30] Even so, my parents decided that I should drop out of the Lingnan Primary School. With the departure of the Frank family and the Chang family, I would have been the only child of the Western staff in my class. (And in any case, I may not have made good on my deficiencies in political studies.) The Bakers, too, withdrew their two young children from the school.[31] Instead, in the fall of 1950 my sister and I were home-schooled by our mother, using the curriculum and texts from the Calvert School of Baltimore. I would have been using sixth-grade materials.

The celebration of October First, the first anniversary of the proclamation of the People's Republic, went off without any outburst of anti-Americanism. According to Acting Provost Arthur Knipp, "Sept. 30th–October 4th was a university holiday. On the afternoon of Saturday, the 30th, about 400 Lingnan bicyclists joined in the bicycle parade in the city. On the 1st many of the students and staff took part in the walking parade on this side of the island [i.e., Ho Nam Island]."[32]

Less than a month later, however, the political atmosphere on the Lingnan campus, which up until then had been remarkably relaxed, tightened up significantly, following China's surprise entry into the Korean War in support of their Communist neighbor and ally. American and UN troops, hoping to wipe out the North Korean regime, had advanced northward up the Korean Peninsula toward the Chinese border at the Yalu River. In response, Chinese troops, who were nominally "volunteers," poured across the border in late October and began pushing the Americans back. China and America were now at war.

A nationwide political campaign to "Oppose America, Aid [North] Korea" (Kang Mei yuan Chao 抗美援朝) was started up. In Guangzhou, classes were cancelled on 3 November and students and teachers, including those at Lingnan, were required to

---

28. James M. Henry to Ethel Montgomery, Hong Kong, 28 November 1950, Box 131, TLUA–HYL; Hahn, Diary Report for December 1950 (also first part of January 1951), p. 10, Maryknoll Mission Archives.
29. "Chen Xujing nianpu jianbian" [A brief chronological biography of Chen Su-ching], in *Zhongguo jindai sixiangjia wenku—Chen Xujing juan* [A library of modern Chinese thinkers: Chen Su-ching], comp. Tian Tong (Beijing: Zhongguo renmin daxue chubanshe, 2015), p. 559.
30. S. C. Chen to Henry C. Brownell, Canton, [October 1950], Folder 38, Box 1, Brownell Papers, University of Vermont Library; Hahn, Diary Report for August 1950, Maryknoll Mission Archives.
31. Baker, *Flowing Ways*, p. 164.
32. Arthur R. Knipp to John A. Christie and Trustees, Hong Kong, 7 October 1950, Box 131, TLUA–HYL.

attend a three-hour citywide mass meeting at a big athletic stadium in the city to listen to the governor of the province, Ye Jianying 葉劍英, hold forth on the current international situation and the aggressive designs of the American imperialists. The forty thousand in attendance responded with loud vows to stop admiring and fearing the United States.[33] At the end of the month, the staff, students, and workers at Lingnan, like those at two other private universities in the city, issued a statement endorsing the campaign. They accused American imperialists of attempting to enslave the Chinese people, much as the Japanese had tried to do. "We teachers, students, staff, and workers must intensify our studies and heighten our awareness."[34] By then, James Henry, still in Hong Kong, had told Henry Frank flatly that "I definitely favor all the Amerfound staff leaving as soon as they get permits." Indeed, at around this time several of Lingnan's Westerners, including Gilbert Baker's family and Lin Gressitt, submitted applications for exit permits.[35] But the permits, even for those willing to leave permanently, were no longer being freely granted.

The authorities in Guangzhou went on a witch hunt for concealed radio transmitters. On the Lingnan campus, according to chemistry professor Frances Spieth, "anti-sabotage posters are the most frequent ones of political import recently—such things as TURN IN YOUR CONCEALED RADIO TRANSMITTER NOW!" In late November, "anyone having a transmitter or parts of one," Father Hahn wrote, was required to register it with the police. In addition, the police conducted a thorough search of the homes of the eleven Western faculty members still on campus. As described by Hahn, the search party, numbering fifteen, was led by a woman cadre. Because it was raining very hard, "[most] searchers stayed at Dr. Rhoads' house and rested, while the girl in charge, an assistant and a guard with a gun made the rounds." Arriving at the house in the Model Village that Hahn shared with Father Putnam, "They examined everything very carefully, tapping the walls, looking through closets, inside of desks, and we wrote down a list of all radio parts."[36] Though I have no recollection of it, presumably their search of our house was no less thorough. The searchers were looking for transmitters; they seemed to have left receivers alone.

It was at the beginning of December that, according to chemistry professor Fred Chang, the anti-American campaign, which "had been mounting in intensity for several weeks without much apparent effect on the campus," really took off. In Guangzhou, the first week of December was declared as "a week to publicize 'Oppose America, Aid Korea'"; it culminated in a big citywide parade on 9 December protesting American imperialism and celebrating the recapture of the North Korean capital, Pyongyang, from the Americans.[37] At Lingnan, classes were repeatedly cancelled to allow students to listen to speeches, to demonstrate, to put up posters, and to denounce their American professors. From 10 December on, the denunciations "began to include poster accusations of individual Americans, gradually including those resident on the campus." Among those

33. Frances [Spieth] to JC [John A. Christie], Canton, 4 November 1950, Box 131, TLUA–HYL; Hahn, Diary Report for November 1950, Maryknoll Mission Archives; "Fan-Mei qinlue dongyuan dahui" 反美侵略動員大會 [A mass meeting to mobilize against American aggression], *Nanfang ribao*, 4 November 1950, p. 2.

34. "Guangzhou gexiao fenfen juxing dongyuan" 廣州各校紛紛舉行動員 [Guangzhou's various colleges one by one initiate mobilization], *Nanfang ribao*, 27 November 1950, p. 1.

35. James M. Henry to ODW, Hong Kong, 15 November 1950 and to Ethel Montgomery, Hong Kong, 15 November 1950, Box 131, TLUA–HYL; Hahn, Diary Report for November 1950, Maryknoll Mission Archives.

36. Frances [Spieth] to JC [John A. Christie], Canton, 4 November 1950, Box 131, TLUA–HYL; Hahn, Diary Report for November 1950, Maryknoll Mission Archives.

37. Fred Chang to ODW, Hong Kong, 10 January 1951, Box 132, TLUA–HYL; *Nanfang ribao*, 1 December 1950, p. 1, and 10 December, p. 1.

accused on the 12th was my father; he, along with William Hoffmann and Lin Gressitt, were criticized "on a large bulletin board" for their "pro-American sentiments." On the 13th Arthur Knipp, Frances Spieth, Joseph Hahn, and Henry Frank were similarly denounced, with Frank singled out as a spy and his predecessor as provost, James Henry, as a super-spy.[38] Henry, who had just left Hong Kong on 10 December to return to the United States, had indeed served in the Office of Strategic Services during the last years of the Pacific War.

Also on 13 December, members of Lingnan's Academic Council (Xiaowu weiyuan-hui 校務委員會), all of them Chinese, issued a statement expressing outrage at a recent speech by Ambassador Warren Austin to the United Nations. In the speech praising "the traditional friendship of the United States for China," Austin had cited as partial evidence "the thirteen colleges established by American Protestant missions," including, specifically, Lingnan University. The Academic Council's statement, while acknowledging the value of friendship between the people of China and the people of the United States, voiced steadfast opposition to American imperialists. It called on all faculty, students, staff, and workers of Lingnan to participate in the Oppose America, Aid Korea campaign. Heading the list of signers of the statement were President S. C. Chen and the Dean of Academic Affairs, P. C. Feng. By this time, according to Acting Provost Arthur Knipp, "We [foreigners] were advised to discontinue meeting with classes. From then on college workmen would do nothing at all for us. Also from then on, except in rare cases, we saw nothing of our Chinese colleagues."[39]

This virulent phase of the anti-American campaign at Lingnan came to a climax with two days of public accusations on 14–15 December. These mass meetings, with reporters and photographers from the city in attendance, were held on the spacious lawn in front of Swasey Hall at the center of the campus and included some 1,700 "students, teachers, workers, and villagers." The first day's meeting opened with a short speech by President Chen, who read out the statement issued the previous day by the Academic Council. Dean Feng followed with a denunciation of American imperialists for various criminal acts and called on everyone to carry out the work of the Oppose America, Aid Korea campaign. Then, according to chemistry professor Fred Chang (based on second-hand reports), "the meeting was thrown open to the public and everyone with a grievance real or fancied against an American or had any knowledge of American 'aggression' was invited to the table [or lectern] to accuse. All the charges which had appeared on the posters were made [again] at this meeting in addition to many more. Dr. [James] Henry got a good share of the mud-slinging told in most fantastically imaginative stories." Also denounced by name at this and the following day's meeting were William Cadbury, Frank Oldt, Henry Brownell, my father, William Hoffmann, Arthur Knipp, Frances Spieth, Henry Frank, and Joseph Hahn, even though Henry, Cadbury, and Brownell were no longer on campus. Not every Westerner on the Lingnan faculty, however, was accused; Maryknoll missionary

---

38. Fred Chang to ODW, Hong Kong, 10 January 1951, Box 132, and Henry Frank, The Past Year at Lingnan, n.p., 26 April 1951, Box 143, TLUA–HYL; Arthur R. Knipp to ODW, Hong Kong, 8 February 1951, Box 132 (microfilm Ms44, Reel 24), Trustees of Lingnan University Archives, YDSL; Hahn, Diary Report for December 1950 . . . , pp. 1–2, Maryknoll Mission Archives.

39. "Dui Aositing wumie ti yanzhong kangyi" 對奧斯汀污衊提嚴重抗議 [Strongly oppose [Warren] Austin's slander], *Nanfang ribao*, 14 December 1950, p. 1; Arthur R. Knipp to ODW, Hong Kong, 8 February 1951, Box 132 (microfilm Ms44, Reel 24), Trustees of Lingnan University Archives, YDSL.

and sociologist George Putnam, who was reputedly well liked by his students, was not, nor were Fred Chang, a Chinese American, and Gilbert Baker, a Briton.[40]

In my father's case, according to the account in Guangzhou's official newspaper, *Nanfang ribao* 南方日報 (Southern Daily), he was identified (as were others) as an "American reactionary professor" and described as "someone who looked down upon Chinese people, especially Chinese women." An engineering student by the name of Mao criticized him for having included "pornography" in his teaching materials. According to Mao, my father had assigned erotic literature in order to dull the students' senses. Mao said that, embarrassed by such shameless pornographic books, he had ripped them to shreds during class. Without offering any evidence, he also accused my father of "frequently beating his Chinese wife." Furthermore, after beating her, my father allegedly demanded, "What equality? How can a Chinese person be equal to me?" After Mao had spoken, a political science instructor named Zhong claimed that my father had made "absurd reactionary" comments, such as "The Communist Party is our enemy; you [Chinese] people cannot win, because we have the atom bomb." In a statement issued at the end of a subsequent accusation meeting, my father was again singled out for denunciation. Here he was criticized for another "absurd reactionary" statement—that Taiwan was not China's and in the past had belonged to Japan.[41]

At the two mass meetings, my father and most of the other American professors were denounced in absentia. Two, however, were hauled before the assembly for direct interrogation. One, at the first meeting, was the entomologist Lin Gressitt, who was quizzed about his work with insects and asked why he had mailed specimens of his insects abroad (to the University of California); he was also criticized for rudeness toward employees at the university's post office. The other person who was interrogated in person was Henry Frank, who, at the second meeting, was asked about the work of the American Foundation, of which he was the resident director. Prior to his appearance, someone from the Medical School had criticized the foundation for providing the Western faculty with living quarters that were "beautiful and spacious" while some of the Chinese faculty had had to rent lodging off campus. Frank was also pressed about his personal views on current East Asian affairs and denounced for having been "an adviser to the [Japanese] puppet provincial government" during the war, perhaps in reference to Frank's membership in the committee that had mediated between the American internees and their Japanese captors at the Stanley internment camp in Hong Kong. In both instances, Gressitt's and Frank's answers, given in English and translated into Chinese, "were shouted down as inadequate or insincere." Neither man, however, was physically abused.[42]

The accusation meetings concluded after two days with a proclamation that henceforth the university would have a new school song, a new school emblem, and a new

---

40. Fred Chang to ODW, Hong Kong, 10 January 1951, Box 132, TLUA–HYL; Hahn, Diary Report for December 1950 . . . , pp. 2–4, Maryknoll Mission Archives; "Lingda zuo kai kongsu dahui" 嶺大昨開控訴大會 [A big denunciation meeting at Lingnan University yesterday], *Nanfang ribao*, 15 December 1950, p. 2, and "Kongsu Meidi fenzi bachi Lingda" 控訴美帝份子把持嶺大 [Denunciations of American imperialist elements dominate Lingnan University], *Nanfang ribao*, 16 December 1950, p. 2.

41. "Lingda zuo kai kongsu dahui," *Nanfang ribao*, 15 December 1950, p. 2; "Lingda quanti shisheng yuangong fabiao liang xuanyan" 嶺大全體師生員工發表兩宣言 [The faculty, students, staff and workers issue two proclamations], *Nanfang ribao*, 16 December 1950, p. 2.

42. "Lingda zuo kai kongsu dahui," *Nanfang ribao*, 15 December 1950, p. 2, and "Kongsu Meidi fenzi bachi Lingda," *Nanfang ribao*, 16 December 1950, p. 2; Fred Chang to ODW, Hong Kong, 10 January 1951, Box 132, TLUA–HYL; Wayne C Gagné, "J. Linsley Gressitt: His Contributions to Science and Conservation" (June 1982), https://scholarspace.manoa.hawaii.edu/bitstream/10125/18436/1/fourth-73-75.pdf (accessed 1 December 2020).

school anniversary, which henceforth would be 14 December, marking the day Lingnan had "turned over" (*fanshen* 翻身) and had thrown off "all US 'domination' and influence." Afterwards, the assembled masses went on a noisy procession around the campus. The demonstrators, "singing Communist songs, and shouting and screaming," made their way to "all the houses of the American staff." At Father Hahn's in the Model Village, "they stopped outside our house, and for about ten minutes kept screaming my name and ordering me out." According to Hoffmann, who lived nearby, "Just ahead of the parade a group of students came with large anti-American posters which were plastered on the doors and windows of all the foreign houses."[43]

The anti-American campaign also targeted some members of the Chinese faculty and staff who were deemed too closely aligned with the Americans. The most prominent Chinese victim on the Lingnan campus was Lee Sing Wah 李聖華, the newly appointed university chaplain. He came under attack beginning on 10 December, when eighteen unnamed but self-styled Chinese Christians wrote to the *Nanfang ribao* exposing him as "an accomplice of the American imperialists and the Chiang [Kai-shek] bandit gang."[44] Also attacked were Tong Fuk Cheung, of the American Foundation office, and Hoh Shai Kwong, of the Chemistry Department. All three men were arrested in December, concurrent with the accusation meetings, and jailed. According to William Hoffmann, writing in late January 1951, "No one has been permitted to see Tong nor Hoh . . . Nobody on the outside knows the charges against them, but many people surmise that it is because they saw Dr. Henry in H.K."[45] My mother had worked under Tong Fuk Cheung when she was James Henry's secretary at the American Foundation in the 1930s. Hoh Shai Kwong was a close family friend and father of my primary school classmate and companion. By this time my parents had told me to stop associating with my Chinese playmates lest I bring more trouble on them and their families. Hoh and Tong at this time were criticized for their associations with the Americans. Later on, Hoh (and perhaps Tong as well) were also accused of having collaborated with the Japanese occupiers during the war. The two men, it may be recalled, had been ordered then by Provost James Henry to remain on the Lingnan campus and "cooperate with the puppets in every way . . . to ensure a minimum of destruction." Hoh was imprisoned for thirty months.[46]

Following the accusation meetings, classes were again cancelled, and the students were required to listen to lectures on land reform, to take part in small-group discussions, and to participate in the sometimes violent program of land redistribution. They were also encouraged to volunteer to fight the Americans in Korea.[47] My cousin Luo Ren, who was now an English major in his first year at Lingnan, was one of those who answered such patriotic calls to service. He and fourteen of his schoolmates (including his future wife) were recruited and sent to a two-year Russian language program in Urumqi to be retrained as translators just as China was embarking on a program of "learning from the

---

43. "Kongsu Meidi fenzi bachi Lingda," *Nanfang ribao*, 16 December 1950, p. 2; Hahn, Diary Report for December 1950 . . . , p. 4, Maryknoll Mission Archives; Fred Chang to ODW, Hong Kong, 10 January 1951, and William E. Hoffmann to Trustees, Hong Kong, 26 January 1951, Box 132, TLUA–HYL.

44. Letter to the Editor, *Nanfang ribao*, 15 December 1950, p. 2; for subsequent attacks on Lee Sing Wah, see *Nanfang ribao*, 16 December, p. 2, 21 December, p. 2, 22 December, p. 1, and 24 December, p. 1. Lee subsequently wrote about the activities that caused him trouble; see Li Shenghua, "Lingnan daxue de zongjiao huodong" [Lingnan University's religious activities], *Guangzhou wenshi ziliao*, no. 13 (1964): 86–101, esp. pp. 98–101.

45. Hahn, Diary Report for December 1950 . . . , p. 3, Maryknoll Mission Archives; William E. Hoffmann to Trustees, Hong Kong, 26 January 1951, Box 132, TLUA–HYL.

46. Au, *Lingnan Spirit Forever*, p. 65.

47. Hahn, Diary Report for December 1950 . . . , p. 5, Maryknoll Mission Archives.

advanced experiences of the Soviet Union." Departing Guangzhou on 2 February 1951, he and his wife were destined to spend the next thirty years in Xinjiang.[48]

The anti-American demonstrations on campus in early and mid-December had made it amply clear, if it had not been clear before, that the Westerners could no longer remain at Lingnan. Recognizing the situation, the Board of Trustees in New York on 5 December sent a cable "instructing" Henry Frank to withdraw "all our personnel" at the "earliest possible" moment.[49] In response, on 11 December, on the eve of the two-day accusation meetings, all those Westerners on the Lingnan teaching staff "who had not already done so"—including us, no doubt—submitted applications for exit permits. The requested date of departure (according to Father Hahn's diary) was 22 December.[50] The day passed without result.

Meanwhile, life for the remaining foreigners, as they waited for their applications for exit permits to be acted on, became quite difficult. Their homes were repeatedly searched. According to Hoffmann, "On Dec. 22 most foreign houses at Lingnan got a thorough searching from members of the Ko On Kuk [公安局, Public Security Bureau]. Prior to that, all but three or four houses were searched by the Ko On Kuk—presumably for transmitting sets. On Dec. 22 they took the radio of Dr. Oldt and also that of Dr. Knipp, but left those belonging to Drs. Frank and Rhoads." At the house shared by the two Maryknoll fathers, the search lasted all day, from 10:00 in the morning until 7:30 in the evening, in the course of which the police "took out desk drawers and looked at the underside of them" in search of contraband (such as radio transmitters and firearms), and they accused and interrogated Father Hahn as a spy.[51]

During one campus search, more than one hundred antique rifles and some hand grenades were discovered in the basement and attic of Grant Hall, which housed the university's administrative offices. (It is possible that these firearms were so useless that they had not been turned in to the authorities earlier.) On 23 December, all the American professors were summoned to President Chen's house; from there, they were marched under guard and "in full view of the students and Chinese faculty" to the university's South Gate, where they were photographed standing behind a big pile of rifles. Afterwards, back at the president's house, a police official demanded that the assembled Americans sign "a paper to the effect that since this was an American university we were responsible for the guns." Provost Frank responded that Lingnan had not been an "American university" since 1928. In the end, the Americans acquiesced to a statement that "it was a criminal offence not to have reported these guns and that Lingnan [not the Americans] was responsible."[52] (The incriminating photograph did not appear in the *Nanfang ribao*; it is unclear if it was ever published.)

---

48. [Luo Ren], "Gan ai he gan fandui: diao aiqi Chen Jielian" 敢愛和敢反對：悼愛妻陳潔蓮 [Dare to love and dare to resist: Mourning my loving wife, Chen Jielian], typescript in my personal collection.

49. Minutes of Semi-Annual Meeting, 5 December 1950, Folder 3244, Box 180, China College Files—Lingnan University, RG 11, United Board Archives, YDSL; ODW to James M. Henry, New York, 5 December 1950, Box 131, TLUA–HYL.

50. Henry S. Frank to Amerfound, 11 December 1950, cablegram, Box 131, TLUA–HYL; Hahn, Diary Report for December 1950 . . . , p. 1, Maryknoll Mission Archives.

51. William E. Hoffmann to Trustees, Hong Kong, 26 January 1951, Box 132, TLUA–HYL; Hahn, Diary Report for December 1950 . . . , p. 7, Maryknoll Mission Archives.

52. Baker, *Flowing Ways*, p. 166; Hahn, Diary Report for December 1950 . . . , p. 9, Maryknoll Mission Archives; Arthur R. Knipp to ODW, Hong Kong, 8 February 1951, Box 132 (microfilm Ms44, Reel 24), Trustees of Lingnan University Archives, YDSL.

It must have been around this time that my father discovered that, though he had turned in to the Communist authorities the rifle he had kept from his days with the OWI, he had failed to turn in all of the ammunition. Instead of confessing to his oversight, which probably would have raised more questions with the Communists, he disposed of the bullets. One night, when it was dark, we stealthily buried them in our yard. They may still be there now.

Finally, on 26 December, the day after Christmas, a slew of "exit declarations" (*lijing shengming* 離境聲明) began appearing in the *Nanfang ribao*. These declarations stated that the named foreigner planned to leave the country "within a few days" and that he or she had applied for an exit permit from the Public Security Bureau of the Guangzhou municipal government. Anyone with a financial or any other sort of claim against the foreigner had seven days from the publication of the notice to come settle it. Each declaration gave the foreigner's name and address. Those posting such declarations included, among the Lingnan contingent, Gilbert Baker, Frank Oldt, and Frances Spieth.[53] Other exit declarations, including my father's, may have appeared in another Guangzhou newspaper, such as the *Lianhe bao* 聯合報 (United Daily).

On 29 December, "the secret police descended upon the campus again." This time, at Father Hahn's house, they discovered a wall safe they had overlooked previously, and were quite angry at the Maryknoll priests. And at Hoffmann's house, "They were watching mostly for incriminating literature and pictures."[54] Also on the 29th, American assets in China were frozen. At Lingnan, according to Father Hahn, "We had to list every article down to the 'last toothpick.' No money could be drawn out of the bank." This came two weeks after a similar move by the US government, which "froze all Chinese communist assets in the United States and made it unlawful to remit funds to mainland China without special license."[55]

At the beginning of January 1951, all the remaining foreigners in Guangzhou (numbering about two hundred) were required to apply for a six-month extension of their residence permits, which had expired at year's end. For this they had to go to the central police station in Guangzhou city, fill out a form (in Chinese), and submit to an interview (conducted in Mandarin Chinese). The summons for the Americans at Lingnan came on 6 January. According to Father Hahn, "Most of the interviews lasted about forty-five minutes, but some lasted several hours." Despite his earlier run-in with Public Security, Hahn himself did not find the interview difficult.[56] Otherwise, they waited. As one of the Americans—possibly Arthur Knipp—wrote his family, "We are residing quietly and normally in our various homes on the campus, having plenty of time for reading and study and walking."[57]

Although their "exit declarations," published at the end of December, had suggested that they would be departing in "a few days," it was not until nearly a month later, on

---

53. *Nanfang ribao*, 26 December 1950, p. 5.

54. Hahn, Diary Report for December 1950 . . . , p. 9, Maryknoll Mission Archives; William E. Hoffmann to Trustees, Hong Kong, 26 January 1951, Box 132, TLUA–HYL.

55. Hahn, Diary Report for December 1950 . . . , p. 9, Maryknoll Mission Archives; Lutz, *China and the Christian Colleges*, p. 467.

56. Hahn, Diary Report for December 1950 . . . , p. 10, Maryknoll Mission Archives; Arthur R. Knipp to ODW, Hong Kong, 8 February 1951, Box 132 (microfilm Ms44, Reel 24), Trustees of Lingnan University Archives, YDSL.

57. Excerpts of a letter from an American staff member to his family, 7 January 1951, reproduced in *Lingnan News Bulletin*, no. 4 (22 January 1951), Folder Last names L, Box 25, Collection No. 1192, Cadbury & Cadbury Papers, Haverford College Library.

20 January, that the first Westerners at Lingnan were actually permitted to leave. (Fred Chang had managed to escape to Hong Kong on his own in mid-December.)[58] The first to go were Martha Baker and her three children and Frank Oldt of the Medical School. (For some reason, Mrs. Baker's husband, Gilbert, was not allowed to leave with her and their children.) They were followed by William Hoffmann and his wife Winifred and Frances Spieth on the 21st, Fathers Hahn and Putnam on the 22nd, and Lin Gressitt on the 23rd. Then, without explanation, the departures ceased, not to be resumed for another ten days, when on 3 February our family, together with Gilbert Baker, were finally allowed to leave. The last to go, the following day, were the two officers of the American Foundation, Henry Frank and Arthur Knipp, who had earlier taken over Frank's administrative duties while Frank awaited his exit permit.[59] Their departures came two days before the Chinese New Year, when, by tradition, accounts were settled.

In those last six or eight weeks before we left, my mother again played an important role as an intermediary, this time between the remaining Westerners and the Chinese authorities, on and off campus. The detention of Tong Fuk Cheung and Hoh Shai Kwong in mid-December was an obvious warning to members of the Chinese faculty and staff to keep away from the Americans. Previously President Chen Su-ching had had cordial relations with his Western colleagues. According to William Hoffmann, "The Pres. and Dr. Frank have got on famously and Dr. Frank has consulted him on everything." But around the time of the denunciation meetings, over the first of which he had presided, President Chen "told Dr. Frank he believed it would be better if they did not see each other any more." (When, however, Frank was about to leave, President Chen did stop by his house to bid him farewell.) Into this breach between Chen and Frank stepped my mother. "Since then," according to Hoffmann, "Mrs. Rhoads has been the go-between, in her usual efficient manner." Frank later confirmed that the work of his office "would have been difficult, if not impossible, to carry on except for her help, as other Chinese persons in Lingnan University were (justifiably) afraid to have contact with me for fear of the possible consequences to them of helping an American whom the students had publicly declared to be an 'imperialist element.'"[60]

Moreover, according to Hoffmann, writing soon after his arrival in Hong Kong, "She also, and particularly recently, has helped much with the details relating to exit permits, etc." Again, Frank confirmed that "all of the Americans who have recently been permitted to come out from Lingnan feel that they owe Mrs. Rhoads a great deal of gratitude for the assistance she gave, under conditions of considerable tension and real risk to herself, in the arrangements necessary for their departure." For example, my mother may have helped them write their Chinese-language "exit declarations" and place them in the news-paper, and she may have translated for them when they were interviewed (in Chinese) for the renewal of their residence permits. Bearing in mind all her assistance, Hoffmann wrote in the days between his departure and ours, "We hope it does not complicate her

---

58. Fred Chang to ODW, Hong Kong, 10 January 1951, Box 132, TLUA–HYL.
59. Hahn, Diary Report for December 1950 . . . , p. 10, Maryknoll Mission Archives; Henry S. Frank to Amerfound, cablegram, Hong Kong, 5 February 1951, Box 132, TLUA–HYL.
60. William E. Hoffmann to Trustees, Hong Kong, 26 January 1951, and Henry S. Frank to American Consulate General, Hong Kong, [Hong Kong], 10 February 1951, Box 132, TLUA–HYL; Austin Frank, personal communication, 2 September 2020.

situation in anyway [*sic*]." Indeed, this may well have been the reason why we were the next to the last, among the Lingnan contingent, to be allowed to leave.[61]

The departure itself from Guangzhou was hurried and hectic. The evacuees, with no advance notice, were given their exit permits the morning of one day and expected to depart the next. Before they could leave their homes, however, their belongings were subject to a search by groups of militant students. In William Hoffmann's case, the evening before his departure, "ever[y] piece of baggage was minutely upset, and everything unfolded, untied, shaken, and otherwise investigated. . . . So we had from 10:00 p.m. till 5:30 the next morning, to repack everything, by lamp light." The luggage was then taken by China Travel Service from the campus to the Guangzhou train station. There the belongings were inspected again before they were allowed to be loaded onto a train.[62] In the case of our family, we had accumulated, as my father put it, "a fair amount of stuff . . . over the past fourteen years," including "a few small pieces of blackwood furniture and some fifty odd pieces of Chinese porcelain and pottery" and "six boxes of books" as well as "the usual collection of blankets, sheets, towels, quilts, etc. for a family of four plus a few household utensils." It is likely that we had transferred some or most of this "stuff" out to Hong Kong prior to our departure from the Lingnan campus. When we eventually left for the States, we shipped altogether "ten [large] nailed boxes in addition to our five trunks and hand baggage."[63]

As the evacuees departed Guangzhou on one of the four trains that went to Shum Chun (Shenzhen) each morning, they passed through (in Gilbert Baker's words) "the familiar landmarks and stations of South China: the lychee trees of Cang Sheng [增城], the great bridge over the East River at Shi Lung [石龍], the rolling hills and the bamboo groves as we approached the border." At Shum Chun their luggage was searched a third time. Only then could they walk across the bridge to Lo Wu and Hong Kong. As Father Hahn wrote, "Rolls of barbed wire stretched across the bridge, with an opening at each end. What a difference to see the nattily dressed Chinese officers on the Hong Kong side compared with the sloppy uniforms of the Communists. It was like coming into a new world."[64]

My parents never said how they felt about leaving China. I don't believe that they shared Father Hahn's apparent relief and happiness to be out of the country. For both my parents the previous fourteen years had been the most exciting and meaningful of their lives. Despite all the wartime trials and tribulations, it had been a good life for the two of them. My father had been held in higher esteem as a college professor and lived in greater comfort than would have been the case had he never left the US. My mother, besides raising two healthy children, had established herself as a much-relied-upon secretary to a succession of important administrators at Lingnan and elsewhere: Provost James Henry, Maritime Customs Commissioner Edgar Bathurst, President Y. L. Lee, and Provost

---

61. William E. Hoffmann to Trustees, Hong Kong, 26 January 1951, and Henry S. Frank to American Consulate General, Hong Kong, [Hong Kong], 10 February 1951, Box 132, TLUA–HYL.

62. William E. Hoffmann to Trustees, Hong Kong, 26 January 1951, Box 132, TLUA – HYL; Arthur R. Knipp to ODW, Hong Kong, 8 February 1951, Box 132 (microfilm Ms44, Reel 24), Trustees of Lingnan University Archives, YDSL.

63. Henry S. Frank, "Confidential Report to the Trustees of Lingnan University," Canton, 31 May 1949, Folder 3243, Box 180, China College Files—Lingnan University, RG 11, United Board Archives, YDSL; HGR to Frank, Hong Kong, 26 February 1951, courtesy of Austin Frank, and to James M. Henry, Yokohama, 30 March 1951, Box 133, TLUA–HYL.

64. Baker, *Flowing Ways*, p. 168; Hahn, Diary Report for December 1950 . . . , pp. 10–11, Maryknoll Mission Archives.

Henry Frank. I believe that if external circumstances had allowed, they would not have left. But of course, when the time came, they had no choice but to leave.

In the case of our family's departure, however, there was one final glitch. At the last minute, at the Shum Chun station, my mother was not allowed to leave with us. It was, I think, my fault. As a Chinese she would not have required an exit permit, but I had heedlessly drawn the attention of the Chinese border guards to her presence. (She would have been keeping her distance from the rest of us.) She and probably also Ah Hoh were, as a result, sent back on a train to Guangzhou, while my father, my sister, and I left China without her on 3 February. A few days later, however, she and Ah Hoh emerged via Macau, escorted by her sister Chi Kin's twenty-one-year-old son (and Luo Ren's older, less politically active, brother), Luo Wen.[65] My mother may have left in the nick of time, for the land border between Guangdong and the outside world was closed on 15 February, "when the requirement that all Chinese obtain permits to leave China went into effect."[66]

In Hong Kong we stayed for a couple of months at the [Anglican] Church Guest House on Upper Albert Road, opposite the Zoological and Botanical Gardens, on Hong Kong Island. Our most pressing issue was the unfinished business of my mother's visa. Her petition for a non-quota immigrant visa had been approved by the US State Department in October, but she still had to apply in person for the actual visa. Henry Frank, in Hong Kong, wrote to the American consulate general vouching for her political rectitude: "She is not, and never has been, a communist sympathizer." She underwent various medical examinations to certify that she was in good health. She also had to get the approval of the consulate to travel to the US without a valid Chinese passport, for her old one had expired and there was no way she could get it re-extended because the passport office of the defeated Nationalist government had been closed in Hong Kong. She finally obtained

Figure 9.6: My parents with Charles Harth, warden of the Church Guest House, and others, Hong Kong, February–March 1951.

---

65. Luo Ji'er, personal communication, 21 January 2015.
66. "Red China Curbs Travel," *New York Times*, 17 February 1951, p. 3; Ethel Montgomery to Mrs. H. C. Brownell, New York, 27 March 1950, Folder 1, Box 2, Brownell Papers, University of Vermont Library.

Figure 9.7: Postcard of SS *President Wilson.*

Figure 9.8: My sister and I aboard the *President Wilson*, March 1951.

this travel approval on 17 March after a personal interview at the consulate.[67] In the meantime, my mother had continued teaching me and getting me ready for my schooling in America.[68]

On 24 March 1951, one week after my mother got her visa, we left Hong Kong aboard not a freighter (as we had previously traveled) but the luxury passenger liner SS *President Wilson* ("Your American Hotel Abroad"). As my father explained apologetically to Henry Frank, "I am sorry that the trip on the 'Wilson' is going to set the Trustees back $2,370, which I agree is a frightful sum, but we have not even had a nibble on any of the lines put out to the agents for the various freighter companies."[69] The ship took us via Yokohama and Honolulu to San Francisco, which we reached on 11 April. This time we were bound not for Philadelphia but for Claremont, California, where in the company of some other Lingnan refugees like the Franks and the Changs we were to ponder our future. As my father explained, "I can see no point in our all going East now, when I have no notion where, if anywhere, I shall find a job."[70]

Neither of my parents ever set foot in Guangzhou again.

---

67. Henry S. Frank to the American Consulate General, Hong Kong, Hong Kong, 10 February 1951, Box 132, TLUA–HYL; CKR, Affidavit in lieu of passport, Hong Kong, 17 March 1951, in my personal collection; HGR to Henry S. Frank, Hong Kong, 11 March 1951, courtesy of Austin Frank.
68. CKR to Martha Frank, Hong Kong, 20 February 1951, courtesy of Austin Frank.
69. HGR to Henry S. Frank, Hong Kong, 11 March 1951, courtesy of Austin Frank.
70. HGR to Henry S. Frank, Hong Kong, 26 February 1951, courtesy of Austin Frank; HGR to Amerfound, cablegram, Hong Kong, 6 March 1951, and CKR to James M. Henry, San Francisco, 14 April 1951, Box 133, TLUA–HYL.

Epilogue

Lingnan University: Its Demise and Revival

In the summer of 1952, a year and a half after the departure of its Western staff, Lingnan University passed from existence; it had lasted sixty-four years (1888–1952). It and the dozen other so-called Christian colleges in China were simply carved up and abolished. In Lingnan's case, the physical campus was turned over to Sun Yat-sen University, which also took over its Arts and Sciences colleges. Lingnan's College of Agriculture became part of the South China Agricultural College, its Medical School became part of the South China College of Medicine, and its Engineering Department became part of the South China Institute of Technology.[1] Lingnan's last president, Chen Su-ching, joined the History Department of Sun Yat-sen University; in 1956, he was appointed a vice president of the university. Ten years later, during the Cultural Revolution, he was denounced as a "reactionary academic authority" and a "traitor." Chen died soon afterwards, in February 1967, and was not posthumously rehabilitated until 1979.[2]

While many members of Lingnan's Chinese faculty stayed on in Guangzhou, others sought refuge in British Hong Kong, where in 1951 they helped found a new post-secondary school, Chung Chi College, with many links to the old Lingnan. Thus, the founding president of Chung Chi, from 1951 to 1954, was Y. L. Lee, the former president of Lingnan, and its third president, from 1960 to 1975, was C. T. Yung, who had been a professor of botany at Lingnan. In 1963, during Yung's presidency, Chung Chi was authorized by Hong Kong's colonial government to join two other colleges to create the Chinese University of Hong Kong as a complement to the English-language Hong Kong University.[3] Chung Chi is now one of the nine constituent colleges of CUHK.

The formation of Chung Chi College notwithstanding, the demise of Lingnan did not sit well with its many former students and graduates. As historian Lutz puts it, when the Christian colleges in China were disbanded and dispersed in 1952, "it was almost impossible for alumni and members of the college community to retain any sense of continuing identity through the successor institutions."[4] The Lingnan alumni in Hong Kong, some of whom had become quite wealthy and influential, felt no sense of identity with Sun Yat-sen University and only some with Chung Chi College.

---

1. Lutz, *China and Christian Colleges*, p. 482; Li and Hill, *Nanguo fenghuang*, p. 108; Au, *Lingnan Spirit Forever*, pp. 7–8.
2. "Chen Xujing nianpu jianbian," pp. 559–561.
3. Lutz, *China and the Christian Colleges*, pp. 484–485; Corbett, *Lingnan University*, p. 164.
4. Lutz, *China and the Christian Colleges*, p. 474.

Figure 10.1: Dedication of Lingnan College, Hong Kong, 19 November 1967. From *Lingnan University, 1888 to Present: A Pictorial History*, commons.ln.edu.hk. To the left of the plaque are President Qian Naixin 錢乃信 and Anglican Bishop Gilbert Baker; to the right, Trustee Kan Koam Ching 簡鑑清. My father is at the extreme right (on edge of photo).

Instead, they worked tirelessly, and with some success, to resurrect the old Lingnan. In 1967, building upon the long-existing Lingnan Middle School in Hong Kong, they founded Lingnan College 嶺南書院 as a private post-secondary school.[5] Twenty-five years later, as the Hong Kong government prepared for the colony's retrocession to Chinese rule, Lingnan College was among five institutions selected to join the ranks of Hong Kong University and the Chinese University of Hong Kong as a university. First, in 1991, it was recognized as a degree-granting tertiary institution; then in 1995 it was relocated from Hong Kong Island to Tuen Mun in the western New Territories; finally, in 1997, it acquired university status and was renamed Lingnan University 嶺南大學. It distinguishes itself from Hong Kong's other universities with its liberal arts curriculum, and it claims to be, via the Lingnan Middle School and Lingnan College, the lineal descendant of the original Lingnan.[6]

Concurrently with their efforts to elevate Lingnan College to a university, Lingnan's Hong Kong alumni, as they did more and more business on the mainland in the post-Mao era, began to press for the resurrection of their alma mater at its original location. Among those active in this movement was my cousin Luo Ren, Ngan Chi Kin's second son, now living in Hong Kong after a long stint in Xinjiang. In 1986 he and a fellow member of the Class of 1953 compiled a pamphlet with numerous essays calling for the "revival" (*huifu*

---

5.   Li Ruiming, *Lingnan daxue*, pp. 230–231; Au, *Lingnan Spirit Forever*, pp. 37–38; *Lingnan College, Hong Kong, Prospectus, 1972–1974*, http://commons.ln.edu.hk/lingnan_calendar (accessed 29 August 2019).

6.   See "Milestones and History" on the website of Lingnan University, Hong Kong, ln.edu.hk (accessed 29 July 2019).

恢復) of Lingnan University in Guangzhou. Their main argument was that Lingnan had been mistakenly classified in 1952 as a "missionary college." Though founded by missionaries, Lingnan was never supported by a missionary board, nor was it affiliated with any particular Christian denomination. Since 1927 it had been registered with the Chinese government, it had had a Chinese president and a Chinese administration, and it had practiced freedom of religion. Also, Lingnan had never been a part of the United Board for Christian Higher Education in Asia. In short, unlike the other Christian colleges such as Yenching and St. John's, Lingnan should never have been abolished.[7]

Though the Chinese authorities rejected out of hand the idea of returning the Hong Lok campus to Lingnan, they did, rather surprisingly, consent to the creation of a separate, semiautonomous unit within Sun Yat-sen University that would be called Lingnan (University) College 嶺南（大學）學院. This arrangement was announced in March 1988, on the one hundredth anniversary of Lingnan's founding. In September 1989, L(U)C held its first classes. Located in the heart of the Hong Lok campus, it has become an international business management school, with English as the medium of instruction.[8] As Lingnan alumnus Lee Sui-ming (Class of 1947) remarked, with the founding of Lingnan University in Hong Kong and of Lingnan (University) College in Guangzhou, the desires of all Lingnan people to "love and cherish" their alma mater have finally been realized.[9]

The Trustees of Lingnan University

Although Lingnan University in Guangzhou ceased to exist after 1952, the Board of Trustees of Lingnan University in New York did not. Independently chartered in New York State in 1893, it continued to operate, although on a much reduced budget. It helped exiled members of the "permanent" faculty (like my father) relocate to the United States and find new employment. It looked after its retirees (like William Cadbury and Henry Brownell). It funded the writing and publication (in 1965) of Charles Corbett's history of the university. And it took an active interest in Lingnan's several successor institutions in Hong Kong and made some financial contributions to programs at Chung Chi College, the Chinese University of Hong Kong, and Lingnan College. But up through the 1970s its ability to do more was constrained by the modesty of its endowment.[10]

Its fortunes changed, however, in 1979. Eight years earlier, the Foreign Claims Settlement Commission of the United States had estimated that when the Communists abolished Lingnan and confiscated all its property, the American trustees had suffered losses totaling $5,700,000. As part of the normalization of diplomatic relations between the United States and the People's Republic of China, the two countries came to an agreement relating to competing property claims. Under one part of the agreement, China would pay "approximately 41 cents on a dollar to American claimants with no interest due," with the payment spread out over several years. Forty-one percent of the $5,700,000 that the Lingnan trustees claimed came to about $2,337,000. The trustees received the first payment, $800,000, in November 1979, and the last payment, $72,000, in July 1990.[11]

---

7. Li Ruiming, *Lingnan daxue*, pp. 219–221; Au, *Lingnan Spirit Forever*, p. 12; Luo Ren and Huang Daren, comps., *Lingnan daxue fuxiao husheng* [Voices calling for reviving Lingnan University] (Hong Kong, 1986).
8. Li Ruiming, *Lingnan daxue*, p. 232; Li and Hill, *Nanguo fenghuang*, pp. 143–251; Au, *Lingnan Spirit Forever*, pp. 80–82.
9. Li Ruiming, *Lingnan daxue*, p. 221.
10. Au, *Lingnan Spirit Forever*, ch. 2–7.
11. Au, *Lingnan Spirit Forever*, pp. 14, 58–59.

The settlement, according to Douglas P. Murray (a former president of the trustees), "almost doubled the organization's endowment." The trustees could now do a lot more toward helping the various successors to Lingnan University. By the late 1990s, "Lingnan's grants had reached approximately one million dollars annually."[12]

In November 1988, in recognition of the reality that they had long ceased to be a degree-conferring university, the trustees of Lingnan University voted to reorganize themselves into what they actually were, a grant-making foundation. The trustees had considered making this change for several years but had been "asked by Lingnan alumni in Guangzhou and Hong Kong to refrain from any change until the matter of re-establishing a Lingnan presence in the People's Republic of China was settled." With the founding of Lingnan (University) College at Sun Yat-sen University in March 1988, the way was clear to make the change. In July 1989 the Board of Trustees of Lingnan University became the Lingnan Foundation.[13] Since then its grants have gone primarily to Sun Yat-sen University (including, of course, Lingnan [University] College) and to Lingnan University Hong Kong. Its assets in 2020 totaled slightly more than $20,000,000.

My Parents and Me

Finally, what of my family and me? When we left China in February 1951, the American trustees, in addition to paying our extravagant fare on the *President Wilson*, found a rental house for us in Claremont, a retirement community in southern California for China missionaries, where some other Lingnan faculty families also landed. According to my father's most recent contract, in the event that he was called home ahead of time, the Lingnan trustees would give him a "regular furlough, of approximately $4,200 a year." We were in Claremont for about a year and a half. My sister and I resumed our (American) schooling, and I entered the seventh grade at the Claremont Junior–Senior High School in mid-year. My mother worked part-time for a local attorney and did some typing for an author.[14] My father, in the summer of 1951, taught an orientation course for foreign students at the Claremont Graduate School.[15] But his main preoccupation was to find permanent employment, which at his age (he was now 51) was not so easy. He was also concerned about the prohibition on interracial marriages in numerous American (usually southern) states—a ban that the US Supreme Court declared illegal only in 1967. In March 1952, however, he landed a job in Springfield, Massachusetts, with the G. & C. Merriam Company, publisher of the Webster dictionaries. He left Claremont for Springfield in mid-March; the rest of the family joined him in August, after school had let out.[16] As their final financial obligation to him, the trustees paid for his and our train fare to the East.

My father worked for the G. & C. Merriam Company (now known as Merriam-Webster) for the next thirteen years. He was a senior member of the team of lexicographers that in 1961 produced the controversial unabridged Webster's Third New International Dictionary. (It was controversial because of its permissive attitude toward usage, such as

---

12. Douglas P. Murray, Preface to Au, *Lingnan Spirit Forever*, pp. vi–vii.
13. Au, *Lingnan Spirit Forever*, pp. 84–86.
14. CKR to Ethel Montgomery, Claremont, 17 April 1952, Folder 276, Box 20, Archives of the Trustees of Lingnan University, RG 14, YDSL.
15. HGR, Curriculum Vitae and testimonials, 28 December 1951, in my personal collection.
16. HGR to Ethel Montgomery, Claremont, 19 March 1952, Folder 276, Box 20, Archives of the Trustees of Lingnan University, RG 14, YDSL.

recognizing words like "ain't.") He had been one of the first to be hired for the project.[17] He retired in 1965, following a heart attack. My mother became an American housewife, doing the grocery shopping, cooking, housekeeping, and laundry. In her spare time, she played the piano and read murder mysteries. While ironing clothes, she listened to radio broadcasts of the New York Yankees baseball games, for, oddly enough, she had become a big Yankees fan. (My father had no interest in sports.) Soon after we moved out to suburban East Longmeadow in about 1961, she became a part-time librarian assistant at the local public library. She was naturalized as a US citizen.

My mother also tried to keep in touch with her relatives, but it was not easy. Her older sister, Ngan Chi Kin, and her husband were living in Guangzhou; because of the then hostile relations between the United States and China, it was impossible to have direct contact with them. She was able, to some extent, to exchange messages and financial aid via her step-siblings in Hong Kong, principally the children of Ngan Heung Cho's third wife, Sam Gwu. She was greatly saddened by the death of her father in Hong Kong in January 1958.

My sister Janet and I went to school in Springfield. I graduated from Classical High School in 1956 and from Yale in 1960. In college, for lack of any other compelling interest, I majored in Chinese Studies. Though growing up in China, I knew very little about

Figure 10.2: My aunt and uncle, Ngan Chi Kin and Loh Ying Ho, and their children and grandchildren, Guangzhou, August 1961. Image courtesy of Luo Ji'er. On right, Luo Wen, with wife and son; at center, Luo Ren, with wife; and on left, Luo Ji'er, with daughter.

17. Herbert C. Morton, *The Story of "Webster's Third": Philip Gove's Controversial Dictionary and Its Critics* (Cambridge: Cambridge University Press, 1994), p. 75.

the country. My mother had tried to keep up my spoken Cantonese, but without success. What little I did remember, however, was of some help in learning Mandarin in college. After Yale, I went on to Harvard for graduate study in modern Chinese history under John Fairbank, my father's one-time boss at the Office of War Information. I managed to avoid military service with a student deferment; I was lucky in that I had been too young for the Korean War and was too old for Vietnam. In 1965 I went to Taiwan for further language training and dissertation research. Toward the end of the year, I learned that my mother was gravely ill with cancer. Cutting short my stay in Taiwan, I left immediately for Hong Kong, partly to do some necessary dissertation research but also to reconnect personally with my maternal relatives. I spent time with my step-grandmother and with her children (my uncles and aunt) and some of their children (my cousins). I also made a semi-successful effort to relearn some Cantonese. I returned to the States at the beginning of 1966. My mother died on 24 February, a few months before my sister graduated from Smith College.

In 1967, I was hired to teach Chinese history at the University of Texas at Austin, where I remained until my retirement in 2003. Also in 1967, my widowed father, who was at loose ends, was persuaded by some of his former students to return to Hong Kong to help the newly founded Lingnan College get underway as Dean of the Faculty of Arts and Professor of English. (See Figure 10.1.) Soon after his arrival and for about a year and a half, he also served as acting president of the college. Living at the Salisbury Road YMCA

Figure 10.3: My step-grandmother, Sam Gwu, and some of the extended Ngan family, with my father, my sister, and Ah Hoh, Hong Kong, January 1969. 1 = my step-grandmother; 2 = seventh Uncle, Po Ming; 3 = fourteenth Uncle, Peter Ki Shun 其信; 4 = seventeenth Uncle, Ki Ping; 5 = eighteenth Aunt, Chi Fai 志嫿; 6 = my father; 7 = my sister, Janet; 8 = her then husband, Andrew Pinkowitz; 9 = Ah Hoh. Photo by fifteenth Uncle, Ki Yee 其義.

in Tsim Sha Tsui in Kowloon, he commuted to work on Hong Kong Island via the Star Ferry. To his former students he was a tangible link between the fledgling college and the old Lingnan in Guangzhou. Among the people my father saw in Hong Kong was Ah Hoh, the housekeeper who had been with us during most of our years in China. Since our departure for the US, she had been living and working in Hong Kong. (My sister, too, saw her, on her honeymoon visit to Hong Kong in 1969; to my regret, I never did.) Though diplomatic relations between the United States and China had begun to improve following President Nixon's 1972 visit and it was now possible for Americans (in organized groups) to visit Guangzhou, my father never took advantage of the opportunity. He said that he did not want to be constrained by guides from going wherever he wanted. He remained with Lingnan College until 1976, when he returned to the United States and came to Austin, where I was teaching and living with my then wife, Suzanne, and our year-old daughter, Jennifer. He died in Austin on 20 November 1983 at age 83.

By then, full diplomatic relations between the two countries had been established. In 1981, out of the blue I received an invitation to attend an international conference in China commemorating the seventieth anniversary of the Republican Revolution of 1911. (I had recently published a book on the revolution in Guangdong and had begun research on the Manchus and the revolution.) It was my first time back to the China mainland since 1951. The conference began in Beijing (with a speech by Party Chairman Hua Guofeng in the Great Hall of the People), continued in Wuhan (where conference participants gave their papers), and finished up in Guangdong (with visits to Sun Yat-sen's

Figure 10.4: Homecoming, Sun Yat-sen University, January 2004.

birthplace and to Sun Yat-sen University). During our visit to the campus of Sun Yat-sen University, I was able to see the Infirmary where I had been born and House No. 47, where we had lived in the late 1940s.

Sometime afterward I ran into Douglas P. Murray, a fellow Yalie who I knew was associated with the trustees of Lingnan University. I told him of my father's association and my own with the old Lingnan; I also inquired whether the trustees would be willing to help me donate my father's collection of books to the general library of Sun Yat-sen University. (They were.) As a result of that conversation, I was invited in 1985 to join the trustees as a board member. I remained a member, off and on, until 2012. It so happened that it was during my tenure that Lingnan (University) College was founded (in 1988), the trustees became the Lingnan Foundation (1989), and Lingnan College became Lingnan University (1997). In January 2004, following a delegation visit by members of the Lingnan Foundation to its various grantee institutions in Hong Kong and Guangzhou, I had the opportunity to meet up, after a break of fifty years, with several of my Lingnan Primary School classmates. After breakfast at a university canteen, we walked around the campus, ending up at the site of the old school. It was a memorable homecoming.

Acknowledgments

This project probably its beginning in the obituary for my father that I wrote for the *Austin American* newspaper in 1983. Its second iteration, twenty-two years later, was a short piece for the *Lingnan University Alumni Association Newsletter* in San Francisco, written at the request of its editor, Warren Achuck, and published in 2005. The third iteration, appearing in June 2013, was a long and hastily prepared paper presented at a small workshop on "Christian Colleges in China: An Experiment in Globalized Higher Education" at the Harvard–Yenching Institute conducted by its director, Elizabeth J. Perry. My thanks to Warren and Liz for their (perhaps unwitting) encouragement to pursue this project.

It is said that "it takes a village to raise a child." This is no less true about writing a book. I owe an enormous debt of gratitude to many, many people. First and foremost are my relatives. They include, on my mother's side of the family, my seventeenth uncle, Ngan Ki Ping; five of my first cousins (Luo Ren [Law Yan] and the late Luo Ji'er, son and daughter of my second aunt; Tony Cheong Shun Ngan and Pauline Chan, son and daughter of my seventh uncle; and Winky Ngan, daughter of my fifteenth uncle); and my nephew, Yi Luo, grandson of my second aunt. For more than a decade and either in person or via email, I have learned from them practically all that I now know about the Ngan family. For example, it was Luo Ren who first told me about the existence of the Ngan ancestral village, and it was Tony Cheong Shun Ngan who, several years later, took me to the village itself.

For my father's side of the family, I am indebted to my sister, Janet R. Pinkowitz, my second cousin, Ray Rhoads, son of the youngest brother of my American grandfather, and another second cousin, Alexander ("Jack") Pugh III, whose mother was my father's first cousin and closest relative. Ray and Jack were extremely helpful in working out the Rhoads genealogy, while Janet and Ray shared with me many old photographs of our ancestors.

Next, I should thank those who have read and critiqued all or parts of the manuscript. Chief among them are my wife, Patricia Stranahan, and my sister, Janet Pinkowitz, who perused the chapters seriatim as they were produced. Janet also helped with the proof reading. Others who have read portions of the draft manuscript are Richard Minear, Arthur Rosenbaum, and David Pong (three old friends in the Asian studies field), and Austin Frank. My thanks, too, to Chi Man Kwong and a second reviewer for Hong Kong University Press. Even if I did not always follow their suggestions, I appreciated all their comments and corrections. Any remaining mistakes (both factual and interpretative) are, of course, my responsibility.

Yet others helped in perhaps less substantial but no less important ways. Several were, like David Pong, fellow Lingnan'ers of my generation: Austin Frank and Marian Zeitlin (children of chemistry professor and provost, Henry Frank) and Fred Chang (son of another chemistry professor, Frederic Chang), who shared with me their own memories of life in postwar Lingnan and answered questions about their parents. Austin, Fred, and I were fellow members of the Lingnan Foundation, as were two others who were helpful: Terry Lautz, who early on passed along Father Hahn's diary of the expulsion of the Americans and alerted me to the Maryknoll Mission Archives, Shirley Mow, who shared several sources with me, and Jane Permaul, who helped find out the death date of one of her relatives.

My thanks go, also, to Bruce Chan (for his knowledge of Cantonese slang terms for "Eurasians"), Matthew Combs (for information about the source of a Chongqing photograph), Geoff Emerson (for taking me on two visits to the grounds of the Stanley Internment Camp), Tisha Goodman (for help in obtaining Gilbert Baker's memoirs in England), Matthew Johnson (for guidance on researching the OWI in China), Ko Tim Keung (for sharing a couple of photographs), Heather Lee and Scott Seligman (for introducing me to the records of the US Immigration and Naturalization Service in Seattle and in New York City), Li Danke (for her knowledge of her native city, Chongqing), Steve MacKinnon (for information about the Bill Holland papers at the University of Massachusetts), Elizabeth Sinn (for telling me about the "old" Hong Kong newspapers that are online at the Hong Kong Public Library), Steve Upton, David Bellis, and Brian Edgar (for informing me about and making available to me an important document from the Hong Kong Public Record Office), Wang Mansheng (for his skill in reading Chinese calligraphy), and Mark Wilkinson (for making available his thesis on the OWI in China).

Special thanks are due to Poon Shuk-wah, at the Chinese University of Hong Kong (and formerly at Lingnan University Hong Kong), who over the years has unfailingly answered my many pleas for bibliographical and other forms of help; to Ada Au-Yeung Pui Man, for the four maps drawn to my specifications; to Matthew Kudelka, for his excellent copyediting, and to Kenneth Yung, Clara Ho, and their colleagues at Hong Kong University Press, who shepherded this manuscript into print.

Then there are the librarians and archivists at the various institutions that I either visited personally or queried remotely, notably, Joan Duffy and Sara Azam (Yale Divinity School Library), the late Ray Lum, Eiji Kuge, and Annie Wang (Harvard-Yenching Library), and Ann Upton and Sarah Horowitz (Haverford College Library). Others include Cara Setsu Bertram (University of Illinois), Betty C. Bolden (Burke Library, Columbia University), Sarah D. Brooks Blair (United Theological Seminary), Don Davis (American Friends Service Committee Archives), Ken Grossi (Oberlin College), Dick Hoffman (Friends Select School), Heather Hoftman (Montana State University), Jane Kjaer (Skidmore College), Donna Miller (St. George's United Methodist Church archives), Fred Nesta and Tommy Yeung (Lingnan University), Ellen D. Pierce (Maryknoll Mission Archives), Eugene Rutigliano (Ohio Wesleyan University), and Wang Lei (Sun Yat-sen University Library). Special thanks to Robert Bickers, at the University of Bristol, for making available to me the official correspondence of the Maritime Customs Service at Qujiang (which is otherwise at the Second Historical Archives at Nanjing, China) and to Janet Bloom, at the University of Michigan, for sharing with me several letters from the Edward Lockwood papers.

I also want to thank various individuals and institutions for permitting me to repro-duce some of the photographs in the book: Christopher J. Anderson and Graziano Kratli (Special Collections, Yale Divinity School Library), Jamie Carstair (University of Bristol), Prudence Doherty (University of Vermont), Cilla Invargsson (Maritime Museum and Aquarium, Gothenburg), Kristin Kay (University of Massachusetts), Meredith McDonough (Alabama Department of Archives and History), John P. C. Moffett (Needham Research Institute), Anne L. Moore (University of Massachusetts Amherst), Zhaohui Xue (East Asian Library, Stanford University), and Chak Yung (City of Vancouver Archives). Thanks, too, to the woman who gave me a copy of Figure 3.6; she and I met at a party in Cambridge in 1962 and discovered that we had crossed paths some twenty-four years earlier and half a world away. I have, unforgivably, forgotten her name, but she's the other baby in the photograph. All other unsourced photos in the book are from either myself or my sister.

Finally, I want to thank the Center for East Asian Studies at the University of Pennsylvania for sponsoring me as a visiting scholar, which gave me access not only to the Penn's own library but also, through Borrow/Direct, to the libraries of many other research institutions.

If there are any "villagers" that I have overlooked, my apologies. Corrections, ques-tions, and comments are welcome; my email address is erhoads@austin.utexas.edu.

Bibliography

Archives

American Friends Service Committee Archives, Philadelphia, PA

General Files 1942–1944—Foreign Service—Country China.

Archives of the Eastern Pennsylvania Conference of the United Methodist Church, St. George's United Methodist Church, Philadelphia, PA

Sarah D. Cooper Memorial United Methodist Church Records, Record of Baptisms.

Boston University, Boston, MA

Christopher Rand Papers, Howard Gotlieb Archival Research Center.

Columbia University, New York, NY

Foreign Missions Conference of North America Records, MRL 12, Burke Library, Union Theological Seminary.

Harvard University, Cambridge, MA

Arthur Greenwood Robinson Papers on the Yung Wing Mission and YMCA Work in North China, Houghton Library.
Trustees of Lingnan University Archives, Harvard-Yenching Library.

Haverford College Library, Haverford, PA

William Warder Cadbury Papers, 1877–1951, Collection No. 1160, Quaker Collection.
William Warder Cadbury and Catherine Jones Cadbury Papers, Collection No. 1192, Quaker Collection.

Lingnan University, Hong Kong

Lingnan Archives, Digital Commons @Lingnan. https://commons.ln.edu.hk/archives.

Maryknoll Mission Archives, Maryknoll, NY

Mission Diaries, 1918–1969—Series 1: China.

Oberlin College Archives, Oberlin, OH

Everett D. Hawkins Papers, 1900–1972, RG 30/130.

Philadelphia City Archives, Philadelphia, PA

Presbyterian Historical Society, Philadelphia, PA

Foreign Missions Conference of North America Records, Record Group 27.
National Archives of the Presbyterian Church in the USA, Board of Foreign Missions, Secretaries' Files: China Mission, Record Group 82.
Pommerenke Family Papers, 1907–1980, Record Group 193.

Second Historical Archives of China, Nanjing

Kukong Semi-Official Correspondence, 1942–1943, 679(1)/32498, and 1943–1946, 679(1)/32499, Maritime Customs Service Archives (on microfilm).

United Methodist Archives Center, Drew University, Madison, NJ

Missionary Files, Methodist Church, 1912–1949, China (on microfilm).

United States National Archives, College Park, MD

Records of the Foreign Service Posts of the Department of State, Record Group 84.
Records of the Office of War Information (OWI), Record Group 208.

United States National Archives, New York, NY

Records of the Immigration and Naturalization Service (INS), Record Group 85.

United States National Archives, Seattle, WA

Records of the Immigration and Naturalization Service (INS), Record Group 85.

United Theological Seminary, Dayton, OH

Dr. Frank Oldt Papers, HC-48, The Center for the Evangelical United Brethren Heritage.

University of Bristol

Chinese Maritime Customs Project, Department of Historical Studies. www.bristol.ac.uk/history/customs.

University of Cambridge

"Joseph Needham in Wartime China, 1943–1946," Needham Research Institute. nri.cam.ac.uk.

University of Massachusetts Library, Amherst, MA

W. L. Holland Papers.

University of Michigan, Ann Arbor, MI

Edward H. Lockwood Papers, 1937–1944, Manuscripts Division, William L. Clements Library.

University of Pennsylvania, Philadelphia, PA

Alumni Records, University Archives.

University of Vermont Library, Burlington, VT

Henry C. Brownell Papers, Special Collections.

Yale Divinity School Library, New Haven, CT

Archives of the Trustees of Lingnan University, Record Group 14, Special Collections.

China College Files—Lingnan University, United Board for Christian Higher Education in Asia Archives, Record Group 11, Special Collections.

China Records Project, Miscellaneous Personal Papers Collection, Record Group 8, Special Collections.

Sarah Refo Mason Papers, Record Group 175, Special Collections.

Trustees of Lingnan University Archives, Film Ms44, Special Collections.

Newspapers

China Mail (Hong Kong)
Hong Kong Daily Press
Nanfang ribao 南方日報 (Southern Daily) (Guangzhou)
New Orleans Times-Picayune
New York Times
Philadelphia Inquirer
Public Ledger (Philadelphia)
San Francisco Chronicle
South China Morning Post (Hong Kong)

Books, Articles, and Websites

Abend, Hallett. *Chaos in Asia.* New York: Ives Washburn, 1939.

Allman, Norwood F. *Shanghai Lawyer.* New York and London: McGraw-Hill, 1943.

Anderson, Mary Raleigh. *A Cycle in the Celestial Kingdom: Protestant Mission Schools for Girls in South China (1827 to the Japanese Invasion).* Mobile, AL: Heiter-Starke Printing Co., 1943.

Anslow, Barbara. *Tin Hats and Rice: A Diary of Life as a Hong Kong Prisoner of War, 1941–1945.* Hong Kong: Blacksmith Books, 2018.

Asano Toyomi. "Japanese Operations in Yunnan and North Burma." In *The Battle for China: Essays on the Military History of the Sino-Japanese War of 1937–1945*, edited by Mark Peattie, Edward J. Drea, and Hans van de Ven, pp. 361–385. Stanford: Stanford University Press, 2011.

Au, Steven Tung. *Lingnan Spirit Forever: A Mission in Transition, 1951–1990; From Trustees of Lingnan University to Lingnan Foundation.* New Haven: Lingnan Foundation, 2002. http://commons.ln.edu.hk/lingnan_history_bks.

Auden, W. H., and Christopher Isherwood. *Journey to a War*, rev. ed. London: Faber & Faber, 1973.

Baker, Gilbert. *Flowing Ways: Our Life in China.* Dorking, Surrey: Joan Baker, 1996.

Banham, Tony. *Not the Slightest Chance: The Defence of Hong Kong, 1941.* Vancouver: UBC Press, 2003.

Barnes, Henry. *Into the Heart's Land: A Century of Rudolph Steiner's Work in North America.* Great Barrington, MA: SteinerBooks, 2005.

Bellis, David. "78 Years Ago: Hong Kong's Wartime Diaries." https://gwulo.com/78-years-ago.

Bickers, Robert. "The Chinese Maritime Customs at War, 1941–45." *Journal of Imperial and Commonwealth History* 36 (2008): 295–311.

Boorman, Howard L., and Richard C. Howard, eds. *Biographical Dictionary of Republican China.* New York: Columbia University Press, 1967–1971.

Briggs, Norman. *Taken in Hong Kong, December 8, 1941: Memoirs of Norman Briggs, World War II Prisoner of War.* Compiled by Carol Briggs Waite. Baltimore: PublishAmerica, 2006.

Brown, Wenzell. *Hong Kong Aftermath.* New York: Smith & Durrell, 1943.

Brown, Wenzell. "I Was a Prisoner of the Japs." *Liberty Magazine*, 10, 17, 24, and 31 October 1942.

Brown, Wenzell. " 'Tell America What They Have Done to Us . . .'." *Saturday Review*, 9 January 1943.

Carlson, Evans Fordyce. *Twin Stars of China: A Behind-the-Scenes Story of China's Valiant Struggle for Existence by a U.S. Marine Who Lived and Moved with the People*. 1940. Reprint, Westport, CT: Hyperion Press, 1975.

Carroll, John M. *A Concise History of Hong Kong*. Lanham, MD: Rowman & Littlefield, 2007.

Chan Sui-jeung. *East River Column: Hong Kong Guerrillas in the Second World War and After*. Hong Kong: Hong Kong University Press, 2009.

Chang, Eileen. *Lust, Caution*. Translated by Julia Lovell. New York: Anchor Books, 2007.

Chang Jui-te. "Bombs Don't Discriminate? Class, Gender, and Ethnicity in the Air-Raid-Shelter Experiences of the Wartime Chongqing Population." In *Beyond Suffering: Recounting War in Modern China*, edited by James Flath and Norman Smith, pp. 59–79. Vancouver: UBC Press, 2011.

Chang Kia-ngau. *The Inflationary Spiral: The Experience in China, 1939–1950*. Cambridge: Technology Press of Massachusetts Institute of Technology; New York: John Wiley & Sons, 1958.

Chen Xiangmei (Anna Chennault). *Chen Xiangmei quanji* 陳香梅全集 [The complete works of Anna Chennault]. Shijiazhuang: Hebei renmin chubanshe, 2000.

Chen Xujing 陳序經. "Youguan Lingda yu Zhong Rongguang de jidian huiyi" 有關嶺大與鍾榮光的幾點回憶 [Some recollections regarding Lingnan University and Chung Wing Kwong]. *Guangzhou wenshi ziliao* 廣州文史資料, no. 13 (1964): 30–51.

"Chen Xujing nianpu jianbian" 陳序經年譜簡編 [A brief chronological biography of Chen Su-ching]. In *Zhongguo jindai sixiangjia wenku—Chen Xujing juan*, compiled by Tian Tong, pp. 542–561.

Chennault, Anna. *A Thousand Springs: The Autobiography of a Marriage*. New York: Paul S. Ericksson, 1962.

Cheyney, Edward Potts. *History of the University of Pennsylvania, 1740–1940*. Philadelphia: University of Pennsylvania Press, 1940.

Chinese Ministry of Information. *China Handbook, 1937–1945: A Comprehensive Survey of Major Developments in China in Eight Years of War*, rev. and enl. ed. New York: Macmillan, 1947.

Chou, Shun-hsin. *The Chinese Inflation, 1937–1949*. New York: Columbia University Press, 1963.

Coble, Parks M. *China's War Reporters: The Legacy of Resistance against Japan*. Cambridge, MA: Harvard University Press, 2015.

Combs, Matthew T. "Chongqing 1943: People's Livelihood, Price Control, and State Legitimacy." In *1943: China at the Crossroads*, edited by Joseph W. Esherick and Matthew T. Combs, pp. 282–322. Ithaca: East Asia Program, Cornell University, 2015.

Corbett, Charles Hodge. *Lingnan University: A Short History Based Primarily on the Records of the University's American Trustees*. New York: Trustees of Lingnan University, 1963.

Cracknell, Phillip G. "The Strange Case of Mr. Kennedy-Skipton" (16 November 2014). battleforhongkong.blogspot.co.uk.

Čulītis, Maksis. "No Pēterpils Līdz Hongkongai" [From St. Petersburg to Hong Kong]. *Jaunā Gaita* [The New Course], no. 80 (1970).

Cunich, Peter. *A History of the University of Hong Kong: Volume 1, 1911–1945*. Hong Kong: Hong Kong University Press, 2012.

Dacun suiyue—Kangzhan shiqi Lingnan zai Yuebei 大村歲月—抗戰時期嶺南在粵北 [The Tai Tsuen years—Lingnan in northern Guangdong during the War of Resistance]. North York, Ontario: "Dacun suiyue" chubanzu, 1998. http://commons.ln.edu.hk/lingnan_history_bks.

Danielson, Eric N. "Revisiting Chongqing: China's Second World War Temporary National Capital." *Journal of the Royal Asiatic Society Hong Kong Branch* 45 (2005): 173–208.

Dew, Gwen. *Prisoner of the Japs*. New York: Alfred A. Knopf, 1943.

Dobson, Richard P. *China Cycle*. London: Macmillan, 1946.

Emerson, Geoffrey Charles. "Behind Japanese Barbed Wire: Stanley Internment Camp, Hong Kong, 1942–1945." *Journal of the Hong Kong Branch of the Royal Asiatic Society* 17 (1977): 30–42.

Emerson, Geoffrey Charles. *Hong Kong Internment, 1942 to 1945: Life in the Japanese Civilian Camps at Stanley.* Hong Kong: Hong Kong University Press, 2008.

Fairbank, John King. *Chinabound: A Fifty-Year Memoir.* New York: Harper & Row, 1982.

Fairbank, Wilma. *America's Cultural Experiment in China, 1942–1949.* Washington: US Department of State, Bureau of Educational and Cultural Affairs, 1976.

Farris, Johnathan Andrew. *Enclave to Urbanity: Canton, Foreigners, and Architecture from the Late Eighteenth to the Early Twentieth Centuries.* Hong Kong: Hong Kong University Press, 2016.

Feng Bangyan 馮邦彥. *Bainian Lifeng* 百年利豐 [A hundred years of Li and Fung], enl. ed. Hong Kong: Sanlian shudian, 2011.

Flath, James, and Norman Smith, eds. *Beyond Suffering: Recounting War in Modern China.* Vancouver: UBC Press, 2011.

Friends' Select School. *The Record* (yearbook). 1949.

"Fuhao pian—Cen Guohua: Guangdongren cong chipin dao haofu de zaoqi renzheng" 富豪篇—岑國華：廣東人從赤貧到豪富的早期認證 [Annals of the rich and powerful—Shum Kwok Wah: The authentication of the early life of a Cantonese who rose from abject poverty to power and fame], *Nanfang dushi bao* 南方都市報 [Nanfang Metropolis Daily], 29 August 2008. http://www.gzlib.gov.cn.

Gagné, Wayne C. "J. Linsley Gressitt: His Contributions to Science and Conservation" (June 1982). https://scholarspace.manoa.hawaii.edu/bitstream/10125/18436/1/fourth-73-75.pdf.

Gao Tianqiang [Ko Tim Keung] 高添強, and Tang Zhuomin 唐卓敏, eds. *Xianggang Rizhan shiqi* 香港日佔時期 [Hong Kong during the Japanese occupation]. Hong Kong: Sanlian shudian, 1995.

Gittins, Jean. *Stanley: Behind Barbed Wire.* Hong Kong: Hong Kong University Press, 1982.

Griggs, D. Thurston. *One Man's Window on the 20th Century* (2002). userpages.umbc.edu/~tgriggs/autobio.html.

Guangzhou True Light High School 廣州市真光中學. "Xiaoyou zhi jia" 校友之家 [List of graduates]. http://www.gztims.com/140/newsdis.asp?id=62.

Guangzhou Xiehe High School 廣州市協和中學. "Xiehe zhi you" 協和之友 [List of graduates]. www.gzxhhs.net/item/131.aspx.

Hagiwara Mitsuru. "The Japanese Air Campaigns in China, 1937–1945." In *The Battle for China: Essays on the Military History of the Sino-Japanese War of 1937–1945*, edited by Mark Peattie, Edward J. Drea, and Hans van de Ven, pp. 237–255. Stanford: Stanford University Press, 2011.

Hahn, Emily. *China to Me: A Partial Autobiography.* Garden City, NY: Doubleday, Doral & Company, 1944.

Hahn, Joseph A. Diary Reports, 1949–51, Folder 2, Box 1. Mission Diaries, 1918–1969—Series 1: China, Maryknoll Mission Archives, Maryknoll, NY.

Han Suyin. *Destination Chungking.* Boston: Little, Brown, 1942.

Hara Takeshi. "The Ichigō Offensive." In *The Battle for China: Essays on the Military History of the Sino-Japanese War of 1937–1945*, edited by Mark Peattie, Edward J. Drea, and Hans van de Ven, pp. 392–402. Stanford: Stanford University Press, 2011.

Harrisburg City Directory. 1876–1877 to 1880–1882.

Hayhoe, Ruth. *China's Universities, 1895–1995: A Century of Cultural Conflict.* New York and London: Garland Publishing, 1996.

He Shiguang (Hoh Shai Kwong) 何世光 and Jia Huilin 嘉惠霖 (William W. Cadbury). "Guangzhou liushou zhi jingguo" 廣州留守之經過 [An account of stewardship in Guangzhou]. In *Kangzhan qijian de Lingnan* 抗戰期間的嶺南 [Lingnan during the war of resistance], pp. 54–55. n.p.: 1946(?). http://commons.ln.edu.hk/lingnan_history_bks.

He Xuehua 何雪華. "Guangdong yijiazu liangdai chule 65-ge daxuesheng 4-wei kang-Ri jiangling" 廣東一家族兩代出了65個大學生4位抗日將領 [A Guangdong family in two generations produced 65 university students and 4 anti-Japanese military leaders]. *Xinxi shibao* 信息時報 [Information times], 31 August 2003. news.eastday.com.

Hepp, John Henry, IV. *The Middle-Class City: Transforming Space and Time in Philadelphia, 1876–1926.* Philadelphia: University of Pennsylvania Press, 2003.

Hill, Max. *Exchange Ship.* New York and Toronto: Farrar & Rinehart, 1942.

History of the West Philadelphia High School, Prepared on the Occasion of Its Fiftieth Anniversary, 1912–1962. [Philadelphia]: West Philadelphia High School Alumni Association, [1962]), in the Historical Society of Pennsylvania, Philadelphia.

Holm, David. "Folk Art as Propaganda: The *Yangge* Movement in Yan'an." In *Popular Chinese Literature and Performing Arts in the People's Republic of China*, edited by Bonnie S. McDougall, pp. 1–35. Berkeley: University of California Press, 1984.

Holm, John Cecil. *Sunday Best: The Story of a Philadelphia Family.* New York: Farrar & Rinehart, Inc., 1942.

Howard, C. W., and K. P. Buswell. *A Survey of the Silk Industry of South China.* Canton: Ling Nan Agricultural College, Canton Christian College, 1925.

Hsieh, Zaza. "My War Years in Hong Kong, China and India." In *Dispersal and Renewal: Hong Kong University during the War Years*, edited by Clifford Matthews and Oswald Cheung, pp. 39–50. Hong Kong: Hong Kong University Press, 1998.

Hsü, Shuhsi. *Three Weeks of Canton Bombings.* Shanghai: Kelly & Walsh, 1939.

Huang Hsing-Tsung. "Peregrinations with Joseph Needham in China, 1943–44." In *Explorations in the History of Science and Technology in China*, edited by Li Guohao et al., pp. 39–75. Shanghai: Shanghai Chinese Classics Publishing House, 1982.

Huang Hsing Tsung. "Pursuing Science in Hong Kong, China and the West." In *Dispersal and Renewal: Hong Kong University during the War Years*, edited by Clifford Matthews and Oswald Cheung, pp. 127–142. Hong Kong: Hong Kong University Press, 1998.

Huang, Rayson. *A Lifetime in Academia: An Autobiography.* Hong Kong: Hong Kong University Press, 2000.

Huang Yanyu 黃延毓. "Mingguo sa niandu zhi sasan niandu jiaowu gaikuang 民國卅年度至卅三年度教務概況 [An overview of academic affairs, 1941–1944]. In *Kangzhan qijian de Lingnan* 抗戰期間的嶺南 [Lingnan during the war of resistance], pp. 32–33. n.p.: 1946(?). http://commons.ln.edu.hk/lingnan_history_bks.

Hucker, Charles O. *A Dictionary of Official Titles in Traditional China.* Stanford: Stanford University Press, 1985.

JamesTalk. "Zhongguo guojiadui shouren duizhang, Li Huitang zhiqiande 'Yuandong qiuwang', Tang Fuxiang" 中國國家隊首任隊長，李惠堂之前的'遠東球王'：唐福祥 [The first captain of China's national team and Li Huitang's predecessor as "Football King of the Far East": Tang Fuxiang] (2019). https://www.dongqiudi.com/archive/953232.himl.

Jansen, E. G. *Jade Engraved: New Zealand Missionaries and Their Chinese Colleagues in Japan's "China Incident".* Christchurch: Presbyterian Bookroom, 1947.

Johnson, Graham E., and Glen D. Peterson. *Historical Dictionary of Guangzhou (Canton) and Guangdong.* Lanham, MD, and London: Scarecrow Press, 1999.

Johnson, Matthew D. "Propaganda and Sovereignty in Wartime China: Morale Operations and Psychological Warfare under the Office of War Information." *Modern Asian Studies* 45 (2011): 303–344.

Karaka, D. F. *Chungking Diary.* Bombay: Thacker, 1942.

Kwong Chi Man, and Tsoi Yiu Lun. *Eastern Fortress: A Military History of Hong Kong, 1840–1970.* Hong Kong: Hong Kong University Press, 2014.

Ladds, Catherine. *Empire Careers: Working for the Chinese Customs Service, 1854–1949.* Manchester: Manchester University Press, 2013.

Lamberton, Mary. *St. John's University, Shanghai, 1879–1951.* New York: United Board for Christian Colleges in China, 1955.

Larsen, Lynn, and Becky Thill. *Dr. Thomas Wynne's Legacy.* New York: TFG Press, 2002.

Lary, Diana. *The Chinese People at War: Human Suffering and Social Transformation, 1937–1945*. New York: Cambridge University Press, 2010.

Launay, Adrien, ed. *Histoire des missions de Chine: Missions du Koung-tong, Monographies des districts par les missionaires*. Paris: Anciennes Maisons Douniol et Recani, 1917.

Leary, William M., Jr. *The Dragon's Wings: The China National Aviation Corporation and the Development of Commercial Aviation in China*. Athens: University of Georgia Press, 1976.

Leck, Greg. *Captives of Empire: The Japanese Internment of Allied Civilians in China, 1941–1945*. [Bangor, PA]: Shandy Press, 2006.

Lee, Edward Bing-Shuey. *Modern Canton*. Shanghai: Mercury Press, 1936.

Lee, Sophia. "Yenching University and the Japanese Occupation, 1937–1941." In *New Perspectives on Yenching University, 1916–1952*, edited by Arthur Lewis Rosenbaum, pp. 107–150. Chicago: Imprint Publications, 2012.

Lee, Vicky. *Being Eurasian: Memories Across Racial Divides*. Hong Kong: Hong Kong University Press, 2004.

Lei Yue Wai and Lei Hei Kit. "Report on a Steam Filature in Kwangtung." *Lingnaam Agricultural Review* 3, no. 2 (1925): 111–112.

Li Guanghe 李光和. "Kangzhan shiqi Rizhan Xianggang de 'guixiang' yundong shuping" 抗戰時期日佔香港的‘歸鄉’運動述評 [A commentary on the "return to the native place" movement during the Japanese occupation of Hong Kong]. *Minguo dang'an* 民國檔案, no. 2 (2010): 109–114.

Li, Lilian M. *China's Silk Trade: Traditional Industry in the Modern World, 1842–1937*. Cambridge: Council on East Asian Studies, Harvard University, 1981.

Li Ruiming (Lee Sui-ming) 李瑞明, comp. *Lingnan daxue* 嶺南大學 [Lingnan University]. n.p.: Lingnan (daxue) choumu fazhan weiyuanhui, 1997.

Li Ruiming (Lee Sui-ming) 李瑞明, and Emily M. Hill. *Nanguo fenghuang: Zhongshan daxue Lingnan (daxue) xueyuan* 南國鳳凰：中山大學嶺南（大學）學院 [A phoenix of south China: The story of Lingnan (University) College, Sun Yat-sen University]. Hong Kong: Commercial Press, 2005.

Li Shenghua 李聖華. "Lingnan daxue de zongjiao hudong" 嶺南大學的宗教活動 [Lingnan University's religious activities]. *Guangzhou wenshi ziliao* 廣州文史資料, no. 13 (1964): 86–101.

Li Shu-fan. *Hong Kong Surgeon*. New York: E. P. Dutton, 1964.

Li Weishi 李威士. "Lingnan daxue gailiang Guangdong siye de yishu" 嶺南大學改良廣東絲業的憶述 [Recollections of Lingnan University's improvements to the silk industry]. *Guangzhou wenshi ziliao* 廣州文史資料, no. 13 (1964): 183–193.

Liang Biqi 梁必騏, and Ye Jinshao 葉錦昭, comps. *Guangdong de ziran zaihai* 廣東的自然災害 [Guangdong's natural disasters]. n.p.: Guangdong renmin chubanshe, 1993.

Lin, Alfred H. Y. "Building and Funding a Warlord Regime: The Experience of Chen Jitang in Guangdong, 1929–1936." *Modern China* 28 (2002): 177–212.

Lingnan College, Hong Kong, Prospectus, 1972–1974. http://commons.ln.edu.hk/lingnan_calendar.

Luk, Bernard Hong-kay. "War, Schools, China, Hong Kong: 1937–49." In *Beyond Suffering: Recounting War in Modern China*, edited by James Flath and Norman Smith, pp. 36–58. Vancouver: UBC Press, 2011.

Luo Ren 羅仁. "Huohong de nianyue" 火紅的年月 [Years and months that were fiery red]. *Binshe* 斌社 [Newsletter of Lingnan University, the Class of 1954] 2 (1998): 5–9.

Luo Ren 羅仁, and Huang Daren 黃達仁, comps. *Lingnan daxue fuxiao husheng* 嶺南大學復校呼聲 [Voices calling for reviving Lingnan University]. Hong Kong, 1986.

Lutz, Jessie Gregory. *China and the Christian Colleges, 1850–1950*. Ithaca: Cornell University Press, 1971.

Macri, Franco David. *Clash of Empires in South China: The Allied Nations' Proxy War with Japan, 1935–1941*. Lawrence: University Press of Kansas, 2012.

McCracken, George E. *The Welcome Claimants, Proved, Disproved and Doubtful, with an Account of Some of Their Descendants*. Baltimore: Genealogical Publishing Company, 1970.

MacKinnon, Stephen R. *Wuhan, 1938: War, Refugees, and the Making of Modern China*. Berkeley: University of California Press, 2008.

MacKinnon, Stephen R., Diana Lary, and Ezra F. Vogel, eds. *China at War: Regions of China, 1937–1945*. Stanford: Stanford University Press, 2007.

Matthews, Clifford, and Oswald Cheung, eds. *Dispersal and Renewal: Hong Kong University during the War Years*. Hong Kong: Hong Kong University Press, 1998.

Meisenhelder, E. W. *The Dragon Smiles*. New York: Pageant Press, 1968.

Melby, John F. *The Mandate of Heaven: Record of a Civil War, China, 1945–49*. Toronto: University of Toronto Press, 1965.

Menon, K. P. S. *Twilight in China*. Bombay: Bharatyia Vidya Bhavan, 1972.

Mitter, Rana. *Forgotten Ally: China's World War II, 1937–1945*. Boston: Houghton Mifflin Harcourt, 2013.

Morton, Henry C. *The Story of "Webster's Third": Philip Gove's Controversial Dictionary and Its Critics*. Cambridge: Cambridge University Press, 1994.

Muscolino, Micah S. *The Ecology of War in China: Henan Province, the Yellow River, and Beyond, 1938–1950*. New York: Cambridge University Press, 2015.

Nanhai xian zhi 南海縣志 [Nanhai County gazetteer]. 1835 ed.

Needham, Joseph. *Travel Journals, South-East China, April 8–July 1, 1944*. nri.cam.ac.uk, website of the Needham Research Institute, University of Cambridge, under "Joseph Needham in Wartime China."

Needham, Joseph, and Dorothy Needham, eds. *Science Outpost: Papers of the Sino-British Science Co-operation Office (British Council Scientific Office in China), 1942–1946*. London: Pilot Press, 1948.

New York City Telephone Directory. Manhattan, White and Yellow Pages, 1926–1927 to 1932–1933.

Ng, Peter Tze Ming. "Nationalism, Democracy and Christian Higher Education in China: A Case Study of Lingnan University, Canton (A Preliminary Report)." A paper prepared for the Workshop on the History of Christian Higher Education in China, Yale University, New Haven, 17 February 1990.

Ng Tze Ming 吳梓明. "Cong Guangzhou sili Lingnan daxue kan jidujiao daxue ying yi hezhong xingshi wei guojia jiaoyu shiye fuwu" 從廣州私立嶺南大學看基督教大學應以何種形式為國家教育事業服務 [How should Christian colleges serve the nation's educational enterprise, as viewed from Guangzhou's Lingnan University]. In *Zhongxi wenhua yu jiaohui daxue* 中西文化與教會大學 [Christian universities and Chinese-Western cultures], edited by Zhang Kaiyuan 張開元 and Arthur Waldron, pp. 241–259. [Wuhan]: Hubei jiaoyu chubanshe, 1991.

Ngan Ki Ping 顏其平. "Zi Yuan" 字緣 [Predestined toward words], an autobiographic sketch written for 皇仁書院1952年畢業班同學會 [Queen's College 1952 Certificate Form Association], 鑽禧專集 [Diamond Jubilee Album]. Hong Kong, 2012.

"Norwegian Merchant Fleet, 1939–1945." warsailors.com.

Pa Chin. *Cold Nights*. Translated by Nathan K. Mao and Liu Ts'un-yan. Hong Kong: Chinese University Press; Seattle: University of Washington Press, 1978.

Pan, Lynn. *When True Love Came to China*. Hong Kong: Hong Kong University Press, 2015.

Pan Xun 潘洵 and Zhou Yong 周勇, comps. *Kangzhan shiqi Chongqing dahongzha rizhi* 抗戰時期重慶大轟炸日誌 [A chronological record of aerial bombardment of Chongqing during the War of Resistance]. Chongqing: Chongqing chubanshe, 2011.

Paton, David M. *R. O.: The Life and Times of Bishop Hall of Hong Kong*. [Hong Kong]: The Diocese of Hong Kong and Macao, and The Hong Kong Diocesan Association, 1985.

Payne, Robert. *Forever China*. New York: Dodd, Mead, 1945.

Peattie, Mark, Edward J. Drea, and Hans van de Ven, eds. *The Battle for China: Essays on the Military History of the Sino-Japanese War of 1937–1945*. Stanford: Stanford University Press, 2011.

Peck, Graham. *Two Kinds of Time*. Boston: Houghton Mifflin, 1950.

"Penn in the Great War: The University's Role in a Critical Time" (2013), archives.upenn.edu.

Pennsylvania, WWI Veterans Service and Compensation Files, 1917–1919, Pennsylvania State Archives, Harrisburg. ancestry.com.

Pepper, Suzanne. *Civil War in China: The Political Struggle 1945–1949*. Lanham, MD: Rowman & Littlefield, 1999.

Personal War Sketches, Grand Army of the Republic, Courtland Saunders Post No. 21, Department of Pennsylvania. Collection No. 1574, Historical Society of Pennsylvania, Philadelphia.

Philadelphia City Directory, 1855 to 1927.

Poon, Shuk-wah. *Negotiating Religion in Modern China: State and Common People in Guangzhou, 1900–1937*. Hong Kong: Chinese University Press, 2011.

Powell, John B. *My Twenty-Five Years in China*. New York: Macmillan, 1945.

Qujiangxian gaikuang 曲江縣概況 [Survey of Qujiang County]. [Qujiang]: Guangdongsheng Qujiangxian zhengfu, August 1941.

Refo, Henry. "Midwest China Oral History Interviews" (1980). *China Oral Histories*, Book 95. https://digitalcommons.luthersem.edu/china_histories/95.

Refo, Muriel Lockwood. "Midwest China Oral History Interviews" (1980). *China Oral Histories*, Book 94. http://digitalcommons.luthersem.edu/china_histories/94.

Rhoads, Ray. "Pennsylvania Family Group Record for Daniel Rhoads (1815–1872) and Susan Russel (1821–1881)." http://www.fgs-project.com/pennsylvania/r/rhoads-d.txt.

Ride, Edwin. *BAAG: Hong Kong Resistance, 1942–1945*. Hong Kong: Oxford University Press, 1981.

Ryan, Thomas F. *The Story of a Hundred Years: The Pontifical Institute of Foreign Missions (P.I.M.E.) in Hong Kong, 1858–1958*. Hong Kong: Catholic Truth Society, 1959.

Rzeznik, Thomas F. *Church and Estate: Religion and Wealth in Industrial-Era Philadelphia*. University Park: Pennsylvania State University Press, 2013.

Sankar, Andrea. "Spinster Sisterhoods—Jing Yih Sifu: Spinster-Domestic, Nun." In *Lives: Chinese Working Women*, edited by Mary Sheridan and Janet W. Salaff, pp. 51–70. Bloomington: Indiana University Press, 1984.

Schoppa, R. Keith. *In a Sea of Bitterness: Refugees during the Sino-Japanese War*. Cambridge, MA: Harvard University Press, 2011.

Scott, Janny. *The Beneficiary: Fortune, Misfortune, and the Story of My Father*. New York: Riverhead Books, 2019.

Sha Dongxun 沙東迅, comp. *Guangdong kang-Ri zhanzheng jishi* 廣東抗日戰爭記事 [A chronology of the anti-Japanese war of resistance in Guangdong]. Guangzhou: Guangzhou chubanshe, 2004.

Silk Association of America. *Annual Reports*, 1923–1924 to 1931–1932.

Situ Yu 司徒昱, and Xu Zhijun 許智君. "Lingdacun shenghuo de pianduan huiyi" 嶺大村生活的片斷回憶 [Fragmentary recollections of life at Ling Tai Tsuen]. In *Dacun suiyue—Kangzhan shiqi Lingnan zai Yuebei* 大村歲月—抗戰時期嶺南在粵北 [The Tai Tsuen years—Lingnan in northern Guangdong during the War of Resistance], pp. 125–127. North York, Ontario: "Dacun suiyue" chubanzu, 1998. http://commons.ln.edu.hk/lingnan_history_bks.

"Siye juzi Cen Guohua zhi nü Cen Yufang huiyi fuqin shengping" 絲業巨子岑國華之女岑玉芳回憶父親生平 [Cen Yufang, daughter of the silk industry giant, Shum Kwok Wah, remembers her father's life]. *Zhujiang shangbao* 珠江商報 [Pearl River commercial news], 9 June 2014. www.sc168.com/pindao/rwsd/content/2014-06/09/content_485620.htm.

Smith, J. L. *Atlas of the 24th, 34th & 44th Wards of the City of Philadelphia* (1911). https://westphillyhistory.archives.upenn.edu/maps/1911-atlas-smith.

Snow, Phillip. *The Fall of Hong Kong: Britain, China, and the Japanese Occupation*. New Haven: Yale University Press, 2003.

Statue of Liberty–Ellis Island Foundation. "Passenger Search." libertyellisfoundation.org.

Sun Xiufu 孫修福, comp. *Zhongguo jindai haiguan gaoji zhiyuan nianbiao* 中國近代海關高級職員年表 [Chronological table of high-ranked staff of the Maritime Service in modern China]. Beijing: Zhongguo haiguan chubanshe, 2004.

Taylor, Jay. *The Generalissimo: Chiang Kai-shek and the Struggle for Modern China*. Cambridge, MA: Harvard University Press, 2011.

Teng, Emma Jinhua. *Eurasian: Mixed Identities in the United States, China, and Hong Kong, 1842–1943*. Berkeley: University of California Press, 2013.

Tian Tong 田彤, comp. *Zhongguo jindai sixiangjia wenku—Chen Xujing juan* 中國近代思想家文庫—陳序經卷 [A library of modern Chinese thinkers: Chen Su-ching]. Beijing: Zhongguo renmin daxue chubanshe, 2015.

Tobe Ryōichi. "The Japanese Eleventh Army in Central China, 1938–1941." In *The Battle for China: Essays on the Military History of the Sino-Japanese War of 1937–1945*, edited by Mark Peattie, Edward J. Drea, and Hans van de Ven, pp. 207–229. Stanford: Stanford University Press, 2011.

Topley, Marjorie. "Marriage Resistance in Rural Kwangtung." In *Women in Chinese Society*, edited by Margery Wolf and Roxane Witke, pp. 67–88. Stanford: Stanford University Press, 1975.

Tsin, Michael. *Nation, Governance, and Modernity in China: Canton, 1900–1927*. Stanford: Stanford University Press, 1999.

United Kingdom, Incoming Passenger Lists, 1878–1960. ancestry.com.

United States, Federal Census, 1850 to 1930. ancestry.com.

United States Patent and Trademark Office. "USPTO Full-Text and Image Database." http://patft. uspto.gov.

University of Michigan, *Register* (Ann Arbor), 1924–1925 to 1926–1927.

University of Pennsylvania, *Catalogue*, 1917–1918 to 1920–1921.

University of Pennsylvania, *The Record* (yearbook), vol. 50 (1920) and vol. 51 (1921).

U.S. World War I Selective Service System Draft Registration Cards, 1917–1918. Pennsylvania, Philadelphia County, Draft Board 19. ancestry.com.

Van de Ven, Hans. "Bombing, Japanese Pan-Asianism, and Chinese Nationalism." In *The International History of East Asia, 1900–1968: Trade, Ideology, and the Quest for Order*, edited by Anthony Best, pp. 99–117. London and New York: Routledge, 2010.

Van de Ven, Hans. *China at War: Triumph and Tragedy in the Emergence of the New China, 1937–1952*. London: Profile Books, 2017.

Vogel, Ezra F. *Canton under Communism: Programs and Politics in a Provincial Capital, 1949–1968*. Cambridge, MA: Harvard University Press, 1969.

Wallace, Franklin. "Midwest China Oral History Interviews" (1977). *China Oral Histories*, Book 76. http://digitalcommons.luthersem.edu/china_histories/76.

Wang, Dong. *Managing God's Higher Learning: U.S.-China Cultural Encounter and Canton Christian College (Lingnan University), 1888–1952*. Lanham, MD: Lexington Books, 2007.

Wang Yidun 王以敦. "Lingda shenghuo sinian de huiyi" 嶺大生活四年的回憶 [Recollections of four years of life at Lingnan University]. *Guangzhou wenshi ziliao* 廣州文史資料, no. 13 (1964): 203–212.

Wang Yidun 王以敦. "Zhanhou Meiguo xinwenchu yu Guangzhou Jidujiao qingnianhui de guanxi he huodong" 戰後美國新聞處與廣州基督教青年會的關係和活動 [The relationship between the USIS and the Canton YMCA and their joint activities in the postwar years]. *Guangzhou wenshi ziliao* 廣州文史資料, no. 28 (1983): 200–207.

Wang Zheng. *Women in the Chinese Enlightenment: Oral and Textual Histories*. Berkeley: University of California Press, 1999.

Wei Yingtao 隗瀛濤, comp. *Jindai Chongqing chengshi shi* 近代重慶城市史 [Modern urban history of Chongqing]. Chengdu: Sichuan daxue chubanshe, 1991.

West China Conference of the Methodist Church. *Year Book & Official Journal*, 1939 (1940).

"West Philadelphia: The History, A Streetcar Suburb in the City, 1854–1907." westphillyhistory. archives.upenn.edu.

Westad, Odd Arne. *Decisive Encounters: The Chinese Civil War, 1946–1950*. Stanford: Stanford University Press, 2003.

White, Theodore H. *The Mountain Road*. New York: William Sloane Associates, 1958.

White, Theodore H., and Annalee Jacoby. *Thunder out of China*. New York: William Sloane Associates, 1946.

Wiest, Jean-Paul. "Catholic Activities in Kwangtung Province and Chinese Responses, 1848–1885." PhD dissertation, University of Washington, 1977.

Wilkinson, Mark Francis. "To Win the Minds of Men: The American Information Service in China, 1941–1945." MA thesis, University of Maryland, 1977.

Wilson, Dick. *When Tigers Fight: The Story of the Sino-Japanese War, 1937–1945*. New York: Viking Press, 1982.

Wright-Nooth, George, with Mark Adkin. *Prisoner of the Turnip Heads: The Fall of Hong Kong and Imprisonment by the Japanese*. London: Cassell, 1996.

Wu Zhande 伍沾德. "Min yi shi wei tian" 民以食為天 [People regard food as heaven]. In *Dacun suiyue—Kangzhan shiqi Lingnan zai Yuebei* 大村歲月—抗戰時期嶺南在粵北 [The Tai Tsuen years—Lingnan in northern Guangdong during the War of Resistance], pp. 55–56. North York, Ontario: "Dacun suiyue" chubanzu, 1998. http://commons.ln.edu.hk/lingnan_history_bks.

Xie Chuning. "China's Casablanca: Refugees, Outlaws, and Smugglers in France's Guangzhouwan Enclave." In *1943: China at the Crossroads*, edited by Joseph W. Esherick and Matthew T. Combs, pp. 391–425. Ithaca: East Asia Program, Cornell University, 2015.

Xie Dingchu 謝鼎初. "Lingda 'Meijihui' de Tang Fuqiang" 嶺大'美基會'的唐富祥 [Tong Fuk Cheung at Lingnan University's American Foundation]. *Guangzhou wenshi ziliao* 廣州文史資料, no. 13 (1964): 125–128.

Xie Qiongsun 謝琼孫. "Li Yinglin xiaozhang yu Lingda" 李應林校長與嶺大 [President Y. L. Lee and Lingnan University]. *Zhujiang wenyuan* 珠江文苑 (March 1985): 33–43.

Yang, C. K. *The Chinese Family in the Communist Revolution*. Cambridge, MA: MIT Press, 1959.

Yang Yimei 楊逸梅. "Li Yinglin shiqi de Lingnan daxue" 李應林時期的嶺南大學 [Lingnan University at the time of Y. L. Lee]. *Guangdong wenshi ziliao* 廣東文史資料, no. 51 (1987): 78–99.

Young, Arthur N. *China's Wartime Finance and Inflation, 1937–1945*. Cambridge, MA: Harvard University Press, 1965.

Yu, Brian. *The Arches of the Years*. Toronto: Joint Centre for Asia Pacific Studies, 1999.

Yu Zhi 余志, ed. *Kangle honglou* 康樂紅樓 [Red Buildings on Hong Lok Campus]. Hong Kong: Shangwu yinshuguan, 2004.

Zhang Genfu 張根福. Kangzhan shiqi de renkou qianyi—jian lun dui xibu kaifa de yingxiang 抗戰時期的人口遷移—兼論對西部開發的影響 [Population migration in the resistance period and its effect on the development of the western regions]. Beijing: Guangming ribao chubanshe, 2006.

Zhang Yucai 張雨才, comp. *Zhongguo tiedao jianshe shilue* (1876–1949) 中國鐵道建設史略 (1876–1949) [A history of the construction of China's railroads, 1876–1949]. Beijing: Zhongguo tiedao chubanshe, 1997.

Zhu, Pingchao. *Wartime Culture in Guilin, 1938–1944: A City at War*. Lanham, MD: Lexington Rooks, 2015.

Zhuang Fuwu 庄福伍. "Xian Yuqing jiaoshou nianpu 冼玉清教授年譜 [Chronological biography of Professor Y. C. Sinn]. *Lingnan wenshi* 嶺南文史, 1994, No. 4.

Zuo Shuangwen 左雙文. *Hua'nan kangzhan shigao* 華南抗戰史稿 [A draft history of the War of Resistance in South China]. Guangzhou: Guangdong gaodeng jiaoyu chubanshe, 2004.

Index